Peirce, Semiotics, and Psychoanalysis

Psychiatry and the Humanities, Volume 15

Published under the auspices of the Forum on Psychiatry
and the Humanities,
The Washington School of Psychiatry

Peirce, Semiotics, and Psychoanalysis

John Muller
Joseph Brent, *Editors*

The Johns Hopkins University Press
Baltimore and London

The Johns Hopkins University Press
2715 North Charles Street
Baltimore, Maryland 21218-4363
www.press.jhu.edu

Library of Congress Cataloging-in-Publication Data will be found at the end
of this book.
A catalog record for this book is available from the British Library.

ISBN 0-8018-6288-4

To Joseph H. Smith, M.D.,
whose vision founded
and for many years sustained
the Forum on Psychiatry and the Humanities

Contributors

Joseph Brent is the author of the biography *Charles Sanders Peirce: A Life* (1993).

James Phillips practices psychiatry in New Haven, Connecticut, where he is an associate clinical professor of psychiatry at Yale University.

John E. Gedo, author of numerous books on psychoanalytic theory and practice, is now retired from his position as Training and Supervising Analyst at the Chicago Psychoanalytic Institute. His chapter, "Protolinguistic Phenomena in Psychoanalysis," was the 1996 Edith Weigert lecture at the Washington School of Psychiatry and was subsequently published in his book *The Languages of Psychoanalysis.*

John Muller, Chairman of the Forum on Psychiatry and the Humanities, is Director of Education and Psychology Training at the Austen Riggs Center and the author of *Beyond the Psychoanalytic Dyad: Developmental Semiotics in Freud, Peirce, and Lacan* (1996).

Jospeh H. Smith is founding editor of the Psychiatry and the Humanities series (1976–92); author of *Arguing with Lacan: Ego Psychology and Language* (1991); past president of the Washington Psychoanalytic Society; and, prior to retirement, Supervising and Training Analyst at the Washington Psychoanalytic Institute.

Wilfried Ver Eecke is a professor of philosophy at Georgetown University in Washington D.C.

Angela Moorjani is a professor and chair of the Department of Modern Languages and Linguistics at the University of Maryland, Baltimore.

David Pettigrew is an associate professor of philosophy at Southern Connecticut State University, coeditor of *Disseminating Lacan* (SUNY), and cotranslator of four books on Jacques Lacan and Martin Heidegger.

Vincent Colapietro is a professor of philosophy at Pennsylvania State University, specializing in American Pragmatism and, in particular, Charles Sanders Peirce.

Teresa de Lauretis is a professor of the history of consciousness at the University of California, Santa Cruz.

Contents

Preface

The renewal of interest in the ideas of Charles Sanders Peirce over the past twenty years has been evident in literary criticism, philosophy, semiotics, linguistics, and philosophy of science, especially in chaos and complexity theory. Such interest has not yet extended into psychoanalysis, but we hope this volume will indicate how psychoanalytic theory and practice can benefit from an understanding of Peirce's ideas.

The Forum on Psychiatry and the Humanities sponsors the Edith Weigert lecture and conducts a seminar in preparation for volumes such as this. Most of our contributors participated in the Peirce seminar, and we believe the reader will come to see what we have found: that the ideas of Peirce are not simply helpful in an auxiliary way, but they illuminate matters at the center of contemporary psychoanalysis—the coherence of the human subject, the role of language in the generation of meaning, the question of truth, the nature of intersubjectivity, the structure of dialogue, the ongoing obscurity of unconscious processes, the ethical link between speech and action, the relation of the individual to the community.

Peirce, Semiotics, and Psychoanalysis

1 A Brief Introduction to the Life and Thought of Charles Sanders Peirce

Joseph Brent

Charles Sanders Peirce (1839–1914) was a singular man—a prodigious, protean, brilliant, and productive intellect who lived a humiliating and tragic life. There is no other quite like him in the history of Western ideas. His life raises the ancient puzzle of the relation of genius and madness. One Peirce scholar, in his review of Peirce's only full-length biography (Brent 1993), gave his impressions of this extraordinary polymath:

> a first ranker in western civilization, pioneer semiotician, innovative historian of science, student of economic theory, hopeless accountant, skilled mathematician, unfaithful husband, initiator of pragmatism, occasional actor, profligate dandy, great logician, brilliant experimental physicist, unlucky speculator, eminent cartographer, student of lexicography, gauche socialite, competent structural engineer, persistent drug-taker, occasional vagrant, student of medicine, nominal Episcopalian, prospective encyclopedia salesman, patentee in chemical engineering, subject of police inquiries, profound philosopher, project procrastinator . . . [Grattan-Guinness 1994]

Germane to the subject of this volume, I add experimental psychology and psychology of the conscious and unconscious mind and of the self and self-consciousness.

The complexity of Peirce's character and his reputation as a broken and dissolute man, despite his recognized brilliance and originality, haunted his reputation during his life and ever since his death more than eighty years ago. Despite his acknowledged genius and accomplishments, he was refused a professorship at Harvard, was fired from his lectureship at the Johns Hopkins University, and was forced to resign from his thirty-year career in geodesy at the United States Coast Survey. A ma-

1

jor Peirce scholar recently wrote that the owners of his papers, the Harvard Department of Philosophy, consistently "acted to obstruct research on Peirce, thus continuing the Harvard vendetta against Peirce which lasted from [Charles W.] Eliot's ascension to the presidency of Harvard in 1889 until the [recent] advent of . . . a new breed of Harvard Professors. The history of the Harvard Department's conduct with respect to the Peirce manuscripts is one of the sorriest tales in American academic history" (Murphey 1993).

Before December 1991, when the department ended censorship of its biographical Peirce material by permitting publication of my biography, with its hundreds of quotations from their biographical manuscripts, it was impossible to attempt well-researched accounts of and explanations for Peirce's extraordinary character and behavior, though there were many guesses based on rumor and privileged information. Driven largely by the desire to hide the often unpalatable facts of his life, this censorship helps to explain Peirce's relative obscurity in the history of Western thought, despite his broad influence.

In the attempt to explain the extremes of Peirce's life, I hypothesize (despite the obvious dangers of historical diagnosis) that Peirce probably suffered from three neurological pathologies, to which he pointed himself. As an adolescent, Peirce began to experience extremely painful episodes of trigeminal neuralgia. These episodes continued throughout his life and often left him prostrate for days, sometimes weeks. His father, who also suffered from a very painful illness, Bright's disease, early introduced him to opium and ether as palliatives for the intense pain.

In his twenties, Peirce began to exhibit the extreme mood swings that are symptomatic of bipolar disorder. The condition worsened with age, and he manifested most of the associated symptoms. On the manic side, he exhibited driven, paranoid, and impulsive actions; extreme insomnia; ecstatic grandiosity and visionary expansiveness; hypersexuality; almost superhuman energy; and had irrational financial dealings, which included compulsive extravagance and disastrous investing. On the depressive side, he had severely melancholic or depressive episodes characterized by suicidal feelings or flatness of mood, accompanied by an inertness of mind, the inability to feel emotion, and an unbearable sense of futility. As an adolescent, Peirce experimented with drugs, and throughout his life he used them with sophistication, both to manage his pain and depression and to enhance the ecstatic creativity of his manic episodes. He was probably addicted to caffeine, alcohol, morphine, and cocaine through much of his adult life. It was these behaviors, in a time when they were believed to be explained only by moral failure, that ruined his personal and professional life.

Peirce was surprisingly unreflective about his own character and did not begin to ponder seriously on the reasons for his disastrous personal and professional failures until his mid-sixties, when he concluded, rightly, that much of the cause was "the poison of biology." He blamed his genetic inheritance for his uncontrollable emotionality, what he called "the criminal trait in the blood," and wrote: "For long years I suffered unspeakably, being an excessively emotional fellow, from ignorance of how to go to work to acquire sovereignty over myself" (MS 848, 905).

Surprisingly, while Peirce gave his uncontrollable emotions and facial neuralgia salient roles in his failures, he gave his left-handedness the most important part to play. In this third diagnosis he proposed—with considerable modern support for his hypothesis—that his left-handedness was an element in a pathological condition caused by differences from the normal in the structure of his brain, which he thought had its most unfortunate effect in his "incapacity for linguistic expression." He speculated that "the connections between different parts of my brain must be different from the usual and presumably best arrangement; and, if so, it would necessarily follow that my thinking should be *gauche*" (MS 632). Peirce always had the greatest difficulty with language of any kind and was constantly reminded that the basis of his way of thinking was diagrammatic, not linguistic. He made it his intention, in all his labored writing, to have the process of thinking laid open to view as "a moving picture of the action of thought" (MS 296, 298, 905; Geschwind and Galaburda 1987). For Peirce, thinking was best represented as the manipulation of diagrams and, in this respect, mathematics was at the root of his philosophy.

In addition to these neurological factors, three other factors deeply influenced his life: his father, Benjamin; his obsession with logic; and religion. Benjamin Peirce was brilliant, profound, facile, and given to outbursts of rage and long bouts of depression. He was powerfully attractive, eloquent, and successful—a loving and overwhelming father, who, from Charles's childhood on, trained his son's intellect for genius, paying little attention to standard curricula, whether it was that of grade school or Harvard University. Recognizing his son's precocity in mathematics, Benjamin concentrated his demanding regimen in that subject, sometimes forcing Charles to play continuous games of double dummy whist through the night, while he criticized every error and its nature. Benjamin rarely provided young Charles with a theorem in mathematics, instead giving him examples or outcomes and requiring him to work out the mathematical principles for himself by the use of diagrams alone. Benjamin also set his son, as an adolescent, to reading such philosophers as Kant, Spinoza, Hegel, Hobbes, Hume, and James Mill. He would then induce Charles to tell him about the "proofs offered by the philosophers, and in a very few words would almost invariably rip them up and show them to be empty" (MS 823). Benjamin was an overpowering and often cruel taskmaster who believed he had sired a genius. He fully intended to make his son a major intellect and the means to the perpetuation of his own philosophical system. When Charles was forty years old, Benjamin declared publicly that "it was a great gratification for [Benjamin] to know that his son would prosecute the work to which he had devoted the latter part of his own life" (Sergeant 1880).

At the same time, the father otherwise allowed the son free rein and even encouraged him to become a connoisseur of wines and to refine his taste for the good things in life. As long as he could afford it, Charles lived an extravagantly luxurious life, in large part to meliorate his suffering. After Charles's death, his nephew wrote, in what the family considered an accurate account, that he became a highly emotional, easily duped, and rather snobbish young dandy who went his own way, indifferent of the consequences (MS 1644). Largely because of his neurological and nervous disorders, his family, particularly his father, indulged and protected him, even when he was in his forties. It is not surprising that this heavily burdened youth publicly avowed his advocacy of the obscure ontological atheism of the nineteenth-century French positivist historian Etienne Vacherot and in other ways paraded his contempt for the hierarchs of Cambridge and Boston. Nor is it unexpected that his wives from both his disastrous marriages became nurses, failed disciplinarians, and scapegoats, as his mother had been.

Charles Peirce began his lifelong obsession with logic when, at twelve, he read his older brother's copy of Archbishop Richard Whately's *Logic*. Apparently what first fascinated him was the uncanny directionality of inference and, later, its puzzling ability to provide and preserve meaning. Around the same time, he discovered his method of constructing a philosophy, which he called "pedestrianism" and later described (at twenty-five), after having mastered the works of Immanuel Kant: "It is necessary to reduce all our actions to logical processes so that to do anything is but to take another step in the chain of inference. Thus only can we effect that complete reciprocity between Thought & its object which it was Kant's Copernican step to announce" (MS 339).

Despite this apparently restricted and inchmeal description, logic is, for Peirce, far more than the cut-and-dried academic discipline: it is the connective tissue of the universe. It is the basis of any thinking having a broadly scientific character, which is to say, of inquiry, generally—which, in Peirce's extended conception of inference, includes not only the deductive and inductive elements usually thought of as making up the discipline but hypothesis, which he calls abduction, as well. Hypothesis is, for Peirce, a form of inference subject to its own rule, which originates knowledge and is how we manage to guess, often fruitfully, the way our world is. Peirce believed this ability to understand our world to be founded in the continuity of mind and nature, in the presupposition that we "have a capacity for 'guessing' right. We shall do better to abandon the whole attempt to learn the truth however urgent may be our need of ascertaining it, unless we can trust the human mind's having such power of guessing right that before very many hypotheses shall have been tried, intelligent guessing may be expected to lead us to the one which will support all test, leaving the vast majority unexamined" (*CP* 6.530).

This step-by-step inferential process also describes Peirce's lifelong manner of philosophizing. He kept at it, scribbling away abstractedly at odd moments, or working with his extraordinary powers of concentration almost without sleep for days, sometimes weeks, even months at a time, a practice he could sustain only with the help of drugs, which included alcohol, morphine, cocaine, and caffeine made from very strong coffee reduced to a syrup. He continued to work this way from the time he was about twenty until the week of his death at seventy-four, despite illness, poverty, and the constant reverses of his life. In 1905, at age sixty-six, he described to the Italian pragmatist Mario Calderoni how he had worked at twenty-eight: "It was in a desperate endeavor to making a beginning of penetrating into that riddle [of human existence, conduct, and thinking, and their relation to God and Nature] that on May 14, 1867, after three years of almost insanely concentrated thought, hardly interrupted even by sleep, I produced my one contribution to philosophy in the 'New List of Categories'" (Peirce 1982).

Three years earlier, in 1902, he had written William James's wife, Alice, while working on his phenomenology: "During the interval, I had not more than a dozen chats with my wife . . . and otherwise hadn't spoken two consecutive sentences to anybody. There were four or five months' silence. It is not an exceptional period. I live always so" (Letter to Alice James [1902]). These illustrations indicate the lifelong interplay of creative obsession and bipolar disorder.

Being born and raised in the long shadow of the Puritan oligarchy made religion a matter of daily importance for the young Peirce, diluted as it was in Benjamin's devout Unitarian faith. Charles's first clear expression of its impact on him was the defiant announcement of his atheism, made when he was an undergraduate. By his mid-twenties, his father's deeply held belief in the underlying harmony of religion and science and his marriage to a clergyman's devout and feminist daughter had convinced Charles of the seriousness, if not the truth, of religion to the point that he joined his first wife in the Episcopal church as her condition for the marriage. Thereafter, his reservations on the subject were largely focused on what he judged to be the dangerous nonsense of theological metaphysics. In 1892, at fifty-three, Peirce had a mystical experience that changed his life. He reported that, after many years of absenting himself from church and communion, in the midst of great personal crisis he felt driven to attend, and one morning, after wandering aimlessly, he entered St. Thomas's Episcopal Church in New York City:

> I seemed to receive the direct permission of the Master to come [to communion] . . . when the instant came I found myself carried up to the altar rail, almost without my own volition. I am perfectly sure that it was right. Anyway, I could not help it.
>
> I may mention as a reason why I do not offer to put my gratitude for the bounty granted to me into some form of church work, that which seemed to call me today seemed to promise me that I should bear a cross like death for the Master's sake, and he would give me strength to bear it. I am sure it will happen. My part is to wait.
>
> I have never before been mystical, but now I am. [MSL 483]

For Peirce, the experience was so important that he said of it, "If . . . a man has had no religious experience, then any religion not an affectation is as yet impossible for him; and the only worthy course is to wait quietly till such experience comes. No amount of speculation can take the place of experience" (*CP* 1.654).

For the mystic, the real is not itself sensible; it is represented by means of sense, in the same manner as an idea is represented by a word, say, *sign.* The word is heard with the ear, but the meaning that it signifies has no more physical properties than a character in *A Midsummer Night's Dream.* From the publication of his first papers in 1867, Peirce held in his doctrine of signs, which he called semiotic, that "we have no power of thinking without signs" (*CP* 5.285) and that "all thought whatsoever is a sign, and is mostly of the nature of language" (420). After his mystical experience, he increasingly treated semiotic as an interpretation of the *logos,* the idea of the world perceived to be God's utterance, the action of signs, or semiosis. In five articles published in the *Monist* in 1891-93 (*CP* 6.7-34, 35-65, 102-63, 238-71, 287-317), which bracket his religious experience, those published before and after it show very clearly in their differences the experience's effect on his thinking. In 1908, Peirce reinterpreted his pragmatism as "A Neglected Argument for the Reality of God" (*CP* 6.452-93).

The mystic will often speak of "the Master" or a similarly reverenced being as the guide to the real. In Peirce's case the "cross like death" was the iron duty "the Master" had bound him to do—the completion of his architectonic philosophy. After his mystical experience of 1892, Peirce, poor, isolated, increasingly sick, and often profoundly depressed and suicidal, wrote more than 80,000 pages of difficult, often brilliant, and sometimes superb philosophical thinking, very little of it published, in trying to do what "the Master" demanded. He died, in 1914, virtually pen in hand.

This volume assumes that Peirce's thought can provide a fruitful basis for the development of psychoanalytic theory. I will now provide an introduction to what is a thoroughly American foundation for a very different way of looking at human psychology, beginning with pragmatism, his theory of inquiry.

Peirce uses the word *inquiry* very broadly to mean the many ways we go about trying to find things out by means of signs and symbols, which are then subjected to logical criticism. He uses the word *inference,* not to stand for the way we presume to think logically, but to point to the fact that when we infer, we are usually giving a reason for what it is that we are asserting. We do this, Peirce held, by using—in various combinations—the three types of inference he distinguishes: deduction, induction, and hypothesis, which Peirce preferred to call abduction. Of the first, he agrees that every deductive inference is already contained in the premises, but he also contends that, even in something so apparently cut-and-dried, there is an experimental element. Induction he calls that type of inference which is concerned with testing, not, as so many philosophers of science have insisted, originating knowledge. But it is Peirce's revolutionary claim that hypothesis or abduction is a third type of inference that is the truly interesting element of his theory of inquiry. Only abduction can originate or advance knowledge, and the difference between induction and abduction is that in induction "we conclude that facts, similar to observed facts are true in cases not examined [while in abduction] we conclude the existence of a fact quite different from anything observed. . . . The former classifies, and the latter explains" (*CP* 2.636). Peirce provides a simple diagram of abductive inference:

The surprising fact, C, is observed;
But if A were true, C would be a matter of course,
Hence, there is reason to suspect that A is true. [*CP* 5.189]

What first strikes the attention is the entirely tentative nature of the conclusion—it is a guess worth considering. Secondly, the schema shows what makes a hypothesis worthwhile or reasonable, whether in everyday life or in science. The diagram says nothing about what would justify or validate the hypothesis. That will be a matter of elaborating the consequences of the hypothesis deductively and then testing it inductively. The only important question concerning any hypothesis is, does it open up a new and unexpected line of thought that leads us to more detailed exploration and test? Here the special importance Peirce attaches to abduction becomes clear; it is the only form of inference which originates knowledge, unlike deduction and induction, which reiterate and test knowledge we already have.

We can now summarize Peirce's view of inquiry as the statement of his pragmatism: it is the logical rule that requires that any genuine hypothesis will lead deductively to consequences that can be tested inductively by experience. Peirce generalized this framework to encompass thought of any kind—perception, emotion, action, inquiry, deliberation, science—and to insist that thought always exhibits the same pattern: the mutual interplay, interaction, and support of the three types of inference he distinguishes. The life of thought he characterizes as the constant formation, reformation, and exercise of habits of inference.

For Peirce, habits of inference take three forms. The first is reasoning proper, the making of fully conscious and, at least in intention, fully worked-out inferences, such as those made by a biologist or clinical psychoanalyst. Reasoning, in this critical sense, is what logicians usually investigate and formalize. The second is what Peirce called *acritical* reasoning (*CP* 5.440). It is the sort of inference that we regularly make in our everyday lives, in conversation, in disciplining our children, in making plans, in arguing for a political candidate, or in any other ordinary pattern of thinking in which we seldom provide our premises or complete an argument. The third form, of particular interest to psychoanalysis, is what Peirce calls "operations of the mind which are logically analogous to inference excepting only that they are unconscious and therefore uncontrollable and therefore not subject to logical criticism" (*CP* 5.108). For Peirce, the most easily identified of these are our perceptual judgments of shape and color, spatial and temporal relations, which are unconscious hypotheses and, therefore, beyond our control.

One way to appreciate the range of Peirce's thought and its application to psychoanalytic theory and practice is to begin with his assault on Cartesianism, one of the origins of modern thinking about inquiry. Peirce understood clearly that Descartes was, as he was himself, trying to grasp the underlying reasons for the success of modern scientific method, and, in his thoroughgoing rejection of Descartes, he invented contemporary logic of science in both its broad and narrow senses. Peirce's criticisms of Descartes also provide the best introduction to his architectonic system of thought. These criticisms are to be found in two papers Peirce wrote in 1868, when he was not yet thirty, "Concerning Certain Faculties Claimed for Man" and "Some Consequences of Four Incapacities," which remained virtually ignored for at least sixty years (*CP* 5.213 - 63, 264 - 317).

Descartes put forward the now familiar idea that we know by means of direct acts of knowledge called intuitions, which are self-evident truths we cannot doubt. These intuitions are absolutely simple, dyadic relations between the knowing mind and what is known, such that the intuition presents a whole truth perfectly circumscribed. Once achieved, the intuition is independent and requires no accounting. Descartes claimed that his methods of investigation give results. He thought that since some of our beliefs may have been constituted nonintuitively, if we are serious inquirers, we must rigorously, at least once in our lives, make the experiment of doubting all our beliefs. What survives will be those simple beliefs that have proved themselves to be intuitions — direct, self-evident knowledge of truth. We, then, individually, build our general knowledge, piece-by-piece in the right order, from these simple intuitions, as in geometry. But it is absurd to ask for justifications of these intuitions, since all investigations depend on them as ultimates beyond explanation.

For Peirce, Descartes' theory of knowledge is an abduction whose consequences must be deduced and then tested inductively. He rejects the Cartesian model of inquiry on several grounds, beginning:

> We cannot begin with complete doubt. We must begin with all the prejudices we actually have. . . . These prejudices are not to be dispelled with a maxim, for they are things which it does not occur to us *can* be questioned. . . . A person may, it is true, in the course of his studies, find reason to doubt what he began by believing; but in that case he doubts because he has a positive reason for it, not on account of the Cartesian maxim. Let us not pretend to doubt in philosophy what we do not doubt in our hearts. [*CP* 5.265]

He goes on to point out that it is a profound mistake to take individual consciousness as our final standard of knowledge. Instead, he holds up the community of inquirers, who can question each other and work toward some agreement as a more appropriate criterion. In practice, Peirce replaces Cartesian intuition with the community of scientific inquirers, who have the hope that, in time, for a given inquiry, one solution will be established as the superior one. Such a tentative, but justifiable outcome is what truth means in science. Finally, Peirce denies that inquiry can be held to justify the Cartesian reliance upon "absolutely inexplicable" intuitions: these, by their very nature, block the road of inquiry.

Peirce deepens his attack on intuition by denying that we have direct intuitive knowledge either of ourselves as unique individuals or of our own inner states and attitudes. He holds that we come to know the important facts about ourselves inferentially; that we first form a definite idea of ourselves as a hypothesis to provide a place in which our errors and other people's perceptions of us can happen. Furthermore, this hypothesis is constructed from our knowledge of "outward" physical facts, such things as the sounds we speak and the bodily movements we make, which Peirce calls signs. The strangeness of such signs is that, while they are purely physical, in order for them to act as signs they must stand in relation to other physical things, and that relation is not physical, but intelligible. This state, in which the suprasensible exists in the sensible, is the commonplace, but seldom noticed, origin of our experience. Peirce, fascinated since boyhood by the intelligibility of relation—by logic and meaning—claims, in W. B. Gallie's words, that "to know, with regard to a succession of physical events, that they make up a series of signs, is to know of the existence of and operation of a mind (or number of minds); and that to be engaged in making or manifesting or reacting to a series of signs is to be engaged in 'being a mind' or, more simply and naturally, to be engaged in thinking intelligently" (1952, 80–81).

We will not see ourselves exactly as others see us, or see them exactly as they see themselves, but we surely see ourselves through our own speech and other interpretable behavior, just as others see us and themselves in the same way. What is important is the commonality of the process, so that whatever else it may be, as Peirce says, "all thinking is dialogic in form" (*CP* 6.338), whether it is intrasubjective or intersubjective. For Peirce, then, the self is a form of dialogue: "One's thoughts are what he is 'saying to himself,' that is, saying to that other self that is just coming to life in the flow of time. When one reasons, it is that critical self that one is trying to persuade; and all thought whatsoever is a sign, and is mostly in the nature of language" (*CP* 5.421). In metaphor, the human self is a nexus actively embodied in an infinite labyrinth of intelligible signs.

In summary, Peirce sets forth the semiotic doctrine that all thought is in signs and, more generally, that in any situation where knowledge is possible, sign action, or semiosis, is its vehicle. While the Cartesian tradition holds that knowledge is essentially direct and dyadic, a two-sided relation between knowing mind and known fact, Peirce insists that knowledge is inferential and triadic in that it always requires three elements, a sign, the object signified, and the interpretant, which may be expressed broadly for any intelligible assertion in the form "A signifies B to C," or, more narrowly, in psychoanalysis, as "A transfers B to C."

Now, a long-acknowledged problem with psychoanalytic theory—its open secret—is that it cannot provide a theoretical basis for "symbol formation," even though analysis is itself carried on exclusively by means of symbols. This failure has meant that the revolutionary discoveries that have been made in clinical practice are disconnected from the theory that is presumed to underlie them. Nevertheless, the language in which such clinical discoveries are expressed is usually the inappropriate language of orthodox psychoanalytic theory. The consequence is fundamental confusion.

Briefly, Sigmund Freud's research, typical of the nineteenth century's obsession with mechanism, was founded on the concept of biological drive, on the presumption that such a foundation would illuminate the depths of human experience by showing how bodily functions generate the energy for and goals of all mental activity. This concentration generally excluded concern with the world of objects and relations between human individuals. Later, when Freud turned to the psychology of the ego as an important part of the problem of relations among objects, he developed a theory of object relations which attempted to preserve his original drive theory by treating the role of objects as the targets of discharge and the inhibition or facilitation of drives. The mind is, thus, an epiphenomenon incapable of causing anything, perhaps even repression, a conclusion that completely vitiates the purposes of psychoanalysis.

The realization that even the most ingenious variations of strictly Freudian ego psychology cannot explain symbol formation (which is to say, effective thought) and are consequently useless in justifying "the talking cure" has led to a profusion of object relations models. In these models, drive theory is either drastically modified or rejected outright by conceptual frameworks in which relations with others are taken to constitute the fundamental elements of mental life. The great clinical significance of object relations, unexplainable by orthodox theory, is that it has been the central conceptual issue in psychoanalysis since 1919, with the early work of Melanie Klein, and became more explicit in the 1940s with the writings of H. S. Sullivan and W.R.D. Fairbairn.

Yet the idea of object relations, although it makes possible significant human intercourse, because of its often explicitly Cartesian dyadic structure represented by the patient-therapist relation and by the generally reductionist tendency of positivism, has proved unable to provide the theory of meaning—"symbol formation"—its clinical findings demand. A few independent theorists, such as Jacques Lacan, have proposed a linguistic psychoanalytic model, but these are the limited beginnings of a semiotic theory.

On the other hand, Peirce's semiotic provides a well-conceived theory of thought-signs, which provides a broad and adequate basis for and development of symbol formation. For Peirce, the universal character of a sign is its triadicity. He holds this position in opposition to the many, originating with Ferdinand de Saussure, who believe that a sign can stand in an essentially dyadic relation, called its meaning, to its object. Peirce points out that this is a fundamental misconception of the nature of a sign because it overlooks that a sign can function only as an element in a working system of signs, which is triadic in nature.

According to Peirce, the irreducibly triadic property of the sign always has three elements: sign (first term), standing for object (second term) to interpretant (third term). Nevertheless, Peirce conceded that, for the sake of analysis, he would allow a sign to be treated only in its relation to the second term, its object. Taken this way, signs are of three kinds: icons, indexes, and symbols. An icon is a sign whose particular way of signifying is by likeness; thus, an ape may serve as an icon of a human. An index signifies by means of an actual dynamic relation to its object. For example, a certain grimace indicates the presence of pain. A symbol is any artificial or conventional sign, so a rose is a symbol of love. Almost all words in a language are symbols in this sense. But neither icon, index, nor symbol actually functions as a sign until it is interpreted, unless semiosis, the action of signs, occurs. It is the fact of evolutionary kinship that makes the ape an icon of the man. Taken by itself, the similarity in appearance of the two beasts means nothing. The independent existence of the grimace and the pain are simply two brute facts, unless we add the doctor's palpating the abdominal lower right quadrant looking for the possibility of appendicitis. And as for the symbol "A rose is a rose is a rose," we may add "sometimes a cigar is just a cigar."

Peirce's idea of the interpretant requires a brief elucidation. We might think wrongly that Peirce intends the word to refer to a person or mind — an actual interpreter. This is wrong because, in the first place, there are kinds of semiosis or sign action that do not involve what we usually mean by minds, such as the communication to be found in a beehive, where one bee is able, by means of signs, to show other bees exactly where nectar is to be found. But more important, this is an incorrect assumption because, as Peirce points out, we do not recognize that a sign has been interpreted by observing a mental action but by observing another sign. To give an example, a person points (index) up at the sky and his companion looks up (interpretant) to see the object of the sign. Someone else might call out, "What do you see up there?" which is also an interpretant of the original sign. For Peirce, any appropriate response to a sign is acting as another sign of the object originally signified. A sunflower following the sun across the sky with its face is also an interpretant. Peirce uses the word *interpretant* to stand for any such development of a given sign.

Freud often gives descriptions of analysis in which he recognizes the actions of signs without naming them as such or considering the possibility of a sign system. In one case of a hysterical patient, Elizabeth Von R., he writes:

> The discovery of the reason for the first conversion opened a second, fruitful period of treatment. The patient surprised me soon afterwards by announcing that she now knew why it was that the pains [sign] always radiated from that particular area of her right thigh [object] and were their most painful there: it was in this place that her father used to rest his leg every morning, while she renewed the bandage around it, for it was badly swollen [interpretant]. This must have happened a good hundred times, yet she had not noticed the connection till now. In this way she gave me the explanation that I needed of the emergence of what was an atypical hysterogenic zone [second interpretant of the original sign]. Further, her painful legs began to "join in the conversation" [semiosis, the action of signs] during our analyses. [*S. E.* 2:148]

Here Freud is clearly aware of the semiotic character of analysis, in particular of its indexical form as symptom, but he develops this thought to further encompass the idea of what I will call *therapeutic semiosis:*

> What I have in mind is the following remarkable fact. As a rule the patient was free from pain when we started work. If, then, by a question or by pressure upon her head I called up a memory, a sensation of pain would make its first appearance, and was usually so sharp that the patient would give a start and put her hand to the painful spot. The pain that was thus aroused would persist so long as she was under the influence of the memory; it would reach a climax when she was in the act of telling me the essential and decisive part of what she had to communicate, and with the last word of this it would disappear. I came in time to see such pains as a compass to guide me; if she stopped talking but admitted that she still had a pain, I knew that she had not told me everything, and insisted on her continuing her story till the pain had been talked away. Not until then did I arouse a fresh memory. [148]

In this passage, the sign is pain, the object is memory, and the interpretant is the therapeutic dialogue between the analyst and patient leading to subsequent semiosis, ending only when the original sign becomes an interpretant and the therapy is complete.

I have only mentioned in passing Peirce's doctrine of universal categories, which underlies his theory of signs and which can be shown to provide a means toward the development of a theory of the unconscious as a system of signs and to account for the development of self-consciousness. This brief and incomplete outline will serve to introduce the man and his thought, so that the essays in this volume may be understood within a framework of connected ideas—the structure of Peirce's architectonic philosophy of inquiry and the problems associated with orthodox psychoanalytic theory.

References

I use the conventional designations to refer to Peirce's works: *CP* 1.1 means *Collected Papers,* volume one, paragraph one; MS or MSL followed by a number means the manuscript or manuscript letter as identified in Robin's *Annotated Catalogue,* cited below.

Brent, Joseph. *Charles Sanders Peirce: A Life.* Bloomington: Indiana University Press, 1993.

Descartes, René. *René Descartes: Discourse on Method, Optics, Geometry, Meteorology.* Translated by Paul J. Olscamp. Indianapolis: Bobbs-Merrill, 1965.

Fairbairn, W.R.D. *An Object Relations Theory of the Personality.* New York: Basic Books, 1954.

Freud, Sigmund. *The Standard Edition of the Complete Psychological Works of Sigmund Freud.* Edited and translated by James Strachey. 24 vols. London: Hogarth, 1953–74.

Gallie, W. B. *Peirce and Pragmatism.* Harmondsworth: Penguin Books, 1952.

Geschwind, N., and Galaburda, A. M. *Cerebral Lateralization: Biological Mechanisms, Associations and Pathology.* Cambridge: MIT Press, 1987.

Goodwin, F. K., and Jamison, K. R. *Manic-Depressive Illness.* New York: Oxford University Press, 1990.

Grattan-Guinness, Ivor. "Beyond Categories: The Lives and Works of Charles Sanders Peirce." *Annals of Science* 51 (1994): 531–38.

Jamison, Kay Redfield. *Touched with Fire: Manic-Depressive Illness and the Artistic Temperament.* New York: Free Press, 1993.

Kant, Immanuel. *The Critique of Judgment.* Translated by J. C. Meredith. Oxford: Oxford University Press, 1952.

Lacan, Jacques. *The Four Fundamental Concepts of Psycho-analysis.* New York: Norton, 1978.

Murphey, Murray. Review of *Charles Sanders Peirce: A Life,* by Joseph Brent. *Transactions of the Charles S. Peirce Society* 29 (1993): 723–28.

Peirce, Charles Sanders. *Collected Papers of Charles Sanders Peirce.* Edited by Charles Hartshorne, Paul Weiss, and Arthur W. Burks. 8 vols. Cambridge: Harvard University Press, 1931–58.

———. Draft letter to Calderoni, late 1905. In "Peirce and the Florentine Pragmatists: His letter to Calderoni and a new edition of his writings," by M. Fisch, and C. J. W. Kloesel. *Topoi* 1 (1982): 68–73.

————. Letter to Alice James, February 12, 1902. William James Collection. Houghton Library, Harvard University, Cambridge.

Robin, Richard S. *Annotated Catalogue of the Papers of Charles S. Peirce.* Amherst: University of Massachusetts Press, 1967.

Saussure, Ferdinand de. *Course in General Linguistics.* Translated by Roy Harris. La Salle, Ill.: Open Court Press, 1986.

Segal, H. *Introduction to the Works of Melanie Klein.* 2d ed. London: Hogarth Press and Institute of Psychoanalysis, 1973.

Sergeant, Mrs. John T., ed., *Sketches and Reminiscences of the Radical Club.* Boston: James Osgood, 1880.

Sullivan, H. S. *Clinical Studies in Psychiatry.* New York: W. W. Norton, 1973.

Vacherot, Etienne. *La Metaphysique et La science.* Paris, 1858.

Whately, Richard. *Elements of Logic: Comprising the Substance of the Articles in the Encyclopedia Metropolitana.* London: J. Mawman, 1926.

2 Peircean Reflections on Psychotic Discourse

James Phillips

It is common knowledge among readers of Peirce that his goal was to develop a general semiotics at a level of abstraction that went well beyond the domain of human psychology. Drawing his semiotic theory back into the territory of human behavior and speech is thus clearly moving in a direction that was not Peirce's primary concern. It is in recognition of this discordance that the current effort to apply Peircean notions to an understanding of psychotic discourse is carried out. That such an application is not where Peirce's interest lay does not in itself gainsay the possibility and potential value of the application.

This Peircean reflection on psychosis will proceed on two levels. The first will be that of Peirce's most general notions regarding the mind and the semiotic process. At this level, what may be said of Peirce might also be said of many other semioticians, with due acknowledgment that Peirce said most of it first. The treatment of semiotics and psychosis at this level will break into two sections dealing with the world and the self in psychosis. At a further level we then enter into the specifics of Peirce's semiotic theory, particularly his notion of the sign as a triadic entity. At this level our discussion will move from general semiotic principles to uniquely Peircean semiotics. Finally, we will end with some suggestions concerning a Peircean contribution to developmental issues in psychosis.

Three further introductory remarks need to be made. First, this chapter is in no way intended to present a comprehensive theory or understanding of schizophrenia and the other psychotic disorders. It is intended rather to suggest what Peircean semiotics might offer for such theory or understanding. Second (and related to the first remark), with the exception of some suggestions regarding psychological development in the final section, the chapter avoids issues of etiology and remains closer to the *form* of psychotic process. The semiotic distortions found in psychosis may indeed be present regardless of the etiology of the particular condition. Third and finally, this chapter ignores the differentiation of the various psychotic conditions. I attempt to look at the semiotic dimensions of psychotic thinking in general, not, for instance, of schizophrenic thinking versus manic psychotic thinking. Indeed, current research points to the nonspecificity of the thought disorders of the various psychotic conditions (Harrow and Quinlan 1985).

Sign and Psychosis

As just indicated, a first level of reflection addresses Peirce's most general statements regarding semiosis and the human subject. In a gnomic utterance (for Short, "a dark saying . . . much beloved by semioticists [that] still passes [his] own understanding" [1992, 124]), Peirce declares that *man is a sign.*

> It is sufficient to say that there is no element whatever of man's consciousness which has not something corresponding to it in the word; and the reason is obvious. It is that the word or sign which man uses *is* the man himself. For, as the fact that every thought is a sign, taken in conjunction with the fact that life is a train of thought, proves that man is a sign; so, that every thought is an *external sign*, proves that man is an external sign. That is to say, the man and the *external sign* are identical, in the same *sense* in which the words *homo* and *man* are identical. Thus my language is the sum total of myself; for the man is the thought. [1868b, 854]

At this level we are not yet considering Peirce's distinctive analysis of the sign as a triadic entity but rather his more global assimilation or identification of mind and semiotic process. The major implication of this identification is that our access to things (and to ourselves) is *by way of* signs and that we ourselves *are* this semiotic process. With this assertion Peirce anticipates and joins company with those of our contemporaries who have also emphasized that there is no "thought" or "mind" behind the articulated thoughts.

What is immediately striking about Peirce's pronouncement that man is a sign is that this is not at all obvious. Indeed, the opposite would seem to be the case. Common sense would declare that we are in immediate contact with things and do not require the mediation of signs. The ordinary condition of signs is thus *transparency.* As we see *through* signs to the world, we do not take note of the signs. Paul Ricoeur reminds us of this transparency of signs: "If, with the ancients and again with the Port-

Royal grammarians, the sign is defined as a thing that represents some other thing, then transparency consists in the fact that the sign, in order to represent, tends to fade away and so to be forgotten as a thing" (1992, 41). The same phenomenon is evoked by Maurice Merleau-Ponty in describing the communicative capacity of language: "When someone—an author or a friend—succeeds in expressing himself, the signs are immediately forgotten; all that remains is the meaning. The perfection of language lies in its capacity to pass unnoticed. *But therein lies the virtue of language:* it is language which propels us toward the things it signifies. In the way it works, language hides itself from us. Its triumph is to efface itself and to take us beyond the words to the author's very thoughts, so that we imagine we are engaged with him in a wordless meeting of minds" (1973, 10).

If the usual fate of signs is to be transparent, to go unnoticed, where does this stop? What are the circumstances in which signs assert their presence? For Peirce they assert their presence when we reflect on the process of thought. As he says in "Questions Concerning Certain Faculties Claimed for Man": "If we seek the light of external facts, the only cases of thought which we can find are of thought in signs. Plainly, no other thought can be evidenced by external facts. But we have seen that only by external facts can thought be known at all. The only thought, then, which can possibly be cognized is thought in signs. But thought which cannot be cognized does not exist. All thought, therefore, must necessarily be in signs" (1868a, 24). Others have focused on the varied circumstances in which the sign quality of thought stands out. Ricoeur continues the statement just quoted: "This obliteration of the sign as a thing is never complete, however. There are circumstances in which the sign does not succeed in making itself absent as a thing; by becoming opaque, it attests once more to the fact of being a thing and reveals its eminently paradoxical structure of an entity at once present and absent" (Ricoeur 1992, 41). As examples of the opaqueness of the sign, Ricoeur highlights speech acts in which the fact of utterance is reflected in the sense of the statement. Thus, when the statement, "the cat is on the mat" is replaced by "I affirm that the cat is on the mat," the sign-making "I" of the second version obtrudes itself on the transparency of the first.

For his part, Merleau-Ponty finds the opaqueness of the sign exposed in poetic language (and even more in painting), with its curious admixture of transparency, mediation, and opacity (1973, 9–46). In the same vein, Jakobson emphasizes that poetry as such foregoes direct referentiality in the service of lingering over the word-signs that comprise the poem (quoted in Ricoeur 1978, 150). And, as is well known, in a movement that extends from Mallarmé to Derrida, the independence of the text from even a necessary *indirect* referentiality has resulted in an acute focus on the sign status of the text. In Steiner's words, "This move is first declared in Mallarmé's disjunction of language from external reference and in Rimbaud's deconstruction of the first person singular. These two proceedings, and all that they entail, splinter the foundations of the Hebraic-Hellenic-Cartesian edifice in which the *ratio* and psychology of the Western communicative tradition had lodged" (1989, 94-95). Finally, in certain poets we find a direct thematizing of the process of poetizing—the use of signs to muse over the use of signs. Thus, for instance, in "The Man with the Blue Guitar," Wallace Stevens writes, "They said, 'You have a blue guitar, / You do not play things as they are.' / The man replied, 'Things as they are/Are changed upon the blue guitar.' / And they said then, 'But play, you must, / A tune beyond us, yet ourselves, / A tune upon the blue guitar / Of things exactly as they are'" (1959, 73-74). And T. S. Eliot in "Four Quartets" writes, "Trying to learn to use words, and every attempt / Is a wholly new start, and a different kind of failure / Because one has only learnt to get the better of words / For the thing one no longer has to say, or the way in which / One is no longer disposed to say it. And so each venture / Is a new beginning, a raid on the inarticulate / With shabby equipment always deteriorating / In the general mess of imprecision of feeling, / Undisciplined squads of emotion" (1962, 128).

These are all circumstances in which signs call attention to themselves in a productive, reflective manner. And this list of circumstances is hardly complete. Others could be mentioned, but it is time to lead the discussion in another direction, that in which the consciousness of signs betokens a crack in the normal semiotic process. Here we begin to speak of a breakdown of the everyday transparency of signs. For the schizophrenic who becomes acutely aware of his or her own words or gestures *as words or gestures,* they suddenly reveal their nature as signs—or semiotic *things.* If, according to Peirce, it is the case that "we are in thought, and not that thoughts are in us" (1868b, 42), the schizophrenic is often not only *in* them, but *engulfed by* them. If the remarkable fact about semiosis is that thoughts as external signs are things and yet transport us beyond themselves, for the schizophrenic this transport often breaks down, and the patient is confronted with word-things that do not assume their usual function. The patient becomes stuck in them. They no longer transport him or her to the object or the other person. Schizophrenic ambivalence, for instance, which Bleuler attributes to loosening of associations and the attribution of both positive and negative feelings to every situation, may also be understood as a paralysis in the normal semiotic process ([1911] 1950, 53-55). Asked to sit on the chair, the patient puzzles, "Chair, what is a chair?" Invited to eat, he pauses over and studies the fork, whose meaning as an implement has ceased to be transparent for him, and he gets caught up in the word-things—fork, food.

For the psychotic, these are not detached reflections or musings on the semiotic understructure of human reality. They are terrifying experiences in which that very structure is breaking down. Certainly the acute anxiety that accompanies psychotic experience is at least in part explained by this collapse of the basic semiotic structuring of human experience. What Freud described as the end-of-the-world experience in psychosis and attributed to a libidinal decathexis of the world (*S.E.* 12:69–71) may thus be reinterpreted from a semiotic perspective. The familiar semiotically structured world is indeed disintegrating.

With the loss of sign transparency in psychosis, the normal semiotic structure of sign, object, and interpretant may be deeply altered. As already suggested, thoughts as sign-things bear a dimension of externality and are not the pure internal presences they are often imagined to be. Peirce emphasized this in the above-cited statement in declaring that man is an *external* sign (1868b, 854). In psychosis, with the disappearance of normal sign transparency, this externality is taken to its furthest extreme, and the thought-signs are materialized into entities of the external world: voices of others, commands from on high, influencing machines, recording machines in the brain, material objects that convey hidden meanings.

It is at this point that the semiotic account confronts the psychoanalytic understanding of psychosis—that is, as loss of ego boundaries in the earlier writers (e.g., Federn 1953; Freeman, Cameron, and McGhie 1958) and as a fusion of self and object representations in later ones (e.g., Kernberg 1975). The psychoanalytic understanding is based on a separation of the internal and the external—self and object, self-representation and object representation—and the blurring of these. The significant reinterpretation that semiotic theory brings to this account is the externality of the sign. If thought already possesses a dimension of externality, it is a shorter step toward full externalization of the thought. The vulnerability of any subject to psychosis is thus exposed.

Among psychoanalysts the externality of the sign has been most clearly recognized by Lacan, who, with his category of the symbolic order, has been particularly sensitive to the semiotic dimension. Working out of a framework that is both Lacanian and Peircean, Muller has explained the breakdown of normal language use in schizophrenia as a failure to use language in its mediating role between the subject and the unarticulated, unsymbolized world—what Lacan terms the Real.

> Now what if language does not function as such a recourse against the Real? What if the Real is experienced without the mediation of language?

> What if words themselves lose their referential context and are experienced as *in* the Real? To say that words are in the Real is to say that words have become like things: whether they come from the therapist or the titles of books or the "internal tape recorder," they can strike the patient's ears, eyes, forehead, chest, like objects. They do not mediate and refer to objects. [1996, 97]

With his understanding of the symbolic order as above, over against, or external to the subject, Lacan offers a unique way of envisioning the externality of the sign. It is thus not surprising that, as Muller explicates, the Lacanian analysis of psychosis emphasizes the thinglike quality of psychotic language.

One patient offers a vivid illustration of the confusion that may occur in connection with the externality of the sign. On the one hand, he is acutely aware of all his mental experiences—thoughts, feelings, sensations, impulses, inclinations—and treats these as external sign-phenomena that have been placed "in" him for some reason. On the other hand, he invests indifferent external communications such as the radio or television with increased and distorted semiotic significance. The internal is thus treated as external and the external as internal. In focusing in this way on this man's profoundly confused use of signs, we are giving a semiotic account of what in general psychiatry would be called thought insertion and ideas of reference.

Another patient illustrates the way in which the externalization of the thought-sign leads to a deeply altered experience in which the world of indifferent things becomes an inexhaustible reservoir of gesture and meaning. A young man with a bipolar disorder would intermittently slip into psychotic thinking in which things everywhere would take on significance. There was not a coherent theme that could be elicited from the abundance of "meanings" and "signs" he would describe. What was paramount was simply that there were signs everywhere. What is suggested in the experiences of such patients is that terror from the collapse of semiotic structure is such that the restitution must involve an overinvestment of the world with meaning.

In this discussion of the severe distortions of normal semiotic processes found in chronic psychoses, one point must be kept in mind. While the usual transparency of signs is abolished in these conditions, this does not generally represent a real self-consciousness of signs on the part of the patient. It is the observer who is made aware of the opacity and externality of signs in the patient's speech through the latter's odd use of them. This is of course a way of distinguishing the poet from the psychotic. In both, signs assert their presence and opacity, but it is the for-

mer who is in control of this process. That said, we may also acknowledge that the statement is an oversimplification of a more nuanced situation. First, there are the psychotics who *are* aware of their semiotic
transformations; then there are those few, for example, Nerval, who simply cover both categories of poet and psychotic.

In this regard it should be acknowledged that in his recently published
Madness and Modernism, Louis Sass has strongly opposed any poet-
versus-schizophrenic polarity of the sort I suggest in this chapter. In what
he calls "autonomization," Sass describes a feature of schizophrenic language that is similar to what is being presented here: "A second characteristic of schizophrenic language involves tendencies for language to
lose its transparent and subordinate status, to shed its function as a communicative tool and to emerge instead as an independent focus of attention or autonomous source of control over speech and understanding"
(1992, 178). Sass does *not,* however, see this autonomization of language
in schizophrenia as *qualitatively* different from what he calls the "apoth-
eosis of the word" in figures like Mallarmé, Barthes, and Derrida. Although there are clearly similarities and overlaps between schizophrenic
and deconstructionist uses of language, and although, as indicated above,
a stark contrast between the two is certainly oversimplified, I would in
the end argue that Sass's argument for a lack of qualitative difference does
not do justice to the disturbed, uncontrolled, and anguished quality of
schizophrenic language and existence.

Signs of the Self

Thus far we have concentrated on the semiotic restructuring (or "de-
structuring") of the *world* in psychosis. Peirce's semiotic description of
the mind was pursued in its implications for how the world is encountered in health and psychosis. The emphasis was on the heightened opacity and externality of the sign in the psychotic's encounter with the
world. We must now shift our focus from the world to the subject itself.
The declaration that a person is a sign was above taken to mean that the
subject is in contact with a coherent world only by way of signs. But this
declaration has a second meaning, namely that the subject relates to *him
or herself* through signs. This is of course the strongly anti-Cartesian bias
of Peircean semiotics. There is no direct intuition or vision of the self.
While in this section we will again witness the problems inherent in the
opacity and externality of signs—now of the self—the emphasis will fall
on the disorder that may follow from the sheer complexity of the range
and structure of signs that define a self.

The loss of Cartesian intuition (and with it the loss of the self as substance in the traditional sense) has become a familiar theme in contemporary thought and has had varying consequences. At the opposite pole from the Cartesian self, in a movement inaugurated by Nietzsche, the loss of the intuited, substantial self has united thinkers from fields as diverse as analytic philosophy, cognitive science, and Buddhism in the conclusion that there is no self. Others, rejecting both the intuited, substantial self of Descartes and the opposite stance of an absence of self, have taken a middle ground, arguing for a self that is real albeit not a substance, a self that can be known not directly but through its effects—and its *signs*. It is in this company that we will locate Peirce. If his contemporary Nietzsche announced the death of the Cartesian substantial self, it was Peirce who proclaimed the birth of a self that could be known indirectly—the semiotic self.

What is this self that is known through its effects and its signs? This is the self of gender, proper name, age and stage of life, profession, avocation, religion—and further, of relationships, marital status, children, and so forth. If I attempt to know myself through pure introspection, the yield is negligible. But if I take the indirect route and approach myself through the series of signs just mentioned, the yield is considerable. I am male, married, middle aged, a psychiatrist, and so forth. To the argument that none of these signs defines the "real" me, there is only one response: With the loss of belief in substance and intuition, we will accept this modest self of indirection, this self of signs.

In addition to the list of categories that mark a typical life, there are two particular classes of verbal signs that signify an identity. The first is that of the personal pronouns. The individual must be able to indicate him or herself as "I," and as Benveniste has spelled out, the use of "I" implies both a "you" and the implicit awareness that the "you" is also an "I" for whom I am a "you." In his words, "The consciousness of oneself is possible only if it is experienced by contrast. I only employ *I* in addressing someone else, who will be in my allocution a *you*. It is this condition of dialogue that is constitutive of the *person*, for it implies a reciprocity in which I become *you* in the allocution of the other who in his turn designates himself by *I*" (1966, 260). Benveniste also points out that the use of personal pronouns is always accompanied by deictic indicators that locate the speaker in space and time (253). As in the above analysis, these personal pronouns, as well the deictic indicators surrounding them, enjoy a large degree of transparency. We are generally not conscious of the sign quality of "I," "you," "here," "now," and so forth.

The second class of self-signifying signs consists of those terms that indicate the material-psychic balance of the human person, the sense of the person as matter and spirit, or body and mind, or as an embodied con-

sciousness. With this class we see a predominance of metaphorical locutions. Since we do not have an adequate language of soul or mind—of
our inner states—we borrow categories of the world and of our bodies
to express the psychological side of our existence. For instance, Lakoff
and Johnson, in a work that develops this use of metaphor in great detail,
describe the use of orientation (e.g., "I'm feeling *up*") and entity (e.g.,
"My mind isn't *operating* today") metaphors—that is, aspects of the material world—to describe states of the mental or psychic world (1980,
14, 27).

To complete this picture of a self known indirectly through its signs,
we must add a final dimension to the categories of signs as just described:
that of the narrative self, the self as evolved over a lifetime, with a past,
present, and future. Narrativity brings to the self the dimensions of tem-
porality and memory, and the integration of these into the more-or-less
coherent story of a single destiny. Each of the categories finds its place in
the life narrative: the child grows into the adult, chooses and develops in
a particular profession, forms relationships and a family, and so forth.

Human identity as narrational is a process, ultimately a reflective
process. At a first level life is simply lived in habit and routine. Yet even
here the unexamined life has, in Ricoeur's terms, a prenarrative or pre-
figured quality (1984). A story is being lived, if not yet told. At a further,
more reflective level, the story embodied in the life is told. The implicit
narrative becomes an explicit narrative. Of course the actual process is
far more complicated. The balance of the lived and the told is always
changing. The average life may have many narratives, and the narrative
of one's own life intermingles with that of the narratives of others. One
is thus a character in one's own narratives as well as in those of others.
In Kerby's words:

> Self-narration, I have argued, is what first raises our temporal existence out
> of the closets of memorial traces and routine and unthematic activity, con-
> stituting thereby a self as its implied subject. This self is, then, the implied
> subject of a narrated history. Stated another way, in order to be we must be
> *as* something or someone, and this someone that we take ourselves to be
> is the character delineated in our personal narratives. The unity of the self,
> where such unity exists, is exhibited as an identity in difference, which is
> all a temporal character can be. [1991, 109]

It should be added, finally, that metaphor is again deeply involved in
the structuring of a narrated life. Such notions as story, character, and narrative are, after all, borrowed from literary genres. And locutions such as
the "passage" or "flow" of life are based on such implicit metaphors as
"life as a river." Ultimately, given the polysemy of signs, most signs of the

self are metaphorical, and we never really transcend this level. Such is the consequence of knowing the self through the indirection of signs.

In view of the complexity of personal identity as a self-narrated network of signs, it is not hard to imagine the difficulties of someone in the course of a psychosis. Since there never was a clear, introspected "I," we cannot technically speak of the loss of this "I" in psychosis. What we look for, rather, is a collapse of the network of signs through which the self is constituted. We regularly see problems with the use of the personal pronouns, as with those patients who use third person locutions to avoid the use of "I" in speaking about themselves. Here the externality of the "I" as sign is transformed into the use of "he" to refer to the self. In this regard, Peirce's remarks about the child's learning to name him- or herself by being named by the parents (Peirce 1868a, 18–21) (and the child's well-known tendency to refer to him or herself in the third person) are apposite. If the child's first experience with the personal pronoun is a self-label learned from another, the externality of the "I" sign is highlighted from the beginning of speaking life. Muller describes a psychotic patient who avoids the use of personal pronouns and other deictic references (1996, 108), and Sass elaborates on this abandonment of deictic indicators in schizophrenia (1992, 177).

The need to use metaphoric expressions to express the psyche-body duality leads to distortions in both directions. A patient in the midst of an acute psychosis and struggling with the material and biological dimensions of his identity said over and over again that he was nothing but a hollow tube in which food entered at one end and shit exited at the other. Not able to tolerate his condition as an embodied, biological organism, he exaggerated this into his entire identity. A contrasting resolution for the same conflict was offered by a psychotically depressed man who insisted that he had no body.

The categories that serve to mark and anchor one's identity into a narrative unity are often employed in a distorted and disorganized manner. A chronically schizophrenic man whom I have known for years has a set of categories with which he attempts to demarcate himself: good student in high school, marine, construction worker, husband, father, unable to work for many years, schizophrenic. These are, however, never ordered in a meaningful way with expectable priorities, hierarchies, and temporal layerings, nor are they narrated into an integrated life. For instance, categories that have not been relevant for decades (e.g., marine, construction worker) are placed alongside contemporary categories, with little sense of current relevance and the temporal passage from one to the other. This man also demonstrates the way in which many patients use the category of "mental patient" or "schizophrenic" as an identity tag that sums up all that is wrong with them in a way that cannot be further articulated.

Finally, the routine use of metaphors to describe aspects of the self offers endless opportunities for confused, psychotic thinking and speech. To take a simple example, Lakoff and Johnson offer the following specimens of "the mind is a machine" metaphor: "My mind just isn't *operating* today"; "Boy, the *wheels are turning* now"; I'm *a little rusty* today"; "We've been working on this problem all day and now we're *running out of steam*" (1980, 27). With each of these statements, taking the expression literally rather than figuratively will lead to the most bizarre notions about one's own mind. Metaphor always operates through a dialectic of similarity and dissimilarity. Thus, each of the above statements has the general form of "my mind is *like* a machine." If the "like" is removed, the result is literal, concrete, metaphoric, and possibly psychotic.

The Triadic Sign and Psychosis

The above discussion has focused on the implications of general principles of Peircean semiotics for an understanding of psychotic thinking and speech. It is now time to concentrate on Peirce's unique triadic conception of the sign to see what further light it sheds on psychotic thought. The line of thought developed in this section is not intended to replace or supersede but rather to extend that developed above. In the varied definitions of the sign he offered over several decades, Peirce always included the triad of sign, object, and interpretant. In Houser's summary:

> In its most abbreviated form, Peirce's theory of signs goes something like this. A sign is anything which stands *for* something *to* something. What the sign stands *for* is its object, what it stands *to* is the interpretant. The sign relation is *fundamentally* triadic: eliminate either the object or the interpretant and you annihilate the sign. This was the key insight of Peirce's semiotic, and one that distinguishes it from most theories of representation that attempt to make sense of signs (representations) that are related only to objects. [1992, xxxvi]

The triadic nature of the sign may be illustrated with one of Peirce's own examples, a thermometer (quoted in Deely 1990, 24). As a physical thing in the natural world, the thermometer's column of mercury is caused to rise by an increase in the ambient temperature. As such, the thermometer is a thing among things and a part of the natural causal order. It is not yet a sign. What transforms this thermometer-thing into a sign is that it "stands *for* something *to* something." It stands *for* its *object,* the ambient temperature, *to* its *interpretant,* the person recognizing the thermometer as a thermometer. One reason for Peirce's neologism, "interpretant," as opposed to "interpreter," is to focus on the fact that the interpretant is more precisely not the "interpreting" person but rather the *thought* generated in the mind of the "interpreting" person or consciousness. The interpretant of the thermometer-sign is thus the idea of such and such ambient temperature in the mind of the observer. The sign is said to mediate between object—the ambient temperature—and interpretant—the *idea* of the ambient temperature. In this example, then, by means of the thermometer-sign, the observer can form an idea of the ambient temperature.

The most commonsense understanding of the Peircean sign is that of the sign as word or gesture, not a thing as in the example of the thermometer. As word or gesture the sign structure is that of one person signifying something about the world to another person. The sign is the statement or gesture of the first person, the object is that about which this person is speaking or signifying, and the interpretant is the second person (or second person's thought) to whom the first person is communicating. The triadic structure in this case would involve one person signifying something to another person about something. In a much-quoted letter of 1908, Peirce described the sign structure in this manner: "I define a Sign as anything which is so determined by something else, called its Object, and so determines an effect upon a person, which I call its Interpretant, that the latter is thereby mediately determined by the former" (1977, 80–81).

Peirce was vigorous in his insistence, however, that the sign need not involve separate individuals in this way. Specifically, the interpretant need not be another person or mind. The above quote is immediately followed by the sentence: "My insertion of 'upon a person' is a sop to Cerberus, because I despair of making my own broader conception understood" (ibid.). Thus, the interpretant may be the thought of another person, but may as well be simply the further thought of the first person. In any process of thought, for example, in any soliloquy, the succeeding thought is the interpretant of the preceding thought. That is, each thought interprets the thought that has preceded it. A particular thought is then both the *interpretant* of the thought that precedes it and the *object* of the interpretant thought that succeeds it.

This generalization of the sign relationship to a process that can take place in one mind and need not involve the participation of two minds, although clearly an abstraction from the more straightforward, two-person notion of semiotic process, is still not the level of generalization that Peirce wished to reach for the sign. In his most abstract, most general understanding of the sign, it need not involve any mind at all. As he wrote in 1902, "If the logician is to talk of the operations of the mind at all . . . he must mean by 'mind' something quite different from the object of study of the psychologist. . . . Logic will here be defined as *formal semiotic*. A definition of a sign will be given which no more refers to human thought than does the definition of a line as the place which a particle occupies, part by part, during a lapse of time" (quoted in Fisch 1986, 343).

As this statement indicates, Peirce was interested in an understanding of logic and semiotics that was wholly independent of psychology. For our purposes, however, we will have to draw him back to psychology—specifically to such questions as to how semiotic processes develop and how they actually work in human beings. For these questions the final abstraction is of limited use, while the less abstract levels of sign process—involving either one or two persons (or minds)—will prove to be of great use. Although for Peirce "the interpretant is deliberately *not* described as being necessarily an idea in the mind of someone" (Colapietro 1989, 7), our focus, remaining as we will at a more psychological level, will be on the interpretant as an idea in the mind of someone.

If we try to imagine actual sign use in ordinary circumstances, we must envisage a complex and changing situation in which the subject may occupy any (or all) of the positions of the sign triad at any particular moment. The subject may thus be the sign, the object (to him or herself or another), or the interpretant (of his or her own thought or that of another). In an encounter between two people, each speaker's utterance will be the sign referring about something, the object, to the other person, the interpretant. But the speaker will at the same time also be the interpretant and object of his or her own ongoing speech, and as well the object in another sense if referring to him- or herself. The situation then quickly reverses as the other begins to speak. And as the dialogue continues and begins to take the form of a single thought process with two voices—a notion with which Peirce was highly sympathetic, referring to us as "mere cells of a social organism" (quoted in Colapietro 1989, 65)—we may say that it becomes a kind of soliloquy. In that event the sign and the interpretant (and at times the object) are at all times both of the speakers. But then recalling that for Peirce, in agreement with Plato, "all thought is dialogue" (quoted in Colapietro 1989, xiv), we conclude that the distinctions between soliloquy and dialogue—between a one-person and a two-person thought process—blur. A dialogue is always a soliloquy and a soliloquy is always a dialogue. In each case the same triadic sign process obtains.

Peirce elaborated his analysis of signs by classifying them into three trichotomies (and then later into a tenfold classification). For our purposes we need only focus on one of the first trichotomies, that of the relation of sign to object, and within that division only the distinction between index and symbol. The indexical sign has an actual connection with its object. As Peirce puts it, "An *Index* is a sign which refers to the Object that it denotes by virtue of being really affected by that Object" (1897, 102). Examples are a footprint in the sand or a rap on the door. In contrast, the symbolic sign has an arbitrary, conventional relation to its object. Again in Peirce's words, "A *Symbol* is a sign which refers to the Object that it denotes by virtue of a law, usually an association of general ideas, which operates to cause the Symbol to be interpreted as referring to that Object" (ibid.). The immediate examples are words, which, except for occasional onomatopoeic qualities, are associated with their referents in a wholly arbitrary, conventional manner.

Appreciating, then, the complexity of the semiotic processes in the most ordinary speech or thought, it is not hard to imagine the range of distortions these processes may undergo in psychosis. In what follows I will first describe some examples of these distortions and then suggest the developmental processes and disturbances that may be related to them.

Let us begin with the patient described above who carefully examines his mental experiences and often overinterprets and misinterprets them. For instance, he experiences a sexual sensation when in the presence of a woman at work. In Peircean terms this sensation is an index of the patient's arousal and of the woman as the object of his desire. Further, we would say that the interpretant of the sign is the further thought that follows the patient's sudden urge, such as a thought that he might like to go out with the woman (or whatever thought occurs in the woman, if he indicates his desire to her). However, things are not so simple for this patient. As soon as he experiences the sensation he quickly concludes (1) that the woman has provoked the feeling, and (2) that she was ordained to do this so that he will have sexual experiences. The sensation has now shifted from an indexical to a symbolic plane. The patient is not simply affected by the object, the woman, which would make his feeling an index. There is an intention from an outside force that is being communicated to him. His feeling thus has the power of a symbolic communication, although not with the full clarity of spoken language. Furthermore, the positions of sign, object, and interpretant become increasingly complex and confused. Since he also assumes that the woman has had desire toward him placed in her, they are each both object and interpretant: objects both for each other and of the outside force, and interpretants of the other's desire as well as of the outside intention.

Another patient asks me to uncross my legs after I have crossed them in the middle of a session. Asked to explain her request, she informs me that she takes the crossing of my legs to be a sexual pass toward her. This woman has taken a rather simple, low-level sign—the leg-crossing as an index drawing attention to me (and possibly of my discomfort or restlessness)—and treated it as a gesture of my desire toward her. Again, there is a shift from index to symbol. The leg-crossing has taken on elaborate symbolic significance. Moreover, she has completely altered the relationships of sign, object, and interpretant. The object—what is represented by the leg-crossing—is no longer my discomfort but is now herself, the object of my desire and gesture. And the interpretant has become herself as the interpreting agent with all the reactions evoked or provoked by my putative advance.

Finally, let me suggest a more complex example, that of the paranoid patient. How may he be analyzed from a semiotic perspective? To begin, he is someone who identifies himself as the *object* of the signifying and interpreting activities of others. They talk and plan *about* him. Sometimes they signify (so he thinks) *to* him. It then becomes his task to *interpret* their communications (about him or to him). He does not really talk to or with anyone; he is unable to assume the position of the signifying agent that would be required for this. Even in an apparent conversation, he is busy placing himself as object and interpreting the hidden meanings of his interlocutor. There is certainly a jumble of sign classes in his distorted thinking. As in the above examples, simple indexes are taken for symbolic communications. The striking effect of these shifts is the way in which he becomes the object and interpretant of signs that in fact have nothing to do with him. Caught in these distorted and exaggerated poles of the sign triad as the object and the interpretant, and never the signifying agent, he loses the freedom that goes with that position.

What emerges from these examples is the generalization that, in psychotic thinking, the specification of the precise Peircean sign category is less important than the recognition that in all cases there is an overinterpretation of simple indexes into symbols. Events in the world that do nothing but call attention to themselves (e.g., a spontaneous cry) or provide information about the object in question (e.g., a weathercock) are taken to mean more than they are. This corrupted meaning always implies some other agency generating the meaning, however anonymous that agency remains; and with that implicit agency there is an improper shuffling of the positions of sign, object, and interpretant. In this psychotic process a rustling of the trees does not remain a simple index of wind and current weather conditions. It carries the symbolic weight of hidden presence and communication, and the psychotic subject is not a neutral observer of the wind but rather the intended object and interpreter of whatever message is carried by the gesturing leaves.

Sebeok has called attention to the importance of indexicality in Peirce's conception of the sign:

> Peirce contended that *no* matter of fact can be stated without the use of some sign serving as an index, the reason for this being the inclusion of *designators* as one of the main classes of indexes. He regarded designations as "absolutely indispensable both to communication and to thought. No assertion has any meaning unless there is some designation to show whether the universe of reality or what universe of fiction is referred to." Deictics of various sorts, including tenses, constitute perhaps the most clear-cut examples of designations. Peirce identified universal and existential quantifiers with selective pronouns, which he classified with designations as well. [1995, 224]

Indexes are deictic indicators that anchor the speaker in the world, the world of this particular here and now and the world of this particular intersubjective situation. The psychotic may simply abandon the use of deictic references (as with Muller's patient, whose speech contained no first-person references [1996, 108]) or, as emphasized in the above examples, confuse index with symbol. The consequence of this confusion is that, in the terminology of Peirce just cited by Sebeok, the psychotic does not offer adequate "designation to show whether the universe of reality or what universe of fiction is referred to." But this is not for lack of designating indexes; it is rather that the psychotic, in confusing index and symbol, has thoroughly confounded the universes of reality and fantasy.

Developmental Considerations

I would like to conclude with some suggestions, obviously quite speculative, concerning developmental processes that might be associated with the psychotic distortions of normal semiotic processes. In this discussion I will pass over the issue of the enormously complex relationship of constitution and development. I will likewise leave undiscussed but will assume what is generally known and accepted about cognitive and psychological development. It is common knowledge that the highly complex semiotic processes that Peirce has illuminated and that are part of ordinary adult thought and speech must be learned by children in the company of correctly thinking and speaking adults. The child development literature is replete with examples of the child's efforts to get its semiosis right. Indeed, Peirce himself offers perspicuous remarks about the way in which the child learns to recognize him- or herself *through* the comments made by adults *about* him or her. The child's sense of self is a product of their testimony: "A child hears it said that the stove is hot.

But it is not, he says; and indeed, that central body is not touching it, and only what that touches is hot or cold. But he touches it, and finds the testimony confirmed in a striking way. Thus, he becomes aware of ignorance, and it is necessary to suppose a *self* in which this ignorance can inhere. So testimony gives the first dawning of self-consciousness" (1868a, 20).

The seminal work in developmental semiotics has been carried out recently by Muller in *Beyond the Psychoanalytic Dyad* (1996). Muller reviews the infant developmental literature extensively and demonstrates that the dyadic relationship of mother and infant is framed and held by the cultural system of signs to which they belong. This system is assimilated by Muller both to Peirce's category of Third as well as to Lacan's symbolic order. Muller shows further that it is the presence of this Third that prevents the mother-infant dyad from sliding into merger and fusion.

> The Third is required to frame the dyad and thereby enable the partners to relate without merging. . . . The complexity of intersubjectivity . . . can best be understood when the dyadic processes of empathy and recognition are taken as operating in a triadic context in which a semiotic code frames and holds the dyad. It is the determining presence of such a code, shaping culture, communication, and context, that makes possible the saying of "I" and "you" whereby the human horizon is opened to the reach of intimacy, both personal and perhaps also transcendent. [1996, 61-62]

I focus on another aspect of development that depends on a different aspect of Third. While in his most general descriptions of the categories Peirce connected Third to mediation and generality, he also applied the categories to specific domains such as that of the sign. On the one hand, the sign plays the mediating role that is associated with Third. In Greenlee's words, "What the sign succeeds in mediating is the object-interpretant relation; for either actually or potentially the sign renders the object available to the interpreter (in whatever way available, whether for thinking, saying, acting, making, etc.)" (1973, 33-34). In this vein Peirce wrote, "In its genuine form, Third is the triadic relation existing between a sign, its object, and its interpreting thought, itself a sign, considered as constituting the mode of being of a sign. A sign mediates between the *interpretant* sign and its object" (1966, 389).

On the other hand, Peirce also brought all the categories to bear on the sign relationship: "A *Sign,* or *Representamen,* is a First which stands in such a genuine triadic relation to a Second, called its *Object,* as to be capable of determining a Third, called its *Interpretant*" (quoted in Anderson 1995, 46). In what follows I will emphasize the actual embodiment of Third in a real person in early development. While this may seem a departure from Muller's understanding of the Third as the symbolic order, there is in fact no real departure, given Lacan's instantiation of the symbolic order in the figure of the father.

Now what might be a Peircean reading of the early development of the triadic sign and its relation to psychosis? Let us begin by recalling that Peirce's unique contribution to semiotics is his insistence on the triadic nature of the sign. "The sign relation is *fundamentally* triadic: eliminate either the object or the interpretant and you annihilate the sign. This was the key insight of Peirce's semiotic, and one that distinguishes it from most theories of representation that attempt to make sense of signs (representations) that are related only to objects" (Houser 1992, xxxvi). The developmental question that inserts itself into this discussion is how the triadic nature of the sign is learned. The suggestion I wish to propose is that in early development—in *learning* semiosis—actual individuals may be important in a way that they are not in adult semiotic process. As was described above, an adult soliloquy is a triadic semiotic process in which sign, object, and interpretant are all present in the single train of thought. (And also, as was described above, because the three components are all present, the soliloquy has qualities of a dialogue.)

The infant, however, does not begin in soliloquy; it begins in communicational interchange with its mother or care giver. What will later be the ability to have a "conversation" with itself must start with a "conversation" with its mother. It is as this conversation is internalized that the internal dialogue can take place. Now, since a dialogue must always involve the three components of the sign—in the straightforward case, one person talking to another about something—might it not be the case that not two but three real people (or more) are necessary to inculcate semiosis at the beginning of life? In other words, at the beginning, each component of the semiotic triad would be embodied in an actual person. Semiotically, the father would represent the critical third in the dialogue of mother and infant. Given Peirce's identification of the interpretant as the third in the sign triad, the paradigmatic case would place the father as the *interpretant* of the mother-infant dialogue. In fact, however, the developing conversation with the infant would entail the usual alternation of roles as each of the three assumed the role of signifying agent, object, or interpretant. Indeed, a critical aspect of the evolution of the mother-infant dyad would be the ability of the mother and father to treat the infant as the object of *their* dialogue, in which case the child would experience itself as *object* of a semiotic process, as well as *interpretant* of the parental dialogue.

Whatever the apportionment of roles at a particular moment, the important point is the need for actual persons representing the three positions in the inculcation of semiosis. This would be the Peircean reading of early development and the tendency for a pathologically exclusive mother-infant relationship to promote psychosis. Adult object relationships require semiotic competence, and the development of semiotic competence depends on early object relationships. If actual people are necessary for early training in the semiotic triad, and a pathologically exclusive mother-infant relationship prevents the entrance of a third into relationship, the result will be a failure to inculcate the mastery of normal semiosis. (It should be noted, finally, that in this discussion I am not insisting on the literal presence of the child's father but rather on the presence of another or others—or even of the father or another as a symbolic presence.)

Among the many possible failure scenarios—or aspects of what is really one failure scenario—in early semiotic development, let me mention three. The first would be that in which the mother's interactions with the infant did not permit the presence of the father (literally or symbolically). In this case, with the father absent both as semiotic object as well as interpreter/interpretant of the mother-infant dialogue, the language would remain highly subjective, and the semiotic object would not achieve independence of subjective meaning. Conversation would never be about something truly exterior to the conversants. The second scenario would be the one in which the parents could not make the infant an object of *their* conversation. In this case the mother would not be sufficiently extricated from the dyadic relationship with the infant, and the infant would not experience itself wholly as object, or as interpreter/interpretant of a conversation about it. The third scenario would be one in which the infant and father could not engage in an interaction that took the mother as object. Here the infant would not have the experience of the mother as object as well as subject, and as in the second scenario, as someone fully separate from itself. Each scenario thus represents a variation on the need for embodiment of the various positions of the semiotic triad in actual persons in the early inculcation of semiosis.

Conclusion

This reflection of Peircean semiotics and psychosis has moved through three stages. In a first stage I focused on Peirce's most general notions concerning the dependence of thought on signs and concerning the externality of the sign. In his or her relationships both to the world and to the self, the psychotic was seen as foundering on the externality of the sign. In a second stage I focused more specifically on Peirce's triadic understanding of the sign. Here the emphasis fell, on the one hand, on the psychotic's conflation of sign, object, and interpretant, and on the other hand, on his or her confusion of index and symbol. In a third and final stage, I questioned the developmental implications of a Peircean analysis, suggesting the need for actual embodiment of the semiotic triad in early development and the failure of this in the potential psychotic.

References

Anderson, Douglas. *Strands of System: The Philosophy of Charles Peirce.* West Lafayette, Ind.: Purdue University Press, 1995.

Benveniste, Émile. *Problèmes de linguistique générale.* Paris: Gallimard, 1966.

Bleuler, Eugen. *Dementia Praecox; or, The Group of Schizophrenias* (1911). Translated by J. Zinkin. New York: International Universities Press, 1950.

Colapietro, Vincent M. *Peirce's Approach to the Self: A Semiotic Perspective on Human Subjectivity.* Albany: State University of New York Press, 1989.

Deely, John. *Basics of Semiotics.* Bloomington: Indiana University Press, 1990.

Eliot, T. S. *The Complete Poems and Plays: 1909–1950.* New York: Harcourt, Brace and World, 1962.

Federn, Paul. *Ego Psychology and the Psychoses.* London: Imago Publishing Company, 1953.

Fisch, Max. *Peirce, Semiotic, and Pragmatism: Essays by Max H. Fisch.* Edited by K. L. Ketner and C.J.W. Kloesel. Bloomington: Indiana University Press, 1986.

Freeman, T., Cameron, J., and McGhie, A. *Chronic Schizophrenia.* London: Tavistock Publications, 1958.

Freud, Sigmund. *The Standard Edition of the Complete Psychological Works of Sigmund Freud.* Edited and translated by James Strachey. 24 vols. London: Hogarth Press, 1953–74.

———. "Psycho-Analytic Notes on an Autobiographical Account of a Case of Paranoia (Dementia Paranoides)" (1911), vol. 12.

Greenlee, Douglas. *Peirce's Concept of Sign.* The Hague: Mouton, 1973.

Harrow, M., and Quinlan, D. *Disordered Thinking and Schizophrenic Psychopathology.* New York: Gardner Press, 1985.

Houser, Nathan. Introduction to Peirce (1992), xix–xli.

Kerby, Anthony. *Narrative and the Self.* Bloomington: Indiana University Press, 1991.

Kernberg, Otto. *Borderline Conditions and Pathological Narcissism.* New York: Jason Aronson, 1975.

Lakoff, G., and Johnson, M. *Metaphors We Live By.* Chicago: University of Chicago Press, 1980.

Merleau-Ponty, Maurice. *The Prose of the World.* Edited by C. Lefort and translated by J. O'Neill. Evanston, Ill.: Northwestern University Press, 1973.

Muller, John. *Beyond the Psychoanalytic Dyad: Developmental Semiotics in Freud, Peirce, and Lacan.* New York: Routledge, 1996.

Peirce, Charles Sanders. *The Essential Peirce: Selected Philosophical Writings.* Edited by Nathan Houser and Christian Kloesel. Vol. 1 (1867–93). Bloomington: Indiana University Press, 1992.

———. "Questions Concerning Certain Faculties Claimed for Man" (1868a). In Peirce (1992), 11–27.

———. "Some Consequences of Four Incapacities" (1868b). In Peirce (1992), 28–55.

———. "Logic as Semiotic: The Theory of Signs" (1897). In *Philosophical Writings of Peirce,* edited by J. Buchler, 98–119. New York: Dover Publications, 1955.

———. *Selected Writings.* Edited by P. Wiener. New York: Dover Publications, 1966.

———. *Semiotic and Significs: The Correspondence between Charles S. Peirce and Victoria Lady Welby.* Edited by Charles Hardwick. Bloomington: Indiana University Press, 1977.

Ricoeur, Paul. "The Metaphorical Process as Cognition, Imagination, and Feeling." In *On Metaphor,* edited by Sheldon Sacks, 141–58. Chicago: University of Chicago Press, 1978.

———. *Time and Narrative.* Vol. 1. Translated by K. McLaughlin and D. Pellauer. Chicago: University of Chicago Press, 1984.

———. *Oneself as Another.* Translated by K. Blamey. Chicago: University of Chicago Press, 1992.

Sass, Louis. *Madness and Modernism: Insanity in the Light of Modern Art, Literature, and Thought.* New York: Basic Books, 1992.

Sebeok, Thomas. "Indexicality." In *Peirce and Contemporary Thought: Philosophical Inquiries,* edited by Kenneth Ketner, 222–42. New York: Fordham University Press, 1995.

Short, T. "Peirce's Semiotic Theory of the Self." *Semiotica* 91 (1992): 124.

Steiner, G. *Real Presences.* Chicago: University of Chicago Press, 1989.

Stevens, W. *Poems.* Selected by Samuel French Morse. New York: Vintage Books, 1959.

3 Protolinguistic Phenomena in Psychoanalysis

John E. Gedo

For an enterprise explicitly engaged in decoding the latent meanings of human communications, psychoanalysis as a discipline has been surprisingly slow to give weight to the subtleties of speech and language. This history is doubly strange considering that Sigmund Freud, before establishing our intellectual domain, wrote a distinguished monograph about the neuropathology of language, *On Aphasia* ([1891] 1953). In much of the psychoanalytic world, through most of our century of existence, and despite the Wittgensteinian revolution in philosophy, the medium of communication employed by the participants in clinical psychoanalysis has been implicitly regarded as if it were a perfectly inert solvent that facilitates chemical reactions without having any direct influence on them—in other words, as if analytic communication took place by way of some totally unambiguous semiotic code, analogous to the operations of a computer.

Only in the past generation have psychoanalysts become alert both to the significance and to the complexities of the *form* of human communications, over and beyond their imprecise lexical content. It must be acknowledged that much of this work originated in France, particularly in the school of Lacan—developments admirably summarized for American readers by Muller and Richardson (1982). Perhaps the most important of these contributions was the differentiation of three registers of experience: first, the active use of concrete signals, as signs or icons; second, the so-called imaginary structure of dyadic mirroring; and last, the later development of symbolic communications (Muller 1996).

In this country, Levin has written most cogently about the line of development of semiotic capacities, basing his schema on evolutionary considerations (1991). According to this schema, the human communicative repertory first includes only the language of affects, which the infant conveys by means of vocalizations and facial expressions. It then expands with the addition of a language of gestures and postures. A third phase begins when words with consensual meaning come to be used to supplement earlier communicative skills. The next increment in these skills involves the use of syntactically organized language, and a fifth phase is reached when the child acquires the ability to construct a coherent narrative. In adults, these communicative skills are organized into an integrated assembly that makes use of various combinations of these five distinct semiotic modes.

From a clinical perspective, the earliest American contributions on the semiotics of psychoanalysis were those of Victor Rosen (1977). My own interest in the subject was an outgrowth of attempts I had made (Gedo and Goldberg 1973; Gedo 1993) systematically to explore the implications of the hierarchical view of developmental psychology that was increasingly becoming the accepted standard following the conceptual work of Rapaport (1959). About fifteen years ago, I committed myself to the proposition that, in response to the ever-shifting developmental levels according to which analysands' psychic operations are organized, the analyst's efforts to communicate in the treatment setting must also make use of distinctive channels and modes of discourse (Gedo 1981, chap. 11).

The crux of my argument has been that, in regressive states, analysands often become unable to process the intended meaning of even syntactically and lexically clear messages—unless those meanings are amplified by paraverbal indications of affect. For many years, in the guise of adherence to the principle of "analytic neutrality," such expressions of the analyst's affectivity had been condemned as taboo: they were seen as evidence for unresolved countertransference problems (for dissenting views, see Stone 1961 and Greenson 1967). Through painful clinical experience I discovered that, whenever an "archaic transference" (Gedo 1977) is manifested, my communications are at risk of being grossly misunderstood unless the music of my speech is congruent with the lexical meaning of my words. In this context, I concluded that, in terms of the music of speech, the lexical content of the message corresponds to melody, its timing to rhythm, its affectivity to sonic intensity, and its cognitive style to tone color. To state the implication of this conclusion in the words of an unusually discerning analysand, treatment sessions should be like the performance of an a cappella choir.

A dozen years ago, Tufts University organized the first American symposium on "Language and Psychoanalysis"; by then, all participants were in consensus about the importance of the nonlinguistic aspects of communication, that is, on Saussure's differentiation between *la langue* (language) and *la parole* (speech). At this event, I proposed a conception of successful analysis as the attainment by the participants of a "shared language"—in analogy with the acquisition of the "mother tongue" in the course of felicitous development (Gedo 1984, chap. 8). In contrast to the teaching-learning situation in childhood, in analysis it is the obligation of the analyst to master the various semiotic codes used by the analysand, no matter how eccentric these may be (for a discussion of the rhetorical choices the analyst must confront in this process, see Gedo 1984, chap. 9; Gedo 1994; and Leavy 1980). Probably the most difficult code to comprehend is the mode of dyadic dramatic enactments, the communication of meanings involving all participants in a pantomime that relives an old scenario, a drama in which any and all parts of the semiotic codes previously learned may be utilized (Gedo 1988, chap. 9).

More recently, I have been interested in the nonverbal or protolinguistic aspects of communication in the analytic situation (Gedo 1996, chap. 1), including both the analysand's frequent uses of other-than-verbal codes, such as music or gesture, albeit in a manner characteristic of a secondary process (*S.E.* 12: 215–28), and primary process codes such as the body language used in various types of "somatization" (Gedo 1988, chap. 6). It is notable that such body language may either constitute actual symbols (this is the case in so-called conversion reactions), or it may consist of concrete signals lacking in symbolic meaning: tics, for instance, signify only whatever the given movement always denotes. In such conditions, only preverbal channels of communication for transmitting certain specific messages are available to the individual (for a discussion of other syndromes in which such conditions prevail, see Gedo 1988, chap. 6, and Lichtenberg 1983).

In this chapter, I wish further to explore clinical contingencies of this kind, especially those in which the loss of ability to use consensual language is more or less veiled by a continuing pattern of speech that, for the most part, consists of *seemingly* meaningful words. Clinicians familiar with the symptomatology of certain types of schizophrenia are well acquainted with paraphasic productions of this kind, which are generally referred to as "word salads." In the era of pioneering attempts to treat the psychoses by means of psychoanalytic psychotherapy, enormous effort was expended on decoding such "language," that is, on trying to translate it into secondary process statements. Although such activities often succeed in building a communicative bridge between therapist and patient, it has seldom been possible to ascertain whether the translator has actually discerned the speaker's intended meaning.

It is most likely that in the great majority of cases, no lexical meaning is actually intended at all; word salads probably betoken regression to the earliest stage of vocalization, in which only the articulation of a succession of phonemes is possible. In this sense, their articulation can be seen as the vomiting of words. This probability does not mean that the schizophrenic's speech is completely devoid of discernible information, but the signals in question have little or no lexical significance—instead they are automatically (that is, on a neural level) correlated with a variety of affective states. In this connection, it is beneficial to recall the work of the Franco-Hungarian linguist Fonagy, who demonstrated such correlations in the speech of children speaking either French or Hungarian (1983). (The children were old enough to speak in a consensually meaningful way, but the phonemic-affective correlations were nonetheless present.) It is also relevant to cite reports about the poetry produced by certain schizophrenics, such as the Swiss artist Adolf Wölfli; the verse consists of lexically unintelligible texts but succeeds *qua* music at the level of the physical properties of the speech necessary to articulate it (Morgenthaler 1992; see also MacGregor 1989). Gilbert Rose has convincingly argued that the power of great art to reach the human depths resides in the correlation of its formal properties (i.e., its physical and hence perceptual organization) with the preverbal affectivity of its creators and consumers (1992; 1995). The word salads of schizophrenics present the same affective universe, albeit almost always artlessly.

Until relatively recently, psychoanalysts have failed to note that (more or less) transient episodes of speech lacking all consensual meaning may also occur in the course of psychoanalysis whenever the treatment induces regression to the earliest modes of psychic organization. I first reported such an event about fifteen years ago in the case of an academic in his mid-thirties, an analysis eventually terminated with a more than satisfactory outcome (Gedo 1981, chap. 11). Because the symptoms involving language were a crucial aspect of the analysis, it is worth emphasizing that, about a dozen years after the termination of the analysis, when he faced a dead end in his academic career, this man began to write poetry, an activity that increasingly came to occupy a central place in his emotional economy. Poetic talent consists, in part, of the ability closely to monitor the sonic properties of utterances.

As I previously reported, the analytic transference in this case relatively quickly tilted in the direction of reliving infantile rage and negativism in response to perceived abandonment (287–96). In this context, the patient seemed to lose the ability to judge whether his communications would be comprehensible to me; when I asked for clarification, his second or third effort to convey his intended meaning was often even more confusing than the first. At the same time, not infrequently, he was also unable to comprehend my communications as I was trying to clear up the confusion. Nor could he grasp that we were talking at cross-purposes; I tended to experience his behavior as provocative. If I chose to wait out such a crisis in a passive mode, my tactic only led to escalation of the impasse, because (with some justification) the analysand would then feel that I was punishing him through deliberate neglect for his conscientious performance of the task of free association.

In time, I was able to distinguish these episodes, precipitated by negativism, from superficially similar events based on the patient's fantasy that I could magically read his mind. When this second eventuality was at issue, I usually did not feel provoked, and the analysand had much less difficulty in regaining the ability to use consensual languages. In instances when he was being negativistic, the most effective way to resolve the impasse turned out to be to express my irritation with unconcealed emotions—or, if I discerned what was about to happen early enough, to issue in urgent tones a warning about impending danger concerning our joint enterprise. This is not the place to elaborate on the technical difficulties of such analytic vicissitudes or their solutions. I wish to focus, instead, on the transference significance of these regressed behaviors.

Needless to say, this person had been subjected to many traumatic changes in childhood. Both of his parents had been immature and impulsive; before the boy reached the age of two, his father had killed himself in an automobile wreck by driving while intoxicated. At that juncture, the child's care was entrusted to his paternal grandparents; when his mother was about to remarry (the patient was then three), she resumed her parental role at the home of the maternal family. With the aid of unusually detailed childhood records, we were eventually able to reconstruct that, on the occasion of each of these traumatic separations, the boy had become rageful and disorganized. At the time of his father's death, he regressed in terms of bowel training; when his mother reclaimed him, his habitual "disobedience" was savagely punished—at times his care givers actually tied him to his crib in a vain effort to control him.

The records contained no information about the vicissitudes of the child's mastery of language, but I think it is safe to assume that it suffered parallel deterioration. Thus, the spiteful abandonment of the communicative functions of speech in the context of an archaic transference (Gedo 1977) seemed to constitute the repetitive reenactment of aspects of the tantrums and negativism characteristic of the analysand's early childhood—or, if you will, the unconscious repudiation of an untrustworthy world of human relatedness.

Lest I give the impression that regression to a preverbal state can only take place in the context of a negative transference, I would like to offer a second clinical illustration (a case I have previously discussed in Gedo 1988, 153–55). The analysand in question began occasionally to speak in an incomprehensible manner in the third year of a lengthy analysis, after considerable improvements had taken place in this day-to-day adaptation. In his case, this pattern of communication very seldom made me feel provoked, and the analysand could always be brought out of his regressed state by an urgent warning that this strange phenomenon had to be understood through collaborative efforts. Eventually, we reached the consensus that the symptom amounted to lapsing into a private language, like the babbling of an infant.

The patient emphasized that this supervened when he felt particularly "relaxed," but *this* phrase also turned out to be misleading, because it was a euphemism for a sense of depersonalization, a loss of the subjective sense of self. Eventually, he was able to recall that he had experienced similar states throughout his childhood, whenever he was not self-consciously engaged in battling care givers. When he was around five years old, he was hospitalized for suspected poliomyelitis because of widespread muscular "paralysis" for which no somatic cause was ever found. Presumably, this was the most severe episode of total aimlessness he ever suffered. As if to confirm that his very identity depended on fighting a hostile environment, the patient's difficulty in using consensual language in the analytic situation disappeared as soon as he encountered the next crisis in his daily life.

Both of my clinical examples to some extent conform to the observations of Freud about the occurrence of speech in dreams (*S.E.* 4:298–304; 5:402–26). It will be recalled that he cautioned the would-be dream interpreter not to accept the overt lexical meaning of these "utterances" at face value. However, Freud pointed out that these sonic manifest contents are associated with unconscious latent thoughts in an associative manner: if they form sentences, they turn out to be quotations and thus merely serve as tags that locate an experience to which the latent thoughts refer. Of course, in the examples I have used, it was not possible to extract any meaning from the manifest utterance, nor did my efforts to discern some latent meaning ever bear fruit. I mention Freud's discovery nonetheless because it does parallel my conclusion about regression to a preverbal state in the sense that neither dreams nor the associations I have highlighted are organized in accord with secondary process mentation.

The foregoing considerations should alert us to the possibility that certain syntactically and lexically comprehensible communications may also be devoid of authentic significance, for example, instances of language that might be characterized as "blathering." (In the dictionary, *blather* is defined as talk that is both voluble and empty—close to *bab-ble*, which denotes not only the meaningless sounds made by infants but also "meaningless chatter.") Although blather may occasionally betray some hidden significance, it is generally intended to cover over an *ab-sence* of meaning. In this sense, its function is analogous to that of "sec-ondary revision" in dreaming (*S.E.* 5:488-508)—to lend a pseudo-rational facade to overt senselessness. The ability to blather *effectively* depends on the individual's linguistic talent in the verbal arena: in my clin-ical work, the best blatherer I ever encountered was a successful televi-sion personality, well known for his mellifluous language.

Although the therapeutic results we achieved were respectable, my attempt to conduct a *psychoanalysis* with this person was utterly de-feated by his inability authentically to convey his inner experience in words (for further details of this treatment, see Gedo 1981, 68-77 or Gedo 1991, 72-78). The patient correctly predicted that analysis would not prove to be feasible for him because he knew that as soon as he tried to articulate what he was experiencing it became falsified by the trans-lation into his sophisticated adult language. In other words, he was aware of his blathering, and he was distressed about this handicap. I have the impression that such insight about the condition is relatively rare.

I do not wish to imply, however, that the appearance of blathering fails to convey any meaning—on the contrary, it is a highly significant analytic finding. It is merely the lexical content of such communications that is lacking in importance; the phenomenon as a whole is an "iconic enact-ment" (Muller 1996) that betrays an urgent need to screen threatening inner developments, usually in the affecto-motor realm. Blathering might well be described as a smoke screen of relatively insignificant verbiage. I have not encountered the phenomenon in a sufficient number of cases to permit forming any hypothesis about what makes it possible for cer-tain individuals to ward off threatened traumatization through the mere distraction of such "whistling in the dark."

In certain analysands with regressive propensities, analogous threats lead not to such "white noise," but to silence. Formerly, interruptions of the stream of associations were routinely classified as manifestations of "resistance," and in some instances, that is what they turn out to be after further investigation. (From a technical viewpoint, it is prudent to ask on every such occasion, "What made you stop talking?") In other cases, si-lence betokens a return to a preverbal universe, often one of inchoate feeling states or "involuntary" motor acts. The one most dramatic incident of this kind that I have witnessed in my consulting room was an episode of Charcot's *grande hystérie,* complete with opisthotonos, convulsions, and the clouding of consciousness. Spontaneous orgasm without prior sexual arousal, the loss of bladder control, and the onset of vomiting or diarrhea are further examples of iconic enactments that usually super-vene in silence. But even without the occurrence of such motoric phe-nomena, the appearance of a "blank space" in inner experience is as pro-foundly significant as is the cessation of sound in the middle of a musical composition. And it is beneficial to remember that the emergence of such primitive phenomena in the analytic situation usually means that some-thing of great importance from the past is being relived in the present—hence, it is seldom properly understood as an untoward development.

Intervals of silence frequently supervene during the terminal phase of successful analyses. In instances of that kind, I have usually felt com-pletely comfortable in joining my analysands in "sessions of sweet, silent thought," to quote Shakespeare, although the only thoughts either of us could capture in these circumstances were retrospective self-observa-tions about having felt comfortable, without "thinking" anything that could be put into words. I experienced such intervals in the last stages of my own analysis; the probability that they represented the repetition of feeling states from the first year of life was suggested by a unique sen-sation that several times "joined in the conversation" (*S.E.* 2:296)—I ex-perienced pronounced aching of the gums, which was presumably a so-matic recollection of the first emergence of teeth and the onset of weaning. For me, it was a dramatic introduction to protolinguistic phe-nomena in psychoanalysis.

Of course, lapses into silence more frequently occur in circumstances that repeat childhood vicissitudes of pathogenic import. I have the im-pression that, whenever it is such an event that is being reenacted, the lapse into silence tends to make both participants more or less uncom-fortable. Analysands who undergo such regressive episodes often appear stunned; upon recovery, they generally describe having felt bewildered or "empty." The most memorable incident of this kind I have witnessed proved to be so contagious that I found my own capacity for reflection to be temporarily almost as impaired as the analysand's. In my own be-wilderment, the only associations I had were snatches of discordant mu-sic. In time, these coalesced into a recognizable melody—part of the great quartet from the last act of Verdi's *Rigoletto.* It then occurred to me that my analysand was reliving the trauma she experienced when, at four years old, she witnessed an atrocity—as does the audience at the climax of the Verdi opera. To be specific, the child was present when her mother mangled her own infant daughter, the child's sister, by running her limbs through a machine for pressing laundry.

Of course, I had for some time known about these historical data, and I had always assumed that the incident had been traumatic. What the mutual regression into a preverbal universe taught me was not a fresh bit of childhood history but something about the depth of the child's regression when the tragedy occurred. It was my inability to "think" (in the sense of "thought" as the processing of abstract symbols) that convinced me that my analysand was suffering from a homologous loss of functional capacity. As a dyad, we were temporarily in a state of complete attunement through the mechanism Kleinians call "projective identification."

Note that my musical associations were at first devoid of symbolic meaning, and, when their significance finally emerged, it was not as symbol but as a concrete sign, a mere *index* to an act of murder. You will recall that, in the opera, Rigoletto hires an assassin who double-crosses him by killing Rigoletto's own daughter. In exact conformity with Freud's claims about the occurrence of speeches in dreams, in quoting music that accompanies certain actions in an opera, I was merely tagging the time when and place where answers to my bewilderment could be found, without as yet having in any way arrived at those answers. To follow this clue and thus to gain the insights I am now able to articulate was a lengthy and tortuous process, but I did ultimately figure out that my analysand felt that she was the true murderer, like Rigoletto. In her view, responsibility was primarily not the mother's; the mother was a mere hireling. At bottom, the "accident" had proved to be severely traumatic because it confirmed the child's fantasy of her own omnipotence.

I do not doubt that the foregoing survey of the protolinguistic phenomena I have encountered in analytic practice leaves many analogous behaviors out of account. Instead of trying for comprehensiveness in the absence of firsthand exposure to a sufficiently broad sample, let me proceed to discuss some conceptual implications of the material I have presented thus far. To begin, I wish to consider how to explain the emergence of such behaviors in either analyst or analysand, individuals whose everyday linguistic repertory outside of the analytic situation continues to meet expectable adult standards. In the case of the analyst, I assume that the ability temporarily to identify with a patient's regression to a preverbal state is one of the requirements of the effective and conflict-free use of empathy in analytic work—the kind of refinement of so-called primitive functional capacities that Kris long ago called "regression in the service of the ego" (1952). The analysand's regression is, in favorable instances, in the service of the therapeutic enterprise, and it is both confined within the analytic setting and (as several of my illustrative accounts suggest) circumscribed to certain specific functions.

The occurrence of regressions limited in extent and duration suggests that, prior to their emergence, the relevant sector of the personality was split off and unable to organize overall behavior. In other words, the safety of the analytic holding environment must account for a relaxation of the defensive operations that otherwise conceal these nuclei of personality organization (Gedo and Goldberg 1973). Hence the therapeutic mobilization of these behavioral potentialities allows them, for the first time, to become integrated with the generally prevalent aspects of self-organization (for a more detailed discussion, see Gedo 1988, chap. 4).

The possibility of abrupt shifts, back and forth between relatively archaic and relatively more mature modes of functioning (also demonstrated in most of my clinical examples), shows that patterns of behavior are never completely lost; in the hierarchical arrangement of behavior regulation, all previous patterns indefinitely coexist, each ready for use whenever it is most advantageous from an adaptive viewpoint. From this perspective, we may infer that protolinguistic phenomena are not necessarily entirely confined to sectors split off from the prevalent self-organization—they may remain readily accessible when needed, as in the case of an analyst at work. This conclusion, in turn, should alert us to the fact that the paraverbal aspect of everyday speech must of necessity consist of the very elements which, when they emerge in pure culture, are seen as preverbal forms of communication.

Let me briefly illustrate this point through the simplest of examples, that of the tempo of the analysand's speech production. It is generally accepted that this may undergo drastic changes without discernible alteration of any other aspect of the linguistic code, and there is also wide consensus about the correlation of marked acceleration of the individual's typical spoken tempo with certain affective states, especially with hypomania or extreme anxiety, and of its marked slowing with other affective conditions, mostly with depression. These correlations with basic moods are already evident in the vocal patterns of young children and, of course, in that the emotional tone of music depends on tempo, from lento to prestissimo.

I shall offer only one additional example, that of iconic gestural communication that overrides the significance of verbal discourse, although this discourse goes on more or less without interruption. In my clinical work, I most frequently observed this state of affairs during the analysis of a young woman who had been trained as a ballet dancer. Without even leaving the couch, she was able to convey certain fundamental matters by way of her posture—for instance, by turning her head to the wall when she unconsciously desired to "turn her back to me." (When she was aware of such a wish, she generally stopped talking—she might then literally turn her trunk away from me or even leave the room for several minutes.) Note that the patient's change of posture had no symbolic significance and that this person, because of her training, was more prone than most to encode meanings in the language of gestures. She turned her head as a signal most would have verbalized by way of an expletive, like "Fuck off!" But she was able to do this, like the ladies of T. S. Eliot, while she continued politely to talk "of Michelangelo."

Let us now turn from describing various protolinguistic phenomena encountered in the psychoanalytic situation to the therapeutic significance of careful attention to their emergence. I have already noted that, at a minimum, the initial appearance of such primitive modes of communication signifies that a therapeutic regression to an archaic state of self-organization has taken place (see Gedo and Goldberg 1973); giving due weight to such an observation should alert the analyst to shift focus to the most regressive aspects of the analytic transaction and to be particularly careful to avoid miscommunicating by overestimating the analysand's current ability to process complex messages. If only the paraverbal aspects of speech are affected, while its lexical and syntactic aspects remain unaltered, calling attention to these specific changes and inquiring into their meaning and genesis generally leads to fruitful results in elucidating the analysand's affective state.

Beyond these generalities, we should note that the specific protolinguistic phenomenon that emerges in the context of the analytic transference is likely to be a reasonable duplicate of an early childhood state of pathogenic import. As all of the clinical illustrations I have provided here exemplify, such a repetition of aspects of the past that have no symbolic encoding in memory is always an optimal—and sometimes the only available—entree through which the past may be recaptured.

Until relatively recently, psychoanalysis could only offer arbitrary interpretive schemata based on unsubstantiated developmental hypotheses as therapeutic tools to deal with preverbal material. Because these matters were and are experienced wordlessly, secure inferences about them must perforce follow not from the lexical content of the analysand's associations but from their *form*. Hence, protolinguistic phenomena constitute our Rosetta stone for the decipherment of these "prehistoric" events.

References

Fonagy, Ivan. *La Vive Voix: Essais de psycho-phonétique.* Paris: Payot, 1983.

Freud, Sigmund. *On Aphasia* (1891). New York: International Universities Press, 1953.

——— . *The Standard Edition of the Complete Psychological Works of Sigmund Freud.* Edited and translated by James Strachey. 24 vols. London: Hogarth Press, 1953–74.

"The Psychotherapy of Hysteria" (1895), vol. 2.

The Interpretation of Dreams (1900), vols. 4, 5.

"Formulations on the Two Principles of Mental Functioning" (1911), vol. 12.

Gedo, John. "Notes on the Psychoanalytic Management of Archaic Transferences." *Journal of the American Psychoanalytic Association* 25 (1977): 787–804.

———. *Advances in Clinical Psychoanalysis.* New York: International Universities Press, 1981.

———. *Psychoanalysis and Its Discontents.* New York: Guilford, 1984.

———. *The Mind in Disorder.* Hillsdale, N.J.: Analytic Press, 1988.

———. *The Biology of Clinical Encounters.* Hillsdale, N.J.: Analytic Press, 1991.

———. *Beyond Interpretation.* Rev. ed. Hillsdale, N.J.: Analytic Press, 1993.

———. "Analytic Interventions: The Question of Form." In *The Spectrum of Psychoanalysis,* edited by A. K. Richards and A. Richards, 111–27. Madison, Conn.: International Universities Press, 1994.

———. *The Languages of Psychoanalysis.* Hillsdale, N.J.: Analytic Press, 1996.

Gedo, John, and Goldberg, Arnold. *Models of the Mind: A Psychoanalytic Theory.* Chicago: University of Chicago Press, 1973.

Greenson, Ralph. *The Technique and Practice of Psychoanalysis.* Vol. 1. New York: International Universities Press, 1967.

Kris, Ernst. *Psychoanalytic Explorations in Art.* New York: International Universities Press, 1952.

Leavy, Stanley. *The Psychoanalytic Dialogue.* New Haven, Conn.: Yale University Press, 1980.

Levin, Fred. *Mapping the Mind.* Hillsdale, N.J.: Analytic Press, 1991.

Lichtenberg, Joseph. *Psychoanalysis and Infant Research.* Hillsdale, N.J.: Analytic Press, 1983.

MacGregor, James. *The Discovery of the Art of the Insane.* Princeton: Princeton University Press, 1989.

Morgenthaler, Wilhelm. *Madness and Art: The Life and Works of Adolf Wölfli.* Vol. 3. Lincoln: University of Nebraska Press, 1992.

Muller, John. *Beyond the Psychoanalytic Dyad: Developmental Semiotics in Freud, Peirce, and Lacan.* New York: Routledge, 1996.

Muller, John, and Richardson, William. *Lacan and Language: A Reader's Guide to Écrits.* New York: International Universities Press, 1982.

Rapaport, David. *The Structure of Psychoanalytic Theory: A Systematizing Attempt.* Psychological Issues, monograph 6. New York: International Universities Press, 1959.

Rose, Gilbert. *The Power of Form.* Rev. ed. Madison, Conn.: International Universities Press, 1992.

———. *Necessary Illusion.* Madison, Conn.: International Universities Press, 1995.

Rosen, Victor. *Style, Character, and Language.* Edited by S. Atkins and M. Jucovy. New York: Aronson, 1977.

Stone, Leo. *The Psychoanalytic Situation.* New York: International Universities Press, 1961.

4   Hierarchical Models in Semiotics and Psychoanalysis

John Muller

Our dominant epistemic rule has become the rule of context: If we wish to understand an adult's actions, how a child learns a new behavior, or the functioning of an organism, we have to situate these in relation to context. As Bateson stated, "Without context, words and actions have no meaning at all" (1980, 16). Such a context-driven approach may appear to contribute to the fragmentation of knowledge, to the postmodernist breakdown of coherence, but an emphasis on context doesn't necessarily lead to isolation and loss of the ability to generalize. Context implies an organization among elements of a system; I would argue, moreover, that it is the hierarchical configuration of these elements that makes possible the delineation of context in relation to which a piece of behavior can be examined. Again, Bateson emphasized "that all communication necessitates context, that without context, there is no meaning, and that contexts confer meaning because there is classification of contexts" (18).

Social psychologist Ken Gergen considers the following example: If you walk into a room and come upon a young man tearing pages out of a volume, what does this behavior mean to you? If the room is a library, you might react differently than if it were the basement of a community hall. If nobody is present in the library, you might think it an act of vandalism or thievery; if the librarian is sitting at the next table, however, you might interpret it as a sanctioned task. The context will govern the meaning of the behavior, and the context can be known by the semiotic code that designates rooms as libraries, delineates functions of librarian and assistant, and defines an action as destroying or preserving. The semiotic code is capable of so delineating a context because it consists of a hierarchical system of relations capable of accounting for any type of relation—at least, this is how I understand the architectonic system of Charles Sanders Peirce (1891).

The rule of context also applies to the data of psychoanalysis. From an anthropological base, Crapanzano argues that the context of the psychoanalytic dyad is semiotic—the semiotic code grounds the dyad as its Third, defining the roles and tasks of each member of the dyad: "The signifying chain, the Symbolic order, culture, and grammar we might say, serves to stabilize the relations between self and other by functioning as a Third" (1982, 197). This emphasis on the Third does not diminish the dyad; I will attempt to show how the dyad has a unique role in transforming a physical state into a sign. In emphasizing the dyad, however, most of contemporary psychoanalytic theory, with the exception of Lacan's (1988) and some recent formulations (Brickman 1993; Ogden 1994; Schoenhals 1995), has overlooked the Third as the grounding context, as if the dyad could ground itself, or provide its own context.

The history of psychoanalytic theory itself shows a failure to take its own context into account, in particular its own clinical context, the specific types of patients or symptoms that give rise to the particular theories. In the hierarchical model of Gedo and Goldberg (1973), further revised and elaborated by Gedo (1993), such clinical contexts are grouped according to a model of epigenetic development, so that the hierarchical relation of their corresponding theories becomes readily apparent. The model aims to show how "a hierarchical arrangement of models, paralleling the hierarchy of modes of psychic functioning, will constitute a supraordinate model of the mind" (Gedo and Goldberg 1973, 10). As far as I am aware, this is the only such comprehensive model that attempts to integrate various models in Freud with Kohut's psychology of the self and object relations theory, and the only such attempt that has received detailed support from research findings (Wilson and Gedo 1993). I hope to show how the architectonics of Peirce's and Gedo's hierarchical models complement each other.

Peirce's architectonic theory establishes a hierarchical relationship among aspects of experience: between signing and what is signable in experience, among the various ways signs are related to their objects in experience, and among the elements within the structure of the sign itself. Peirce carefully traces a triadic structure through all of this, a structure built on the foundation of his three categories of relation: firstness, secondness, and thirdness, defined by him as follows: "First is the conception of being or existing independent of anything else. Second is the conception of being relative to, the conception of reaction with, something else. Third is the conception of mediation, whereby a first and second are brought into relation" (1891, 296).

Firstness embraces quality: this is the familiar notion of qualia, that aspect of consciousness made up of determined, sensuous features. In firstness, however, quality is neither determined nor identified, and is not given as an object for a subject. Firstness is the realm of the unbounded, undifferentiated state, a state of potential. As I have tried to point out elsewhere (Muller 1996), firstness is correlated with Lacan's register of the Real. Distinct from reality, which is a social construction, the Real is that aspect of experience beyond an epistemological frontier, that aspect of experience without a name and without an image.

Secondness for Peirce is the dynamic category of force and impact, in particular the kind of impact that takes place in a dyadic relation. Secondness puts a boundary around firstness and, in the case of human subjects, defines qualia as pertaining to a particular consciousness, usually of an object, as caused by a prior action or state of mind, and as leading to a particular outcome. It corresponds to Lacan's register of the Imaginary, that sensuous aspect of experience marked by one-to-one correspondence between an object and its image, or between the subject's ego and the consciousness of his or her object of desire.

Thirdness is the category of generality and habit or law, required for thinking, self-reflection, and any experience of continuity and community. It is that generalization yielded when seconds are assessed and understood. With such understanding we see how quality is governed by habit or law so that specific impacts are produced in specific ways. The three terms are summarized by Brent: "While the absolute present and immediate, unthought, unconscious experience describe Firstness, and existence and the compulsion of external reality, of brute fact, of the blank resistance we find everywhere in our experience — the Outward Clash — describe Secondness, Thirdness is that which mediates between the two and gives meaning, order, law, and generality" (1993, 334).

Peirce's triadic structure applies with great specificity to the realm of signs. Signs consist of certain qualities related to their objects; these relationships between signs and their objects become known through the signs' interpretants. This mediation can take place in three ways, in terms of a hierarchy of relationships between signs and their objects. In the category of firstness, signs relate to their objects by way of resemblance through qualitative similarity; such signs that relate to their objects by way of resemblance are known as icons. In the realm of secondness, signs relate to their objects existentially, by way of contiguity or causal impact; such a sign that bears a contiguous or causal relation to its object is known as an index. Indexes also have qualities and may indeed bear a specific resemblance to their objects, but their specific sign function is not through resemblance but through contiguity and causality. In the field of thirdness, signs have a relationship to their objects solely through a convention; such signs are known by Peirce as symbols, and their relation to their objects is determined not through resemblance nor through causality but through a type of agreement or conventionality that becomes habitual. The use of symbols depends on the operation of a semiotic code.

Indeed, some such code is required for the uses of signs based on resemblance as well as on contiguity. Neither an icon nor an index may be registered *as a sign* unless a semiotic code is operating that interprets it, that lifts the sign onto a signifying plane. Icons are pervasive in nature, and for Peirce are the basis of all learning. The index as evidence of contiguity or causality is the basis of all judgment, especially judgments that make predictions. The conventional sign, however, and, in particular, the system of conventional symbols known as language, is essential for modeling experience, constructing hypotheses, and thereby obtaining patterns within experience for the occurrence of icons and indexes.

Interpretants, mediating between signs and their objects, have three distinct levels in a hierarchy: feelings, actions, and concepts or habits as responses to a sign. Dewey noted how "emotional interpretants," in their suddenness, are initially in the category of firstness, as if "just there": "The 'interpretant' of an iconic sign, as a form of Firstness, is emotional" (1946, 92). Enactments that occur in the course of psychoanalytic treatment rely on icons for their effects. Such iconic features, the constituents of what Johansen has called "enacted iconicity" (1993, 139), are not generally perceived as iconic by the recipient of the enactment nor by the one acting, who is blind to the action's meaning or to its status as a repetitive icon. Modell describes such repetitive aspects in the transference as "the iconic transference" (1993, 49) and writes of the transference repetition as "the unconscious attempt to manipulate the secondary object through the affects induced in the countertransference" (1984, 35). These iconic features of a repetition are usually available for interpretation only by a third, whose position is distinct from the dyad; this, indeed, defines the unique position of the analyst, who is simultaneously a member of the archaic transference dyad, which establishes the conditions for the reappearance of the archaic behavior.

Peirce's notion of the sign embraces feeling and action as preliminary if not immediate aspects of the sign's significance. The feeling interpretant, the sign's initial impact on the receiver, which is a form of coerced mirroring, is an ongoing feature of any analysis, and, indeed, as recent research has shown, of any perception whatsoever (Spielman, Pratto, and Bargh 1988). This initial impact may lead to action—what Peirce called the dynamic interpretant of the sign—or the sign's actualized, pragmatic meaning. The abstract meaning of the sign, what Peirce called the logical interpretant, is a generalization requiring the use of verbal symbols and is a further development of semiosis in the hierarchy of iconic, enactive, and symbolic communication. In semiosis the sign stands for something by producing in its receiver (who may not be conscious of it) its significance. This significance is its interpretant, which Peirce intended to be distinct from its interpreter. Signs were so foundational for Peirce that he argued, as did Lacan after him, that the interpreter does not produce the sign's significance or its interpretant. Rather, the sign, in a given context and according to a specific code, produces an interpretant in a receiver who thereby, and in no other way, may become an interpreter in a working system of signs.

Observations from psychoanalysis as well as the investigations of the iconic, face-to-face interactions of mothers and infants, share a common complexity: the data emerge only in dyadic interaction, in which what we observe is always the interpretant of a preceding sign, attesting to the operative effects of intersubjective dynamics, including the elusive variables of intention and interpretation (Wolff 1987, 262). As Balint wrote, with infants and severely regressed patients "a highly important constituent of what we observe is our own contribution" (1959, 70); or, as Gedo concludes, "The specific transferences evoked in psychoanalysis are codetermined by the analyst's technical convictions and his or her actual characteristics as a person and a personality" (1991, 95). Such technical convictions, what Peirce would call habit, may evoke different transferences in different contexts and in different levels of patient function. This, however, is often forgotten. Because the dyad exercises such evident developmental and transferential influences, we may be led into conceptualizing the dyad as a complete system, to the neglect of the Third, which is understood in Lacan's framework as the Symbolic register and in Peirce's terms as the semiotic practices that organize and frame the interaction. This point is stated directly by Kirshner: "This symbolic framework, in fact, is the prerequisite for the basic maternal function in human development" (1994, 241). The neglect of this Third hampers thinking in both psychoanalysis and infancy research.

An early, vigorous attempt to counteract reductionism to dyadic forces appeared in the framework known as general system theory (von Bertalanffy 1968), with its emphasis on interactive complexity, hierarchies, and cybernetic codes. Its task, as von Bertalanffy defined it, was "to study general system characteristics and to concentrate on those aspects of reality which are inaccessible to conventional scientific treatment." He continued:

> The goal of general system theory is clearly circumscribed. It aims at a general theory of wholeness, of entire systems in which many variables interact and in which their organization produces strong interactions. It does not deal with isolated processes, with relations between two or a few variables or with linear causal relations. These are the domain of classical science. The development of such a theory became possible only after we had overcome our mechanistic prejudices and had abandoned mechanistic metaphysics. [[1972] 1975, 162]

In this broad approach, the investigative focus shifts from a mechanical, linear, causal model to a semiotic, interactive, probabilistic one in which codes play a central role. There is more to a system than its semiotic code, but, without taking the code into account, the system's behavior is not intelligible.

General system theory offered comprehension of a broad range of disciplinary domains: "Its applications range from the bio-physics of cellular processes to the dynamics of populations, from the problems of psychiatry to those of political and cultural units" (ibid.). From this viewpoint it is crucial to specify the context, the level of the system under discussion, and to affirm "what is species-specific for man and his behavior." On this point von Bertalanffy was unequivocal: "As a biologist I have found that the specificity of human behavior can best be formulated by means of the concept of *symbol* and *symbolic activities*" (164). For this reason, semiotics has a special relevance for understanding the data of psychoanalysis, data which are never simply "found" but come to light in response to the theory at work:

> Facts, observations, data, and protocols are not simply "given" as ultimate raw material of science. They not only are selected from an unlimited number of possible and actual observations, but are created in accordance with an accepted conceptual universe. Any perception and any scientific observation is already an interpretation. . . . What observations are relevant and how they are organized depends on conceptual schemes that cannot be derived from those same observations. [168]

I propose that the general conceptual scheme provided by the semiotic theory of Charles Sanders Peirce suggests a hierarchical system and supports a hierarchical model that can usefully organize the emergent data of psychoanalysis.

Sebeok has noted how Peirce's structuralist features, as exemplified in his triadic notions, resonate with Freud's (1983, 6). These categories are an attempt to structure relations, to see how relationships themselves follow from the affirmation of positions. I believe such an attempt must be made today in psychoanalysis in order to contextualize and embrace in a more comprehensive way the problematic prominence of the dyad. As a reaction to the perceived intrapsychic emphasis of early psychoanalytic theory and practice, the proponents of object-relations theory and self-psychology have so emphasized the "relationship" that context, code, task, and role are either ignored or seen as subservient to the requirements of establishing and maintaining a "relationship." The phenomenology of transference/counter-transference experience is so developed that we are led to believe that "the relationship" and its development can provide a comprehensive view of psychoanalytic theory and practice.

The notion of *relation* is as complex as expected. The word *relate* essentially means two things: to narrate and to be connected to. The Latin origin of the word means a "carrying back," from *"refero,"* and includes the notion of a report (itself a word meaning "to carry back"). To carry back, to narrate, to be connected to, these all presume that at least two positions have been differentiated, and this, in turn, requires that there be a third, a code, to define differences and to mediate between positions—that is, to give meaning.

Such a mediating function for relations Peirce assigns to the category of thirdness, the category that Wilden sees as congruent with Lacan's Symbolic register: "Firstness seems to be related to the Real, and Secondness to the Imaginary, for where Thirdness is the domain of mediated triangular relations, Secondness is ontologically the domain of the apparition of what is other, and psychologically is the domain of reaction, struggle, and duality" (1984, 267). Pharies writes that of the three, the most difficult to conceptualize "is firstness, because it represents pure feeling, the naked potential input to all mental operations, before perception and before cognition." For Pharies, the "requirement that firsts be unrelated to anything else has some rather bizarre consequences" (1985, 10). This is not surprising, because what Peirce attempts to describe is, I think, Lacan's register of the Real; for "the Real," Lacan stated, "is absolutely without fissure" (1988, 97). Peirce writes:

> The idea of the absolutely first must be entirely separated from all conception of or reference to anything else; for what involves a second is itself a second to that second. The first must therefore be present and immediate, so as not to be second to a representation. It must be fresh and new, for if old it is second to its former state. It must be initiative, original, spontaneous, and free; otherwise it is second to a determining cause. It is also something vivid and conscious; so only it avoids being the object of some sensation. It precedes all synthesis and all differentiation; it has no unity and no parts. It cannot be articulately thought: assert it, and it has already lost its characteristic innocence; for assertion always implies a denial of

something else. Stop to think of it, and it has flown! What the world was to Adam on the day he opened his eyes to it, before he had drawn any distinctions, or had become conscious of his own existence—that is first, present, immediate. [1887–88, 248]

As we shall see, the category of firstness may be taken as the domain of states of psychotic merger, of severe fragmentation anxiety, of psychic dissolution. In the category of secondness we encounter difference. In the category of thirdness is given the means to relate. Pharies writes, "The essence of thirdness is mediation," quoting Peirce to state that it "consists in active power to establish connections between different objects" (1985, 12).

Peirce summarized his three categories of experience as follows: "Immediate feeling is the consciousness of the first; the polar sense is the consciousness of the second; and synthetical consciousness is the consciousness of a Third or medium" (1887–88, 260). These three categories may be understood as corresponding to a developmental hierarchy of iconic, enactive, and symbolic communication in which each type of sign determines its corresponding type of interpretant. In iconic communication, as between mothers and infants or in psychotic dedifferentiation, icons produce, as their immediate significative effects, feeling interpretants, correlative affect states (what I have called "coerced empathy"), and even iconic physical correspondences. In enactive communication, indexes affect the other member of the dyad to produce dynamic interpretants in what are called enactments. In symbolic communication, symbols determine other symbols ("logical interpretants") that bring what is absent into symbolic presence and promote conscious understanding and insight regarding the effect of iconic displays and the significance of indexes, especially those of affective arousal.

The movement from enacted iconicity to symbolic mediation constitutes a semiotic line of development and a developmental achievement. For Peirce (as for Hegel), it amounts to letting go of the notion that the individual has the truth and affirming that truth lies in the developing community of investigators. For Lacan, the oedipalization of the subject and acceptance of limit, specifically the impossibility of being the all-fulfilling object of another's desire, brings about the shift from duality to plurality. For Gedo, development ranges from apraxia to creativity by means of a series of differentiations, beginning with the earliest self/other distinction.

In a recent work Gedo shows how semiotic transformation occurs in the analytic dyad, which, one could say, acts as a solution converting a physical state into a sign (1996). Such conversion is achieved, for example, when the analyst articulates the meaning of strange gestures as representations of unconscious attempts to evade attack. The shift from physical state to psychoanalytic sign may also take place as the patient brings a physical symptom (a seasonal allergy) into the transference and, as Freud and Ferenczi noted earlier, it joins in the conversation as a "conversion" symptom. Such a conversion symptom, once common in hysterical disorders, is constituted as a substitute sign representing a repressed sign of some sort of conflict. Gedo writes of his patient:

> After several years of analytic work, when an erotic transference to an older brother came into focus, she experienced several asthmatic attacks in the analytic setting. These turned out to represent the repetition of highly charged physical encounters in latency, in the course of which her brother literally smothered her as the climax of these covertly sexual battles. When the symptom was interpreted as symbolic fulfillment of a wish to experience similar tussles with me, these *hysterical* episodes came to their end. [1996, 28]

The asthma becomes a hysterical symptom *in* the transference dyad, the archaic dyad experienced by the patient.

In hypochondriasis, "a condition in which the physician finds neither physiological alteration nor symbolic significance . . . the only message communicated is a concrete one, that of sensing an abnormality" (30). This abnormality is coded at a presymbolic level, not in words. Decoding this message requires a semiotic partner, such as the analyst, whose attentive presence in the dyad facilitates a potentially useful regression to an archaic dyad; the transference dyad thereby becomes "representative of conditions at the very beginning of the first phase of development" (33). Such somatic symptoms amount to "a resort to potential communications that are encoded in relatively primitive ways" and may be understood as "a failure in achieving full-fledged psychic elaboration in the sense of symbolic thought" (35). The analytic act here is overtly semiotic and deals with blocked, disjointed, or displaced semiosis: "When, in the clinical situation, we succeed in attaching verbal symbols to what was previously confined to concrete bodily processes, we have filled in a deficit through direct, remedial instruction" (ibid.). It should be emphasized, however, that such remedial intervention can be effective only in the dyadic transference insofar as it recapitulates the archaic dyad in which the very first semiotic transformations took place.

We can see how Peircean semiosis works in Gedo's examples: "As in the case of the patient with dermatitis, so in that of the man with this Raynaud's syndrome; an expert observer should be in a position to use the physical evidence to initiate the symbolically encoded exchange of information about the putative emotionality that gave rise to these phenomena" (34). The physical evidence functions as a sign, an index, whose interpretant, the symbolically encoded exchange of information, denotes its object, the putative emotionality, as cause of the sign. The triadic structure of the semiosis may be indicated as follows:

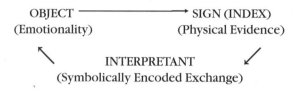

OBJECT ———————————→ SIGN (INDEX)
(Emotionality)   (Physical Evidence)

INTERPRETANT
(Symbolically Encoded Exchange)

In semiotic terms, the analytic process enables the patient (or, more precisely, the patient's blocked semiosis) to move from degenerate secondness (the bodily state as a somatic index of unknown origin and meaning) to thirdness (the somatic sign whose object is a particular emotional state) via the secondness of the transference dyad in which the interpretation as third raises the index to a rule.

In keeping with his hierarchical model, Gedo proposes "a developmental line concerning somatization, one based on the underlying capacities for increasingly complex intrapsychic and interpersonal communication" (31). This developmental line draws on Levin's schema for communication in which five modes of communicative competence (affect, gesture, words, syntactical organization, and coherent narrative) are correlated with the hierarchical model's five modes of psychic functioning (1991). Somatization, as "one facet of affective expression," stress-induced and therefore akin to trauma, is characteristic of mode I. In semiotic terms, the extreme result of trauma is akin to Peirce's category of firstness as undifferentiated quality. In Lacanian terms, this corresponds to the register of the Real as that which has no name and no image, no mediated relation.

Somatizations in analysis are often aspects of enactments which may be preverbal or prelinguistic, but not presemiotic. What is being enacted constitutes a repetition and is therefore iconic of the earlier experience. Enactments usually herald the return of archaic features of the earliest dyad and call attention to the role of mirroring in the dyad. Johansen proposes that "iconicity lies at the very core and at the very beginning of the acquisition of the semiotic function" (1993, 139), while Morris claims that "enactment is a constitutive element of a dialogic structure at the basis of psychoanalytic understanding" (1993, 34 – 35). As I have noted elsewhere, we can discern the occurrence of an enactment in the oddities of the behavior or in our reaction as the interpretant of the sign (1996). As Peirce comments, "My Dynamical Interpretant consists in direct effect actually produced by a Sign upon an Interpreter of it" (1958, 413).

The preceding remarks suggest how Peirce's semiotic framework can organize the data of psychoanalytic work. With regard to a hierarchical structure, we can now attempt to map his categories onto the hierarchical model. This model may be understood as a semiotic code that provides both a guide to assessment as well as a norm for analytic intervention. Gedo (1991) acknowledges the influence of Erikson's epigenetic schema (1963), but without its preformational aspects. As Gedo and Goldberg stated, development is not the unfolding of pre-given structures but rather self-organizing processes that result from interactions with the environment: "Epigenesis views the formation of structure as the result of successive transactions between the organism and its environment; the outcome of each phase is understood to depend on the outcomes of all previous phases. Each new phase integrates the previous phases and has a new level of organization and regulation" (1973, 12).

Such integration is not continuous but rather marked by the kind of discontinuities and phase transitions associated with complexity theory, as formulated, for example, by Thelen and Smith (1994) and Thelen (1995). Fogel and Thelen, in their review of infancy research, conclude that development is not controlled by "an epigenetic ground plan"; they attribute development to small changes in the values or relations of certain "control parameters" such as motoric strength, communicative competence, or environmental scaffolding. Infant, context, and environment form a complex dynamic system in which "a small change in the control parameter can reverberate and result in major consequences for the entire system" (1987, 750). Such small changes in control parameters, I would suggest, include the differentiation of phonemes (listening), pointing behavior (motoric indexing), the capacity to recognize one's image in a mirror (visual self-identification), and the discrimination of one's spoken name (social address), all of which take place in the first six months of infancy (Muller 1996) and enable the infant to sustain secondness, to shift from iconic to enactive, and eventually to symbolic, communication.

Whereas Peirce intended his category of firstness to include members without relationship to anything else, I would like to interpret this clinically as the category of severe regression and loss of boundaries in which one's fragile coherence as a separate person cannot be sustained. This would then be the category of "self-state" concerns as described by Kohut (1977; 1984), including susceptibility to anxiety about fragmentation, profound disorganization due to extreme trauma, and the contact with the unnameable in Lacan's category of the Real. Included in firstness would also be alexithymia (McDougall 1974) and psychosomatic ailments, which, Lacan claimed "are at the level of the Real" (1988, 96). As noted earlier, in a developmental hierarchy of functions, the category of firstness would correspond to the hierarchical model's mode I, which Gedo locates prior to neocortical functioning and gestural communication and describes as follows:

> Prepsychological era; sensorimotor organization; needs
> Inability to distinguish one's own person from the milieu
> No active defenses available; necessity for external assistance
> Danger of disorganization or traumatization
> Regulation through principle of avoidance of unpleasure [1993, 160]

The typical problem for mode I functioning is "overstimulation (or traumatization)," for which "pacification" is the most useful intervention (18).

In mode II "the single most characteristic feature of functioning" is "the simultaneous presence of. . . mutually contradictory attitudes, without felt discomfort about this dissonance (i.e., without intrapsychic conflict)" (Gedo 1987, 564). Gedo classifies various kinds of "transitional" behaviors in mode II, including "somatizations that constitute concrete communications, without symbolic referents," displaying "the coexistence of significant splitoff realms of mentation; it is this lack of self-cohesion that I look upon as the most salient characteristic of mode II" (1996, 32). He describes this mode as follows:

> Transition to experiential and subjective; symbolic functions
> Personal aims uncoordinated; independent volition of others not recognized
> Typical defense: projection
> Danger of "separation" or threats to self-cohesion
> Regulation in terms of organismic integration [1993, 160]

In Peirce's categories, mode II is the realm of "degenerate secondness"; consciousness of a particular state, without knowing its cause, takes it out of the realm of firstness. Such a state may be painful or ecstatic, there may be no sense that it will ever end, and there may be no specific object in consciousness. Such a state of mind is a second without its second and functions as an index, pointing to an unknown, often prompting an appeal for relief. Gedo states that the typical problem for this mode of functioning is "disruption of self-cohesion," with appropriate treatment "via unification of self-organization" (18).

The threat of self-fragmentation of the newly constituted self calls for the reliance on mirroring icons to maintain cohesion. The interventions of "pacification" for mode I, together with "unification" for mode II, make use of icons, empathic mirroring responses, and also what Peirce means by an index: a sign with a causal-contiguous relation to its object, a sign of the active, containing presence of the analyst. The principal function of the soothing self-object, the analyst experienced precisely not in a relationship but as a function of the self, is to produce an effective index of de-arousal and coherence. Such analytic interventions are still signs, operating according to a code, but their efficacy lies not in the use of verbal symbols but rather in the way iconic mirroring can produce a unified, iconic response, and in how the indexical gesture sets a limit, bounding and holding the fragmenting self. Such analytic action makes use of the enactive mode proper to this level of communication. In order to assist patients in restoring felt coherence, we work with them in modes I and II "sitting up," face-to-face, precisely because the human face is so richly iconic and icon-inducing. For the same reason, in the routine analytic practice that assumes higher modes of functioning, the patient on the couch as well as the analyst have only partial access to the sight of the human face, because its iconic properties would constrain them and narrow the field of associations.

Mode III is characterized by stable self-cohesion, the development of affective communication, and is "the realm of early childhood illusions or mentation characterized by the primary process" (Gedo 1987, 560). Gedo describes it as follows:

> Era of subjective wishes
> "Object constancy"; recognition of separateness of aims
> Typical defense: disavowal
> Danger of parental sanctions
> Regulation in terms of pleasure principle [1993, 160]

This mode has narcissistic features that take the form of magical illusions about one's parents and about oneself, the pursuit of narcissistic completion in the other through the disavowal of limits. Since the typical problem is the "persistence of illusions," the necessary analytic intervention is "optimal disillusionment" (18), typically through a refusal of iconic signs. Treatment crises often develop when the patient takes or demands a response as iconic mirroring of his or her state and the analyst maintains differentiated limits in order to challenge the patient's primary defense of disavowal. The disavowal of limits may take the form of claiming certainty, especially in a dyadic relationship; the task, as Wright states, is to assist the patient to move "from dyadic certainty to triadic relativism" (1991, 221). As Gedo reiterates, to take this step the patient may need instruction, especially about how to learn; such instruction, I think, consists primarily in how to recognize and use indexes.

In Peirce's terms, this would be the category of secondness, which, as noted earlier, includes members of dyads. The mode of relating dyadically is marked by oscillations between iconic mirroring and struggles to negate the other. Peirce wrote, "The second category . . . is the element of struggle. . . . By struggle I must explain that I mean mutual action between two things regardless of any sort of third or medium, and in particular regardless of any law of action" (quoted in Wilden 1984, 266). In the category of secondness, the responses of each are primarily defined by the other through intense self-other identifications and antagonisms.

Also in this category we encounter difference: "To the mind, Secondness appears as otherness" (Pharies 1985, 11). The challenge to the emerging self is to tolerate otherness in the other and thereby affirm the boundaries of the self. This category includes Lacan's rendition of the dyad as caught in the imaginary register of point-to-point correspondences, the second position in his structural analysis of "The Purloined Letter," the position that rests secure in believing it knows what the other knows (1988, 191).

In mode IV, we find "symbols of a more abstract sort, which obviate the need for somatization" (Gedo 1996, 32). In Peircean terms, this would be "degenerate thirdness," where the object of the symptom is a repressed sign, signifying intrapsychic conflict and, more likely, fear of interpersonal conflict and punishment. Gedo describes this mode of functioning as follows:

> Internalized morality; ego vs. id
> Typical defense: repression
> Danger of moral anxiety
> Regulation via reality principle [1993, 160]

The typical problem for mode IV is "intrapsychic conflict" whose solution requires "interpretation" (18). This is the most commonly discussed analytic response that attempts to make what is unconscious conscious. Conversion symptoms in hysteria, verbal slips, and compulsive rituals are conscious symptoms, signs whose objects are unconscious signs, repressed or otherwise unavailable to consciousness. Through interpretation, conscious signs are brought into relationship with unconscious signs: this is usually effected by means of an act of translation.

Mode V functioning is "the condition in which symptom formation of any kind is unnecessary" (Gedo 1996, 32). Gedo characterizes this mode as follows:

Preconscious vs. unconscious
Renunciation
Reality dangers
Creativity [1993, 160]

The typical problem for mode V functioning is "frustration," the solutions for which are pursued "via introspection" (18). Thirdness is proper to this mode, but thirdness is involved in both modes IV and V insofar as they are based on triangulation and oedipal structure. The patient functioning at these levels suffers from conflict over guilt and confusion of priorities, and has neurotic symptoms that require interpretation of symbolic, unconscious communication. Symbolic, metaphoric interventions are most effective at this level in addressing what lies beyond the repression barrier.

Peirce's category of thirdness includes all mediating functions of the code, defining the position that provides a lawful perspective on the dyad. This is the field of Lacan's Symbolic register, in which symbols mediate experience by generating interpretants of objects. The Third includes culture and society as the field of ritual and symbolization. In Lacan's terms, it is the place of the barred Other, the place of the analytic function, the place where "the name-of-the-father" signifies the laws of nature and of discourse. The Third provides a place for the shared task and context that relativizes the dyad.

The following table suggests the hierarchical organization of Peirce's semiotic categories as well as levels of functioning with the corresponding analytic interventions:

Categories:

First	Second	Third
Quality	Fact	Relation
Feeling	Action	Law

Signs:

Icon	Index	Symbol

Relation to Object:

Similarity	Contiguity	Convention

Problems:

Fragmentation	Splitting	Repression
Foreclosure of the sign as signifier	Disavowal of the interpretant	Displacement of the sign from the object

Analytic Interventions:

Create a sign to mark a boundary	Confront disavowal through indexes	Interpret signs as substitute symbols

The most common type of nonverbal analytic intervention uses mirroring responses as iconic signs to forestall fragmentation.

If the above affords a tentative, coherent integration at the level of practice, it may also extend to the level of theory and psychopathology. As Gedo and Goldberg emphasize, hierarchical models require different things from theories at each level. Firstness would then include self-state theories, dealing with how the self is differentiated and maintained. Basic self-analysis, understanding of physiological processes as well as basic differentiation of affective states, the role of boundaries at the edge of the Real, and such topics as religion and art would constitute some of the essential material for study in this category. Basic psychopathology in this category would include psychotic fragmentation, psychosomatic illness, alexithymia, and major depression.

Secondness would include object-relations theories, self-psychology, empathy, and aspects of the infant-mother dyad. Major psychopathology in this category would include serious characterological disturbance, including narcissistic and borderline personality disorders as well as severe perversions. Regression to archaic demands and gratifications in dyadic relations would be viewed in relation to the refusal of the place of the Third, of standards, of ideals rooted outside the dyad.

Thirdness includes the semiotic code that governs relationships, as well as the general system and family therapy theories that account for the dynamics of triangulated relationships. This category would include the theory of interpretation in relation to mirroring, containment and holding, and enactment, defining much of the psychoanalytic literature on technique. All forms of triangulated psychopathology would fall in this category.

With such a triadic structure of theory and practice, there is no opposition between intrapsychic and interpersonal, between intersubjective and systems theory, between soothing and interpreting—it all depends on what position we operate from, where we think the patient is functioning, which category we wish to emphasize at the moment and for what assessment reasons, and at what level we are working with a patient in a particular session. Using the hierarchical model, Holinger has usefully distinguished psychotherapy from psychoanalysis on the basis of such an assessment (1989).

A hierarchical semiotics provides an encompassing tool to embrace and codify whatever occurs in analysis. A hierarchical psychoanalytic model can then be seen to function as a semiotic code ordering the data of assessment and specifying the type of intervention in response. Such a semiotic perspective can have an integrative effect on psychoanalytic theory and practice at a time when disparate, fragmented theory and practice are pervasive.

References

Balint, Michael. *Thrills and Regressions.* New York: International Universities Press, 1959.

Bateson, G. *Mind and Nature: A Necessary Unity.* New York: Bantam Books, 1980.

Brent, Joseph. *Charles Sanders Peirce: A Life.* Bloomington: Indiana University Press, 1993.

Brickman, Harry. "Between the Devil and the Deep Blue Sea: The Dyad and the Triad in Psychoanalytic Thought." *International Journal of Psycho-Analysis* 74 (1993): 905-15.

Crapanzano, Vincent. "The Self, the Third, and Desire." In *Psychosocial Theories of the Self,* edited by B. Lee, 179-206. New York: Plenum Press, 1982.

Dewey, John. "Peirce's Theory of Linguistic Signs, Thought and Meaning." *Journal of Philosophy* 63 (1946): 85-95.

Erikson, Erik. *Childhood and Society.* 2d. ed. New York: Norton, 1963.

Fogel, Allen, and Thelen, Esther. "Development of Early Expressive and Communicative Action: Reinterpreting the Evidence from a Dynamic Systems Perspective." *Developmental Psychology* 23 (1987): 747-61.

Gedo, John. "Transference Neurosis, Archaic Transference, and the Compulsion to Repeat." *Psychoanalytic Inquiry* 7 (1987): 511-67.

——. *The Biology of Clinical Encounters: Psychoanalysis as a Science of Mind.* Hillsdale, N.J.: Analytic Press, 1991.

——. *Beyond Interpretation: Toward a Revised Theory for Psychoanalysis.* Rev. ed. Hillsdale, N.J.: Analytic Press, 1993.

——. "The Primitive Psyche, Communication, and the Language of the Body." In *The Languages of Psychoanalysis,* 26-36. Hillsdale, N.J.: Analytic Press, 1996.

Gedo, John, and Goldberg, Arnold. *Models of the Mind: A Psychoanalytic Theory.* Chicago: University of Chicago Press, 1973.

Holinger, Paul. "A Developmental Perspective on Psychotherapy and Psychoanalysis." *American Journal of Psychiatry* 146 (1989): 1404-12.

Houser, Nathan. Introduction to Peirce (1992), xix-xli.

Johansen, Jorgen. *Dialogic Semiosis: An Essay on Signs and Meaning.* Bloomington: Indiana University Press, 1993.

Kirshner, Lewis. "Trauma, the Good Object, and the Symbolic: A Theoretical Integration." *International Journal of Psycho-Analysis* 75 (1994): 235-42.

Kohut, Heinz. *The Restoration of the Self.* New York: International Universities Press, 1977.

——. *How Does Analysis Cure?* Edited by Arnold Goldberg and Paul Stepansky. Chicago: University of Chicago Press, 1984.

Lacan, Jacques. *The Ego in Freud's Theory and in the Technique of Psychoanalysis.* Bk. 2 of *The Seminar of Jacques Lacan* (1954 - 55). Edited by Jacques-Alain Miller and translated by Sylvana Tomaselli. New York: W. W. Norton, 1988.

Levin, Fred. *Mapping the Mind: The Intersection of Psychoanalysis and Neuroscience.* Hillsdale, N.J.: Analytic Press, 1991.

McDougall, Joyce. "The Psychosoma and the Psychoanalytic Process." *International Review of Psycho-Analysis* 1 (1974): 437 - 59.

Modell, Arnold. *Psychoanalysis in a New Context.* New York: International Universities Press, 1984.

——. *The Private Self.* Cambridge: Harvard University Press, 1993.

Morris, Humphrey. "Narrative Representation, Narrative Enactment, and the Psychoanalytic Construction of History." *International Journal of Psycho-Analysis* 74 (1993): 33 - 54.

Muller, John. *Beyond the Psychoanalytic Dyad: Developmental Semiotics in Freud, Peirce, and Lacan.* New York: Routledge, 1996.

Ogden, Thomas. "The Analytic Third: Working with Intersubjective Clinical Facts." *International Journal of Psycho-Analysis* 75 (1994): 3 - 19.

Peirce, Charles Sanders. *The Essential Peirce: Selected Philosophical Writings.* Vol. 1 (1867 - 93). Edited by Nathan Houser and Christian Kloesel. Bloomington: Indiana University Press, 1992.

——. "A Guess at the Riddle" (1887 - 88). In Peirce (1992).

——. "The Architecture of Theories" (1891). In Peirce (1992).

——. *Selected Writings.* Edited by Philip Wiener. New York: Dover Publications, 1958.

Pharies, David. *Charles S. Peirce and the Linguistic Sign.* Philadelphia: John Benjamins Publishing, 1985.

Rodgers, Terry. "The Clinical Theories of John Gedo: A Synopsis." *Psychoanalytic Inquiry* 14 (1994): 235 - 42.

Schoenhals, Helen. "Triangular Space and the Development of a Working Model in the Analysis." *International Journal of Psycho-Analysis* 76 (1995): 103 - 13.

Sebeok, Thomas. "One, Two, Three Spells UBERTY." In *The Sign of Three: Dupin, Holmes, Peirce,* edited by Umberto Eco and Thomas Sebeok, 1 - 10. Bloomington: Indiana University Press, 1983.

Spielman, Lisa A., Pratto, Felicia, and Bargh, John A. "Automatic affect." *American Behavioral Scientist* 31 (1988): 296 - 311.

Thelen, Esther. "Motor Development: A New Synthesis." *American Psychologist* 50 (1995): 79 - 95.

Thelen, Esther, and Smith, Linda. *A Dynamic Systems Approach to the Development of Cognition and Action.* Cambridge: MIT Press, 1994.

von Bertalanffy, Ludwig. *General System Theory: Foundations, Development, Applications.* New York: George Braziller, 1968.

——. "The History and Development of General System Theory" (1972). In *Perspectives on General System Theory: Scientific-Philosophical Studies,* edited by E. Taschdjian, 149 - 69. New York: George Braziller, 1975.

Wilden, Anthony. *System and Structure: Essays in Communication and Exchange.* 2d ed. London: Tavistock Publications, 1984.

Wilson, Arnold, and Gedo, John, eds. *Hierarchical Concepts in Psychoanalysis: Theory, Research, and Clinical Practice.* New York: Guilford Press, 1993.

Wolff, Peter. *The Development of Behavioral States and the Expression of Emotions in Early Infancy: New Proposals for Investigation.* Chicago: University of Chicago Press, 1987.

Wright, Kenneth. *Vision and Separation: Between Mother and Baby.* Northvale, N.J.: Jason Aronson, 1991.

5 Feeling and Firstness in Freud and Peirce

Joseph H. Smith

In the first phase of psychoanalytic theory, affect, according to David Rapaport, was equated with psychic energy (1953, 480). In 1894 Freud wrote that "in mental functions something is to be distinguished—a quota of affect or sum of excitation—which possesses all the characteristics of a quantity (though we have no means of measuring it), which is capable of increase, diminution, displacement and discharge, and which is spread over the memory-traces of ideas somewhat as an electric charge is spread over the surface of the body" (*S.E.* 3:60).

In the second phase of psychoanalysis, Freud understood affect to be the product of the discharge of part of the accumulated drive cathexes when direct discharge in action could not take place. Rapaport termed this the "conflict theory" of affects and mentioned that it was advocated also by, among others, John Dewey, who wrote, "When there is no inhibition there is no overflow and no affect" (1894–95).

Although these phases are less sharply delineated than this quick summary would suggest, in the third phase, with *Inhibitions, Symptoms and Anxiety* (1926), Freud conceptualized affect as conscious ego response to inner and outer events, and the emphasis was on signal affect in response to *anticipating* situations—anxiety, for example, in response to anticipating dangers. It is this signal function of affect, already acknowledged in chapter 7 of *The Interpretation of Dreams* (1900), that "provides the thought process with its most important signposts" (*S.E.* 5:602).

At first glance, with affect as consciously inaccessible charge in the first phase, as manifestation of conflict in the second, and as what could be taken as mediator of response to stimulus in the third, it might be tempting to interpret these not just as levels of theory but as levels of affect in accord with the Peircean categories.[1] I shall here refrain from so sweeping an identity in favor of first pursuing the questions of what affect is and what the signifying role of affect might be. Freud and Peirce, I believe, offer the best chance of approaching those questions.

First of all, let me assert that the reason philosophic and psychoanalytic understanding of affect remains so murky has something to do with an evanescence inherent in affect. I refer not just to what Peirce called feeling as firstness but also to the ephemeral quality of conscious feelings as response, affect as secondness, and, even, feelings as thirdness, as in Peirce's example of sympathy.[2] Affect (or feeling, or emotion, terms I use interchangeably) does not so much lend itself to definition as to evocation. Freud's definitions, for instance, of affect as quantitative charge, which Rapaport attributes to his first phase, and second-phase affect as the product of conflict (and again as a quantity capable of being dammed up or discharged), could not be more untrue to the nature of affect. In fairness to Freud, taking his lines cited above about "something . . .—a quota of affect, a sum of excitation—which possesses all the characteristics of a quantity" to be a statement of his first theory of affect was a Rapaportian mistake. "Affect" was thrown into those speculations about a "something" as a metaphor at hand to represent psychic energy and to occupy the gap that was to be filled later by the conceptualization of drive cathexis. The metaphor of affect "spread over the memory traces of ideas," although less charming, is about on the level of Peirce's suggestion that consciousness arises as "a sort of public spirit among the nerve cells" (*CP* 1.354).

Freud himself qualified this statement by saying that "this hypothesis . . . can be applied in the same sense as physicists apply the hypothesis of a flow of electric fluid. It is provisionally justified by its utility in coordinating and explaining a great variety of psychical states" (*S.E.* 3:61). Of course, the hypothesis better fits the "energy—the cathexis—of the instinctual drive" (Rapaport 1960, 874). As Rapaport observed, in the first phase, affect was equated with psychic energy. "Indeed," he wrote, "the use of the term affect as though it were psychic energy (cathexis) . . . persists in psychoanalytic literature to our own day" (1953, 481). I can avow that his 1953 statement still obtains in 1996.

Affect theory of the third phase—affect as quality, as signal, as always and only conscious arising in response to present, remembered, or anticipated situations—is a theory that is both viable and, I believe, compatible with Peirce's thought. Rather than quantitative charge, the first phase of affect theory in Freud should be taken in terms of his discussions of consciousness and quality in the *Project* and in chapter 7 of *The Interpretation of Dreams*. The apparatus of consciousness, Freud believed, is like the surface sheet of a magic writing pad; in order to be always accessible to fresh impressions it is incapable of memory. Affect and perception are or have qualities, and it is only by virtue of quality that anything is accessible to consciousness. "Consciousness," Freud wrote, "which we look upon in the light of a sense organ for the apprehension of psychical qualities . . . can receive excitations from the periphery of the whole apparatus, the perceptual system, and in addition . . . excitations of pleasure and unpleasure . . . [from within] the apparatus" (*S.E.* 5:574). Consciousness begins in an affective and perceptual blur and affect continues as the ongoing matrix of consciousness. Recall Peirce's statement "To be conscious is nothing else than to feel" (*CP* 1.318).

Taken in this way, Freud's first theory of affect is closer to the third (affect as conscious ego response) than to the second (affect as quantity capable of being dammed up or discharged). In fact, as stated above, the third-phase signal function of affect was already stated in chapter 7 of the Dream Book. The problem for current thought is not just that affect of the second phase was taken as a quantity; the more insidious effect was the persistence of reifying metaphors in the third phase. Rather than remaining true to the idea of affect as conscious ego response, Freud of the third phase still often wrote of affect produced or reproduced by the ego, or of affect transformed into another affect as opposed to a new, fresh, and different affective response arising with a change of the situation. Freud was repeatedly drawn into these misleading and reifying metaphors, and repeatedly felt called upon to correct them (Smith 1970).

The main turning point toward Freud's final theory of feeling was *Inhibitions, Symptoms and Anxiety* (1926). It was in this work that he moved away from the idea that anxiety, like vinegar from wine, was "spoiled" libido — libido transformed because repressed. Repression was no longer the cause of anxiety: the formula was reversed. Repression occurs because of danger signaled by anxiety. Needless to say, at that point psychoanalysis became far more complex than simply cure by catharsis, cure by lifting repression so that repressed affects could be abreacted.

But, Freud wavers. At one point he writes, "It seems as though the longing turns into anxiety" (*S.E.* 20:137). At another, he writes of transformation of an impulse (and implicitly an affect) but actually accounts for a different affective response on the basis of regressive degradation. As he phrases it, "One might say that the impulse had been transformed into its opposite" (133). It is not clear whether he means affect is "transformed," or whether the tentativeness indicated by "it seems" and "one might say" means that affect might appear to be transformed to superficial observation. Such ambiguity runs throughout *Inhibitions, Symp-*

toms and Anxiety. Freud renounces the idea of affect being transformed in favor of a changed affective response to a changed situation. "The problem," he wrote, "of 'transformation of affect' under repression disappears" (91). Yet he keeps returning to the idea that affect *may,* in certain instances, be a product of transformed libido (109). It was at the conclusion of such a passage that he wrote "*non liquet*" (110).

While at times he wrote of repressed and unconscious affect, Freud took pains to explain that such phrases should be understood as referring to the fresh affective response to what had been repressed that occurs when repression is lifted, and not as implying that repressed unconscious affect had been there, along with unconscious ideas, all the while (*S.E.* 14:178). That caveat was expressed succinctly in *Civilization and Its Discontents* (1930): to have a clear "psychological conscience," he there wrote, "we cannot speak of unconscious anxiety" (*S.E.* 21:135; cf. *S.E.* 19:22–23). However, Freud's reifying metaphors, along with the tendency of everyone else to reify, along with the evanescence of affect itself, along with the difficulty beyond poetry, art, music, and the immediacy of human response to render in words what affect is—all of these led to the forgetting of Freud's caveats. I in no way exaggerate in estimating that psychoanalysts who assume that affects can be repressed and have unconscious existence would rank somewhere above the ninety-ninth percentile.

Feeling as Firstness in Peirce

Houser writes that feeling as firstness "is discovered only by logico-phenomenological analysis, and *cannot be conceived of distinctly.* . . . The feeling of . . . [firstness] is independent of being perceived or remembered, it is not related to anything. Pure feeling *is not felt,* where 'to feel' means 'to be aware'. . . . In its immediacy, unanalyzed and perfectly alone, feeling is not consciousness, but is an element of consciousness" (1983, 333). As Houser notes, Peirce wrote that feeling as firstness "is not a psychological datum. . . . We can no more start with immediate feelings in psychology than we can start with accurate places of the planets, as affected by parallax, aberration, refraction, etc. in astronomy. We start with mediate data, subject to error, and requiring correction" (*CP* 7.465).

The idea that consciousness begins as an undifferentiated affective and perceptual blur, inaccessible as such to consciousness, would not have been a point of disagreement between Freud and Peirce. Although he may have had a different set of ideas in mind, Freud did assert that "everything conscious has an unconscious preliminary stage" (*S.E.* 5:612). This is not to say there is any certainty that Freud would have accepted Peircean feeling as firstness in toto. Peirce wrote, "The first . . . must be initiative, original, spontaneous, and free; otherwise it is second to a determining cause" (*CP* 1:357). But he also wrote, "By a feeling, I mean an instance of that kind of consciousness which involves no analysis, comparison or any process whatever, . . . which has its own positive quality which consists in nothing else, and which is of itself all that it is, *however it may have been brought about*" (*CP* 1:306; my italics). I take this to mean that quality, feelings as firsts, and what Rorty calls "unsensed *sensibilia*" (1961, 202), characterize the immediacy of consciousness, which is inaccessible to consciousness just because of its immediacy. The idea of quality as such is arrived at by abstracting a "feeling that retains its positive character but absolutely loses all relation" (*CP* 8.267). By feeling as firstness, Peirce, following Tetens,[3] means "whatever is directly and immediately in consciousness . . . without regard to what it signifies, to what its parts are, to what causes it, or any of its relations to anything else" (*CP* 7.540).

While feeling is here defined aside from relations, such references to causes can be taken as Peirce's acknowledgment that even the immediacy of consciousness has some sort of promptings, even though not the kind of definitive response we take the conscious experience of feelings as secondness to be. The problem in comparing Peirce and Freud here may reside in the different meanings they attach to "experience." Peirce often means that which we consciously encounter as facts.[4] For Freud anything conscious, preconscious, repressed (unconscious but potentially capable of being brought into consciousness), or unconscious in principle (like instincts or the mental apparatus as such) are aspects of what a person experiences.

The point of agreement about quality being the requisite for conscious accessibility left both Freud and Peirce with the task of accounting for how the complexity of consciousness arises from the primitive affective and perceptual blur. This is to say, beyond affects, beyond percepts, and beyond primitive ideation as hallucinatory memories of percepts, how do thoughts achieve conscious accessibility? Freud, after hitting on the idea that quality was achieved by thing-representations becoming associated with word-representations, stayed with that position throughout, or almost throughout, his life, only to retract it in the posthumously published *An Outline of Psycho-Analysis* (*S.E.* 23:162). His final conclusion was that instead of preconscious functioning being solely dependent on word-representations, the latter were indicators that preconscious organization and functioning had been established.

Ideas and Affect

The implication is that thinking in images precedes language as such. Thinking in images, to paraphrase Lacan, is structured like a language. In the beginning, the image-idea shifts for the word. The cathected memory traces are the enduring marks, the lasting structures that facilitate the paths or habits of thought. On facilitation Freud and Peirce (and also Derrida) are in agreement. Recall that an idea is the cathexis of a remembered percept. If the idea arises in a hungry infant as an image of the remembered and anticipated mother, would not that situation itself structure the implicit sentence, "I want you"? Consciousness, then, beyond the primitive, is consciousness of relationships (Rapaport 1951, 422; 1950, 320).

Freud's original position on ideation and affect was that the idea and affect arise as representatives of instinctual drive. Both the idea/image and the affect represent or indicate need as danger. Initially, the affect of distress more directly indicates need and danger whereas the idea is a turning away from need toward an image of the object promising resolution of need.

The cry can be taken as a cry for the mother and also as a crying out against the danger of need. Since the need is that which is inner and the object promising resolution is outer, if faith is not established in the object, crying against the inner need, rather than crying for the mother, becomes dominant. This can become established as a pattern of turning inward in self-attack, the seeds of what Freud called the death instinct, the source of the negative therapeutic reaction, masochism, the repetition compulsion, and the various modes of self-defeating, self-destructive behavior (Smith 1986; 1992; 1995b; 1996). Such lack of faith would be reflected not only in negative affect but in altered patterns of ideation and thought. It is likely that in ideation there would be a turning away from an image of the mother, or the experience of perverse and monstrous rather than happy images of her and of her return.

But the point I want to emphasize is that in either event, in the case of predominantly positive or predominantly negative experience, ideas— not affects—are the building blocks of psychic structure or, in Peirce's terms, habit formation. Affects, always arising anew, may guide this process but, in and of themselves, have no permanence. Memory traces endure.

Regarding thought and qualities, Peirce wrote, "Thoughts are neither qualities nor facts. They are not qualities because they can be produced and grow, while a quality is eternal, independent of time and of any realization. Besides, thoughts may have reasons, and indeed, must have some reasons, good or bad. But to ask why a quality is as it is, why red is red and not green, would be lunacy" (*CP* 1.420). Regarding ideas and affects, Freud wrote, "The whole difference arises from the fact that ideas are cathexes—ultimately of memory traces—whilst affects and emotions correspond to processes of discharge, the final manifestations of which are perceived as feelings. In the present state of our knowledge of affects and emotions we cannot express this difference more clearly" (*S.E.* 14:178). Even though I submit this 1915 statement as matching Peirce's, it is drenched, to be sure, with the overemphasis on economics and suggestions of the quantitative that characterized Freud's thought in that era. In a self-correcting move of 1926, Freud wrote,

> How is it possible, from an economic point of view, for a mere process of withdrawing of a preconscious ego-cathexis, to produce unpleasure and anxiety, seeing that, according to our assumptions, unpleasure and anxiety can only arise as a result of an *increase* in cathexis? The reply is that this causal sequence should not be explained from an economic point of view. Anxiety is not newly created in repression [a reference to the earlier view of anxiety as the wine-into-vinegar transformation of repressed libido]; it is reproduced as an affective state in accordance with an already existing mnemic image. [*S.E.* 20:93]

Lingering on, even here, are the quantitative metaphors of affect "created" or "reproduced" rather than affect as a fresh, new response to a present situation in accord with the memory of prior situations. In the light of this second passage, nevertheless, I submit that the first Freudian passage and also the passage from Peirce on thought and qualities can be condensed into the statement that ideas are the structuralized aspect of ego response to inner and outer events and affects the unstructuralized response (Smith 1970, 542). Ideas last. For Peirce, firstness is the *quality* of immediate consciousness (*CP* 1.343). Qualities, in Peirce's terms, are eternal, but our experience of the eternal is ephemeral.

Consciousness

To retrace some of Freud's steps to account for complex consciousness, I return to his beginning—to his account of primitive consciousness—and some of the connections with the thought of Peirce. Memory at this primitive level, the blurred hallucination of a prior experience of feeding, is the identity of perception, meaning that there is as yet no differentiation of idea and percept. It would not, of course, be marked in the mind of the infant as a memory. It *is,* nevertheless, a memory, and also, since it is a memory arising with renewed hunger, an *anticipation* of the mother's return. While the mind of the neonate is unstructured, the situation *is* structured in terms of exigent need, the capacity of the infant to image a prior feeding, and a delay, followed by a return of the mother. This structure of the situation, as I have suggested, allows for structuralization of the mind of the infant.

It is the mother—the object—that comes into view before the self. Of course, recognition of an other, as Peirce noted, involves the simultaneous existence of a recognizing "I," even if the "I" remains, initially, more murky than the object it beholds. "We become aware of ourselves," Peirce wrote, "in becoming aware of the not-self." Peirce makes the point in a variety of ways:

> The typical phenomenon may be described as follows. From the general mass of consciousness, as yet void of any marked determination, suddenly a more definite idea, the *Object* or *Not-Me,* separates itself like a crystal from a clear solution, and like a crystal *grows,* while the rest of consciousness—the mother liquor, so to speak—the *Me,* seems, as it were, to boast of the new birth, as *Its Own,* oblivious of the seminal suggestion that must have been present as a nucleus. [quoted in Houser 1983, 342; see also Peirce 1992, 18–19; Peirce 1958, 223; and Colapietro 1989, 70]

Peirce also referred to this theme elsewhere, as Houser notes, when he questioned the practice of claiming personal possession of one's mind: "One must not take a nominalistic view of Thought as if it were something that a man had in his consciousness. Consciousness may mean any one of the three categories. But if it is to mean Thought it is more without us than within. It is we that are in it, rather than it in any of us" (quoted in Houser 1983, 345).

Those familiar with Lacan will immediately recognize the closeness of the first Peirce passage to Lacan's mirror stage and the second passage to Lacan's concept of the Other. As for the first, however, the *Me* that Peirce writes of would be a not-yet "*Me.*" It would not so much boast of the object as the new birth of "*Its Own*"; it would not so much own or have, but rather *be* the object. The first developmental task is to differentiate the identity of perception (the object as hallucinated) from the identity of thought (the mother as real object of satisfaction). This is a first step in accomplishing the second task, which is to differentiate self and object— to accomplish selfhood in the sense of having a mother rather than being the mother.

The Pleasure Principle

My aim here is to focus on the place of affect in consciousness and as consciousness, and on affect as providing thought with "its most important signposts." As indicated above, repression is not instituted merely to avoid anxiety. Freud wrote, "This does not go deep enough. It would be truer to say that symptoms are created so as to avoid a *danger-situation* whose presence has been signalled by . . . anxiety" (*S.E.* 20:129). Similarly, imaging the object is not merely a quest for pleasure. It is, instead, a quest for the object. That refinding the object is pleasurable does not mean that the fundamental aim is the achievement of pleasure. Nor is remembered pleasure—the memory of an affect—the guide toward the object. The guide toward the object is, instead, the memory of the experience of satisfaction which takes the form of an image of the anticipated object of satisfaction and evokes the vividness of an immediate affect, not just the pale memory of an affect. That the object provided an experience of satisfaction, initially the resolution of exigent need, is what stamps the memory of that experience with a positive valence, not simply that it was pleasurable.

The pleasure principle, "the most frequently and most radically misunderstood psychoanalytic concept" (Rapaport 1960, 875), a principle having nothing to do with pleasure per se (Rapaport 1957–59, 1:74), refers to the direction of psychic activity away from a point of disequilibrium or imbalance and toward equilibrium or balance (Smith 1977; 1991, 32–35; 1995a). The parallel Peircean passage is as follows: "Now it is precisely action according to final causes which distinguishes mental from mechanical action; and the general formula of all our desires may be taken as this: to remove a stimulus. Every man is busily working to bring to an end that state of things which now excites him to work" (*CP* 1.392).

The pleasure principle (just as is Peirce's statement) is a general principle that includes activity referred to by Freud as the reality principle. While in and of itself a principle of tension reduction, the work that is excited by a danger or imbalance encounters delays, obstacles, and facilitations whereby that which constitutes imbalance or balance changes. In Peirce's terms, in the process of work, habit formation occurs. In psychoanalytic terms, in the process of work, tension maintaining structure formation occurs.

Peirce's own arguments against pleasure (rather than object) as goal include his conviction that "it is a great mistake to suppose that the phenomena of pleasure and pain are mainly phenomena of feeling" (*CP* 5.122); "*pleasure and pain are more than pure monadic feelings*" (*CP*

8.75, Peirce's italics). He also believed that "the position of the hedonists is preposterous, in that they make mere feelings to be active agencies, instead of being merely conscious indications of real determinations of our subconscious volitional beings" (*CP* 1.333).

I assume that no consciously experienced affect is purely monadic. There are different kinds of pleasure and different kinds of pain. In any event, pleasure and pain, as is the case with virtually all affects encountered in psychoanalytic texts, are pleasure and pain in *response* to remembered, presently encountered, or anticipated experience—in that sense, feelings as secondness. That affects have a role in mediating change and enlarging understanding of one's self and one's situation (as in sympathy and as in signaling either danger or the object of desire) is affect as thirdness. Affect as thirdness also goes counter to pleasure as such being a goal.

Desire and the Object

The goal of thought is the object through which the aim of satisfaction can be achieved. But in the development of the subject—or, in Peirce's terms, the growth of the subject—aims and objects change (*S.E.* 14:122–23). In trying to think Peirce, Freud, and Lacan together, and in trying to think the difference between animal instinct and human instinctual drive, change of object is a crucial issue.

According to Rapaport,

> the defining characteristic *object* is the outstanding conceptual invention in Freud's theory of the instinctual drive. One of the basic problems of all psychology is how to resolve the paradox that as a science it is to give an explanation, in terms of causes, of behavior, which is a purposive, i.e., teleological, phenomenon in its very nature. Freud's solution of this paradox is to postulate the object as a defining characteristic. [1960, 877–78]

Recall Peirce's statement above, "Now it is precisely action according to final causes which distinguishes mental from mechanical action" (*CP* 1.392). Add to that Freud's statement, "The object . . . is what is most variable about an instinct" (*S.E.* 14:122). Add further that the establishment of human selfhood coincides with the establishment of temporal dimensions. The human remembers and anticipates the object, comes to know the object in ways other than just as an object of need, and is capable of change of object.

Having an image of the object is already a step toward self/object differentiation. It is the establishment of a capacity to delay and a primitive mode of remembering and anticipating the object rather than peremptorily hallucinating the object as present.

Let us also add to these considerations Lacan's thought on demand and desire. For Lacan, demand, although a specific wish, is always also a demand for unconditional love; satisfactions of such specific wishes are taken as tokens of such love (1977, 265, 286, 311), tokens, that is, of impossible love, love as permanent presence, love as remerger with the other. Between the time of being able to take the satisfaction of any need as token of having it all, and the time of being able to own lack and finitude, the satisfaction of any wish, by comparison with all that it "ought" to betoken, is itself a crushing disappointment. In Lacan's words, "Demand annuls the particularity of everything that can be granted by transmuting it into a proof of love, and the very satisfactions that it obtains for need are reduced . . . to the level of being no more than the crushing of the demand for love" (286).

It is in this interval of lostness, between assuming continuous merger and owning lack, that desire comes to be. But desire for what? The crushing of demand implies an initial lack of aim and object. This nothingness at the core of desire Lacan named the *objet petit a* (1978, 180).[5] The initial lack of aim and object both differentiates desire from instinctual drive and also allows for change of object of instinctual drive and the metonymic changes of aims and objects of desire.

According to Lacan, desire is that of which the *objet petit a* is the cause, and the ultimate guilt is in response to ceding one's desire (1992, 319). Desire beyond demand, desire hollowed out of demand, desire recognized as remaining when any specific demand is met, is a first lighting up of the subject, a first owning of demand as "mine," and thus a crucial step in recognizing the separateness of self and other.

Demand is demand for the impossible, not yet recognized as impossible. Desire encounters the impossible. Primitively, the law comes into being as the impossible, as the no-saying impossibility of remerger with the original object. To encounter such impossibility, however, is to encounter also the otherness of the other which opens the possibility of refinding the object as other and the possibility of change of object. The encounter that says no to remerger is, at once, the encounter that institutes a call not to cede one's desire. The object of desire changes, is elevated, from the previous quest for remerger to a quest to refind the object as other. The "no" to remerger establishes an opening for new objects.

The quest for the original object shapes every subsequent quest. But the proximal source of desire is not the bodily disequilibrium of the instinctually driven original quest. The self comes into being with a concern for itself. The proximal sources of desire arise from disequilibria within that self. It is not only the object that changes: change of object coincides with the change from merger to separateness of the self.

Objects of Danger and Objects of Desire

As emotional interpretants, feelings are an initial indicator of the established valency of that to which they respond. The signifying role of feelings is, initially, to guide one toward experience anticipated as positive and away from experience anticipated as negative. When certain experiences continue to be endowed with a positive valence, structure building or habit formation is established. If that which evokes affective response is or becomes a negative experience the response is anxiety, signaling the necessity of avoidance, including avoidance by means of repression. With further development and experience, however, avoiding danger is not by automatic repression. The object of danger becomes known, and a judgment is made as to whether it is to be avoided or faced. The same possibilities for decision open up regarding the object of desire.

That consciousness as such—consciousness beyond feeling as first-ness—is consciousness of relationships is an idea that has an important bearing on the different fate of affect in hysterical and obsessional disorders. In hysteria, the affect is said to be displaced, that is, some insignificant item stands for a repressed, significant item and thus evokes the affective response that the latter, if unrepressed, would itself evoke. In obsessional disorders, the affect is said to be isolated. But what this means is that relationships, the connection between ideas, and thus the significance of certain objects of danger and desire are deleted from awareness so that their presence in consciousness signals neither danger nor desire.

In the primitive state, *what* one approaches or *what* one avoids would not yet be known. With differentiation of objects of danger and objects of desire and with knowledge of relationships established by virtue of language as a system, subtler and more various affective responses appear. The capacity for more nuanced affective response is secondary to more nuanced discriminations of thought, even though affective response may have initially led to the establishment of those discriminations. The defining statements of affect here gleaned from Freud and Peirce are that feeling is always and only conscious; feelings are evanescent and always a fresh response to that which ideation and thought reveal; primitive feelings more directly represent, and in that sense are truer to inner need and danger than ideation, which turns away from need in an image of the object promising resolution of need; and, accordingly, affect is more directly associated with the development of the subject while ideation leads more directly to the constitution of the object.

Beyond Pleasure

Regarding affectivity and change of object, Peirce wrote that feelings form "the warp and woof of cognition" (quoted in Buchler 1955, 96). He also wrote of quality as ground and quality as a general attribute (*CP* 1:551), and that "whatever is in the mind in any mode of consciousness there is necessarily an immediate consciousness and consequently a feeling . . . [and] every operation of the mind, however complex, has its absolutely simple feeling, the emotion of the *tout ensemble* . . . a secondary feeling or sensation excited from within the mind" (*CP* 1.311).

With the "manifold of impressions," Peirce wrote, "we have a feeling of complication or confusion, which leads us to differentiate this impression from that, and then, having been differentiated, they require to be brought to unity. Now they are not brought to unity until we conceive them together as being *ours,* that is, until we refer them to a conception as their interpretant" (*CP* 1.554). The idea of a simple feeling in response to the manifold of inner and outer impressions, a kind of integrate affective response to the manifold, always there afresh at every step of the way, would suggest a role of affect in guiding thought toward such an interpretant.

Peirce believed that "conduct controlled by ethical reason tends toward fixing certain habits of conduct, the nature of which . . . does not depend upon any accidental circumstances, and *in that sense* may be said to be *destined*" (*CP* 5.430). Peircean pragmaticism "does not make the *summum bonum* to consist in action, but makes it to consist in that process of evolution whereby the existent comes more and more to embody those generals which . . . [are] *destined,* which is what we strive to express in calling them *reasonable*" (*CP* 5.433). Through time and the generations, "by virtue of man's capacity for learning, and by experience continually pouring over him" (*CP* 5.402 n. 2), civilization moves toward clearness of apprehension and reasonableness. According to Peirce,

> Every object that has ever been proposed as desirable in itself without any ulterior reason belongs to one or the other of three classes. Namely it either consists
> A. in superinducing upon a feeling a particular quality, say pleasure; or
> B. in extending the existence of some well-known thing, whether one's own life, or some known creed or community, or what not; or
> C. in furthering the realization of some ideal description of a state of things. [*CP* 8.136]

Beyond choice of object for the sake of pleasure (A), and beyond, for example, preservation of the imaginary unity of one's self or of one's kind (B), for Peirce, the direction of human evolution and the tendency of individual development are toward the realization of clarity (C), a belief anchored in a "deep impression of the majesty of truth, as that to which, sooner or later, every knee must bow" (*CP* 8.136).

Notes

1. For a concise statement of the Peircean categories, see Brent (1993), 70.

2. "Sympathy, flesh and blood, that by which I feel my neighbor's feeling, is third" (Buchler 1955, 80). "Intellectual sympathy . . . is a consciousness belonging to the category of Representation, though representing something in the Category of Quality of feeling" (*CP* 5.113). For Peirce, "thirdness . . . is only a synonym for Representation (*CP* 5.105; 1.338–39). "*CP*," followed by volume and paragraph numbers, refers to *Collected Papers of Charles Sanders Peirce.*

3. Peirce writes that Kant borrowed from "his master Tetens" the idea of "Feeling, Knowledge, and Will . . . as the three classes of states of mind" (*CP* 7.540). Kant, however, departed from Teten's understanding by limiting "the word Feeling to feelings of pleasure and pain" (ibid.; see this entire paragraph for a clear statement of what Peirce means by "feeling as firstness").

4. "I call such forcible modification of our ways of thinking the influence of the world of fact or *experience*" (*CP* 1.321; see also *CP* 1.328, 335, 336, 427, 537).

5. Lacan states, "This object, which is in fact simply the presence of a hollow, a void, which can be occupied, Freud tells us, by any object and whose agency we know only in the form of the lost object, the *petit a*" (1978, 180).

I have suggested (1996) that this nothingness is not only an emptiness but also the clearing in which language and the specifically human arise. Being true to one's desire does not mean being insistent on the fulfillment of desire, let alone the fulfillment of any particular desire. Trueness to one's desire is recognition that lack of any total fulfillment is the essence of being human and that that lack, if not foreclosed, remains the clearing and source from which renewal is always possible.

References

Brent, Joseph. *Charles Sanders Peirce: A Life.* Bloomington: Indiana University Press, 1993.

Buchler, Justus. *Philosophical Writings of Peirce.* New York: Dover Publications, 1955.

Colapietro, Vincent M. *Peirce's Approach to the Self: A Semiotic Perspective on Human Subjectivity.* Albany: State University of New York Press, 1989.

Dewey, John. "The Theory of Emotion." *Psychological Review* (1894–95): 1:553–69, 2:13–32.

Freud, Sigmund. *The Standard Edition of the Complete Psychological Works of*

Sigmund Freud. Edited and translated by James Strachey. 24 vols. London: Hogarth, 1953–74.

"Neuro-Psychoses of Defense" (1894), vol. 3

The Interpretation of Dreams (1900), vols. 4, 5.

"Instincts and Their Vicissitudes" (1915), vol. 14.

"The Unconscious" (1915), vol. 14.

The Ego and the Id (1923), vol. 19.

Inhibitions, Symptoms and Anxiety (1926), vol. 20.

Civilization and Its Discontents (1930), vol. 21.

An Outline of Psycho-Analysis (1940), vol. 23.

Houser, Nathan. "Peirce's General Taxonomy of Consciousness." *Transactions of the Charles S. Peirce Society* 19, no. 4 (1983): 331–59.

Lacan, Jacques. *Écrits: A Selection.* Translated by Alan Sheridan. New York: W. W. Norton, 1977.

―――. *The Four Fundamental Concepts of Psycho-Analysis.* Edited by Jacques-Alain Miller and translated by Alan Sheridan. New York: W. W. Norton, 1978.

―――. *The Ethics of Psychoanalysis, 1959–1960.* Bk. 7 of *The Seminar of Jacques Lacan.* Edited by Jacques-Alain Miller. Translated, with notes, by Dennis Porter. New York: W. W. Norton, 1992.

Peirce, Charles Sanders. *Charles S. Peirce: Selected Writings (Values in a Universe of Chance).* Edited, with an introduction and notes, by Philip P. Wiener. New York: Dover Publications, 1958.

―――. *Collected Papers of Charles Sanders Peirce.* Edited by Charles Hartshorne and Paul Weiss. 8 vols. Cambridge: Harvard University Press, 1931–58.

―――. *The Essential Peirce: Selected Philosophical Writings.* Vol. 1 (1867–93). Edited by Nathan Houser and Christian Kloesel. Bloomington: Indiana University Press, 1992.

Rapaport, David. *The Collected Papers of David Rapaport.* Edited by Merton M. Gill. New York: Basic Books, 1967.

―――. "On the Psychoanalytic Theory of Thinking" (1950). In Rapaport (1967).

―――. "The Conceptual Model of Psychoanalysis" (1951). In Rapaport (1967).

―――. "On the Psychoanalytic Theory of Affects" (1953). In Rapaport (1967).

―――. "Seminars on Elementary Metapsychology" Mimeographed copies of seminars held at Austen Riggs Center, edited by S. Miller. 3 vols., 1957–59.

―――. "On the Psychoanalytic Theory of Motivation" (1960). In Rapaport (1967).

Rorty, Richard. "Pragmatism, Categories, and Language." *Philosophical Review* 70 (1961): 197–223.

Smith, Joseph. "On the Structural View of Affect." *Journal of the American Psychoanalytic Association* 18 (1970): 539–61.

―――. "The Pleasure Principle." *International Journal of Psycho-Analysis* 58 (1977): 1–10.

―――. "Primitive Guilt." In *Pragmatism's Freud: The Moral Disposition of Psychoanalysis,* edited by Joseph H. Smith and William Kerrigan. Psychiatry and the Humanities, Vol. 9. Baltimore: Johns Hopkins University Press, 1986.

―――. *Arguing with Lacan: Ego Psychology and Language.* New Haven, Conn.: Yale University Press, 1991.

————. "Ambivalence, Instincts, and Mourning." *Common Knowledge* 1, no. 2 (1992): 97-109.

————. Review of *Pleasure beyond the Pleasure Principle: The Role of Affect in Motivation, Development, and Adaptation,* edited by Robert A. Glick and Stanley Bone. *Psychoanalytic Quarterly* 64 (1995a): 359-65.

————. "Death and Deconstruction." *Clinical Studies: International Journal of Psychoanalysis* 1, no. 1 (1995b): 53-66.

————. "Original Evil and the Time of the Image." *Journal for the Psychoanalysis of Culture and Society* 1, no. 2 (1996): 35-46.

6   Peirce and Freud
The Role of Telling the Truth in Therapeutic Speech

Wilfried Ver Eecke

Psychoanalysis attempts to help people who are caught up in dead-end strategies. It uses language to liberate them from these strategies. In this chapter I turn to Freud, structuralism, and Peirce to clarify the liberating function of language. The idea in Freud's work that I concentrate upon is his demand for telling the truth. I then argue that structuralism is capable of highlighting very well the differentiating function of language which helps the mentally ill person to liberate herself from the domination of unmediated images, but that this theory is not as well equipped as Peirce's semiotic view of language to deal with the demand for truth-telling in the therapeutic process. In discussing Peirce's view of language, I also discuss how his view of the relation between talk and action differs from that of Freud.

The Liberating Function of Language in Freud

In therapy, not all talk is liberating. For an illustration of what kind of speech liberates human beings, one might look to Freud's papers on technique. In his "Further Recommendations on the Technique of Psychoanalysis," Freud writes about the fundamental rule of psychoanalysis when he admonishes his patients:

> What you tell me must differ in one respect from an ordinary conversation. Ordinarily you rightly try to keep a connecting thread running through your remarks and you exclude any intrusive ideas that may occur to you and any side-issues, so as not to wander too far from the point. But in this case you must proceed differently. You will notice that as you relate things various thoughts will occur to you which you would like to put aside on

the ground of certain criticisms and objections. You will be tempted to say to yourself that this or that is irrelevant here, or is quite unimportant, or nonsensical, so that there is no need to say it. You must never give in to these criticisms, but must say it in spite of them—indeed, you must say it precisely *because* you feel an aversion to doing so. Later on you will find out and learn to understand the reason for this injunction, which is really the only one you have to follow. So say whatever goes through your mind. Act as though, for instance, you were a traveller sitting next to the window of a railway carriage and describing to someone inside the carriage the changing views which you see outside. Finally, never forget that you have promised to be absolutely honest, and never leave anything out because, for some reason or another, it is unpleasant to tell it. [*S.E.* 12:134–35]

At the end of his statement, he splits the recommendation in two parts, linguistically separated by the word "finally." The first idea is a description of a process crucial to obtaining access to the unconscious. The second idea is a promise of absolute honesty.

The first idea deals with the process that alone gives access to the unconscious: saying whatever comes to one's mind. Freud contrasts such manner of speaking with ordinary speech. Normally, he says, we "try to keep a connecting thread running through [our] remarks and . . . [we] *exclude any intrusive ideas that may occur to [us] and any side-issues* (ibid.; my italics). Normal speech excludes. The purpose of the exclusion is to keep the unity of the story; however, it restricts the revealing process. Letting go of our control, responsible for producing unity in our story, so that indefinite revelation may occur in speaking is a process that Freud called free association (*S.E.* 20:40–47).[1]

This therapeutic method took the place of hypnosis, a technique that Freud had used in making symptoms disappear. When Freud noticed that patients treated by means of hypnosis created substitute symptoms, he at first used the technique of pressing his hand to his patients' heads while asking them what came to their minds. Later he introduced the method of having his patients lie on a couch to talk about anything that came to mind. The significant change from the first to the third (and last) method was that talking was now done without hypnosis and thus with the patients' full consciousness and full possession of will. With use of this last method, Freud left his patients with the ability to decide on their own what statements to make. Under the first method, hypnosis deprived his patients of such a choice.

It is this opportunity for choice, flowing from his new technique, that Freud addresses in the second idea by insisting that his patients *promise* absolute *honesty* (Thompson 1994, 167–70). Freud thus makes a double moral demand: first, honesty and second, a promise to another person. Why this double moral demand? An explanation can be found in a footnote to Freud's text: "Later, under the dominance of the resistances, obedience to it [the fundamental rule] weakens, and there comes a time in every analysis when the patient disregards it" (*S.E.* 12:135n). Here, Freud tells us that absolute honesty is impossible. Now, the honesty in question concerns honesty in revealing information about one's own person. Thus, the honesty requested by Freud is a moral demand that concerns solely the patient's attitude toward him or herself. However, Freud adds a second moral demand, one about an interpersonal relationship: the promise to be honest. Freud therefore makes the patient, from the beginning of the therapy, not only a moral agent (an honest talker), but also a moral coworker (someone who has made a promise to someone else).[2]

Let us analyze the implications of the double moral request. The first, the request to be honest, appears as a request by an outsider (the therapist) to a person with psychological difficulties. The request for honesty implies that the therapist affirms certain fundamental capacities in the patient, such as his ability to have a moral attitude toward words and persons. The patient is thereby credited with the capabilities to say true or false things to another and to judge the truth and falsity of his or her own statements. In addition, the patient is also granted the privilege of deciding whether or not to tell the truth, because Freud advises therapists not to try to confirm or disconfirm information given by the patient by checking with family members, friends, or acquaintances. Freud thus makes the word of the patient the highest authority for establishing the truth about him- or herself. At the same time, the fact that the therapist must explicitly ask the patient to be honest is a warning that there is difficulty in eliciting honest talk about oneself. Freud points out that the patient will be tempted to deceive him- or herself by creating apparently legitimate excuses for not telling the complete truth. He therefore presents the patient with a conscious tool (the therapist's explanation of why truth-telling will be difficult) to help him or her be more honest than he or she normally would be. Freud's request for honesty thus affirms the patient's abilities, but also warns and gives the patient a conscious tool to help increase honesty.

Freud does not stop here, however, but goes on to make a second request. He asks that the patient make a *promise* to the therapist to be honest. Freud states explicitly why that second demand is necessary. He claims that at one point or another, resistance will lead all patients to disregard the demand to be honest. Freud seems convinced that the conscious warning and the conscious tool given to the patient will be insufficient, though he does not seem prepared to say that his patients will become liars. Rather, Freud seems to say that his patients will be unable to remain truthful because unconscious forces will try to prevent the revelation of truth.

I interpret Freud's demand for a promise to tell the truth as an attempt to mobilize additional resources to deal with unconscious resistance to the revelation of truth. One possible way to clarify the meaning of these additional resources is to argue that a promise to another involves the hope for recognition by that other. As the promise requested is a promise to be moral, the hope for recognition present in this promise must be understood as a hope for recognition as a moral agent by another moral agent.

Clearly, these two moral demands made by the therapist cannot be made gratuitously, as they in turn commit the therapist as well. The first demand for honesty is normally understood to commit the therapist to the moral duty to keep all information provided by the patient secret. The second demand exacting a *promise* to be honest commits the patient to a moral pact with the therapist and, in my view, obliges the therapist to accept the moral dimension of the therapeutic relation (*S.E.* 12:161).

According to the above analysis, therapeutic speech aims at truth. It is made difficult and sometimes impossible by resistance to telling the truth. I wish to explore in the remainder of the chapter how semiotics can explain better than, for instance, structuralism the demands made by Freud of the therapeutic process: telling the truth and overcoming the resistance to telling the truth.

Understanding Different Dimensions of Language
THE STRUCTURALIST INTERPRETATION OF LANGUAGE

Jacques Lacan has relied upon a structuralist interpretation of language in order to highlight the help that speaking can provide in dealing with resistances originating, for instance, in unconscious unmediated images (the imaginary). He articulates a helpful destructive function of language.

The structuralist view of language, introduced by Ferdinand de Saussure, stresses the idea that language is not possible without difference. That difference is present in the basic building blocks of language—sounds (phonemes)—but it is also present in words and their meanings. At the level of sounds, language is not possible if one cannot recognize the difference between different sounds. Spanish speakers do not recognize the difference between the sounds *b* and *v*. Under such a condition, one cannot use the English words *bow* and *vow*. People from East Asia speak languages where the difference between *r* and *l* is not recognized. Under that condition, the words *red* and *led* could not be used as meaningful words.

The idea of difference is also central in the structuralist explanation of meaning. One of the phenomena that the structuralists want to explain is that a word can have different meanings over time, between different authors or between different languages. Therefore, Saussure objected to the theory that the meaning of a word is a fixed idea (Saussure 1959, 116). Instead, he defined the meaning of a word (the signified) as a chunk of the universe of all meaning. The chunk of meaning attached to a word is the meaning left over by all the other signifiers. Thus, the presence of two words in English, *mutton* and *sheep,* where French only has one word, *mouton,* means that the English word *mutton* has a different meaning than the French word *mouton,* even though they have the same root. The meaning of words consists in the differences imposed on the universe of meaning by the presence of all signifiers. The meaning of words is thus established by a system of differences. That system is not fixed — it is flexible, even floating.

This theory can be applied, for example, to the floating meaning of the word *courage* in American English. Thus, as the word *aggressivity* loses its negative meaning and comes to mean *being assertive,* or *being active,* it starts appropriating meanings that in other languages are attached to the word *courage* (or its translation). Thus, using a word implies that the speaker asserts a chunk of meaning left over by the meaning associated with other words. Speaking thus requires making differences, requires making a cut in the universe of meaning and reserving a chunk of meaning to the word that is used.

Motivation is often guided by images. A mother says that she made her son a lawyer. Her somewhat passive son might fuse in the image that sustains his decision to remain a lawyer not only the desire of the mother but also all kinds of reasons: it is a profession in which one is allowed to talk a lot, one earns a good income, one's good income is earned legally, one's Saturdays are spent pleasantly, and one can easily change jobs in and out of public service. When the young person is asked, however, to *say* why he wants to be a lawyer, he is not able to present, all at once, the total attractiveness of the image of being a lawyer. Rather, he must start cutting up the attractiveness of the image and he must select specific reasons for the desirability of being a lawyer. The young person must start with a reason connected with *either* the income received by lawyers, *or* the Saturday habits of lawyers, *or* the opportunity to talk that lawyers have. Speaking (i.e., using language) thus imposes on the speaker the necessity of making differences, of cutting up what is a vague unity in the form of an image.

Lacan uses the structuralist interpretation of language to explain the liberating capability of language. In their capability of fusing, images can become illusionary and captivating. Language, by requiring the use of difference, breaks up, cuts up. If the patient is asked to talk about his or her captivating images, then we understand that the use of language is almost mechanically liberating (Muller and Richardson 1982, 8-9).

By presenting the helpful function of language as its ability to cut up the vague unity present in images, the helping function of language is, in my view, reduced too much to a negative task. The more positive function of language is suggested by what might next happen to the young lawyer in his therapy sessions. He might start "giving involuntarily indices [about the role of his mother] which the astute analyst will seize upon in order to transform unconscious representations into language" (Vergote 1997, 56). I will, therefore, look for a way to better understand the positive contribution made by speaking in a psychoanalytic context. A positive function of speaking and of language is suggested by the two moral demands by Freud: honesty and the promise to be honest. Lacan himself understands the need for a positive function of language and formulates that need in the same moral vocabulary that Freud did: "The unconscious is that chapter of my history that is marked by a blank or *occupied by a falsehood:* it is the *censored* chapter. But *the truth can be rediscovered:* usually it has already been written down elsewhere" (1977, 50; my italics).[3]

The Freudian demand for honesty, like Lacan's call for truth, requires that we also look for a theory of language that explicitly addresses the possibility for truth and thus honesty. I believe that Peirce's view of language can better articulate than structuralism that kind of positive contribution language can make in the therapeutic process.

A POSITIVE CONTRIBUTION OF LANGUAGE

In this section I relate, first, the Freudian demand for honesty to Peirce's theory of induction and abduction (hypothesis), and second, the Freudian demand that the patient be a moral coworker in the achievement of true self-revelation to Peirce's theory of the interpretant.

Freud's demand for honesty. Freudian therapy is not a philosophical technique. It does not rely upon the formulation of general rules, such as "human beings are mortal" or "pain is unavoidable." Freudian technique is concerned with labeling the particular. Take Freud's example: "You ask who this figure in the dream can be." The reported answer is: "It's *not* my mother" (*S.E.* 19:235). Another of Freud's examples is that of his friend saying: "Well, something *has* come into my mind . . . but it's too intimate to pass on. . . . Besides, I don't see any connection, or any necessity for saying it." Freud retorts, "You can leave the connection to me. Of course I can't force you to talk about something that you find distasteful; but then you mustn't insist on learning from me how you came to forget your *aliquis*" (*S.E.* 6:11). In my view, this request for honesty makes no sense without supposing that truth about particulars is possible. But how is truth about particulars possible? The skeptic trend in Anglo-American philosophy initiated by Hume has a predilection to present arguments against the possibility of induction. This is normally interpreted as an attack against conceptual insights (e.g., clouds cause rain). I interpret Hume's sceptic views on induction as also undermining the possibility of simple linguistic statements about particulars (e.g., this is a table). Peirce is one philosopher who clearly sees the problem of talking about particulars but also argues explicitly against this sceptic tradition, as is clear from the following text:

> Looking out of my window this lovely morning I see an azalea in full bloom. No, no! I do not see that; though that is the only way I can describe what I see. *That* is a proposition, a sentence, a fact; but what I perceive is not proposition, sentence, fact, but only an image, which I make intelligible in part by means of a statement of fact. This statement is abstract; but what I see is concrete. I perform an abduction when I [do so much] as express in a sentence anything I see. The truth is that the whole fabric of our knowledge is one matted felt of pure hypothesis confirmed and refined by induction. Not the smallest advance can be made in knowledge beyond the stage of vacant staring, without making an abduction at every step. [quoted in Brent 1993, 72]

In the above quotation Peirce draws attention to the problem of knowing (labeling, describing) particulars—as Hume would—but also hints that such knowing is possible because of the processes of induction and hypothesis or abduction. In order to solve the problem of how truth about particulars is possible, I will therefore need to clarify Peirce's ideas about the processes of both induction and hypothesis or abduction. An induction is the intellectual act of seeing some characteristic in many cases and concluding that that characteristic must be the case as a general rule for a class of objects, even for those members of the class not yet observed. Peirce says it succinctly: "By induction, we conclude that facts, similar to observed facts, are true in cases not examined" (*CP* 2.636). Applying the definition of induction to Peirce's case of azaleas, that would mean that, in order to be able to say that a bush is an azalea, one *must* be convinced that unobserved azaleas will truly have a number of characteristics, such as twiglike branches, mostly dark green leaves if the plant is healthy, a specific kind of flower, etc. Peirce himself gives as an example of an induction the ability to *transform the observation* that the letters *e, t, a, s,* etc., approach 11¼ percent, 8½ percent, 8 percent, 7½ percent, etc., of all the letters in English texts *into the rule* that it must be so (Peirce 1992, 32).

To grasp what Peirce means by hypothesis or abduction, consider the following:

> By hypothesis, we conclude the existence of a fact quite different from any-thing observed, from which, according to known laws, something observed would necessarily result. [*CP* 2.636]

or

> Long before I first classed abduction as an inference it was recognized by logicians that the operation of adopting an explanatory hypothesis—which is just what abduction is—was subject to certain conditions. Namely, the hypothesis cannot be admitted, even as a hypothesis, unless it be supposed that it would account for the facts or some of them. The form of inference, therefore, is this: The surprising fact, C, is observed; But if A were true, C would be a matter of course, Hence, there is reason to suspect that A is true. [*CP* 5.189]

A hypothesis or abduction, therefore, is the ability to conclude from observing in one object a number of characteristics that this object is a member of a certain class having a number of additional characteristics, some of which are not immediately visible but for which evidence can be found. Thus, if a bush has a number of characteristics, I can conclude that it is an azalea and from that first conclusion I can draw further conclusions, for example, that it is a plant and needs water and sunlight in order to flourish. Or a text is observed to have letters occurring with the frequency noted above. The text is by abduction or hypothesis then said to be an English text (Peirce 1992, 33–35). It therefore follows that the text will be understood by an English-speaking person and that I will not need to find a French speaker to translate it.

Truth, then, for Peirce, is something that one arrives at by means of interpretative activity using knowledge of laws about the objects experienced. Saying something truthful is therefore something like a process, a communal process, even. It is a process because it requires the acquisition of knowledge of particular characteristics of concrete objects (e.g., azaleas, English texts). It is a process, too, because one must learn what other, less visible characteristics those objects have (azaleas are plants and thus carry out photosynthesis). It is a communal process because an individual is guided by others in discerning what bushes can properly be called azaleas and why. It is also a communal process because the discovery of the hidden characteristics of an object cannot possibly be the project of one individual alone—it is too infinite a task. More profoundly, it also involves the discovery of *necessary* hidden characteristics. Such necessary hidden characteristics Peirce calls laws of nature. They are true if they lead to successful actions in the world. The search for more successful actions requires the formulation of more adequate rules for action, which in turn give us a better understanding of the nature of the object under study. Both the need for more successful action and the creative effort to formulate more adequate rules are not solely individual events but communal ones as well. Both also rest upon the testimony of others (Colapietro 1989, 72).

It is by connecting the demand for adequate rules of possible action to the requirement of correctly labeling objects (particulars) that Peirce overcomes Hume's problem of induction and becomes able to argue that human beings can reach the truth. His argument is twofold. First, the correctness of an intellectual statement is not reduced to observation, but includes successful action rules (Peirce's energetic interpretant) (35). Second, Peirce claims that the mind, as part of nature, is adapted to nature and is thus capable of comprehending the world in the sense that the mind can find out how to interact properly with the world. As the proper interaction with an azalea by a specialized biologist is much more demanding than the proper interaction by a weekend gardener, labeling a plant an azalea has a different meaning for the two. But both can label it correctly.

Peirce's claim that human beings are capable of correctly labeling particulars makes us realize the sensibleness of the Freudian demand for honesty. Peirce's view that labeling particulars *includes* rules of appropriate behavior lets us see that correct labeling suggests or even demands certain actions, even if they are painful. Freud's demand for honesty is a demand for a virtue. Honesty, like all virtues, can carry burdens. Honesty is the willingness to carry the difficulty and the pain of knowing particulars (e.g., acknowledging first that the female figure wears a blouse like one's own mother, and thus that this domineering female is one's mother, and, second, that one needs to protect oneself against domineering persons, even if they are one's relatives).

The idea that truth is possible, that it rests on a process, and that it can be painful can be used to understand one fundamental aspect of the therapeutic process, namely, the partiality or distortion in the revelation of truth. Thus, Freud interprets a denial as a half-truth, because it labels the repressed and then marks it with a negation (*S.E.* 19:235–36). Elsewhere, he interprets a negation followed by either new material or an indirect confirmation (associations of similar nature, etc.) as a confirmation of the partial truth of the negated interpretation (*S.E.* 23:262ff.).

In his study "Negation," Freud describes the moment in which he appeals to the honesty of the patient in order to move beyond the denial and thus to establish a more complete truth. He confesses, though, that such an intellectual acknowledgment is not the solution to the patient's problems yet, because intellectual truth is here separated from emotional acceptance. Intellectual truth does not lead to proper action (*S.E.* 19:236) and can therefore not be considered the highest form of truth.

Freud's report about the two phases in denial and his judgment that intellectual acceptance alone is insufficient can be clarified by Peirce's above explained theory of knowledge of particulars. Intellectual acceptance of a dream content often takes the form of, "I guess I have to conclude that this domineering figure in my dream is my mother, because the hair, the blouse, the bracelet, the shoes all belong to my mother." The intellectual acceptance of a dream content does not take the form of, "Yes, this domineering woman is my mother and domineering women must be avoided." Intellectual acceptance of a dream content is connecting a new string of characteristics with an old string that was firmly action-guiding without allowing the new string of characteristics the right to become a guide for action (for an additional example, see Ver Eecke 1984, 145). Emotional acceptance of a dream content is allowing the new string of characteristics the right to become a guide for action. The two strings of characteristics are summarized by two different labels, or in the language of Peirce, two different interpretants: the old string results in the interpretant *mother,* whereas the new string results in the interpretant *domineering.* If one keeps in mind the action-oriented aspect of labeling particulars (of using interpretants), then the difference between intellectual and emotional acceptance of a dream content is the difference between saying that the female figure in one's dream is my domineering *mother* or my *domineering* mother. The first method of labeling gives no guide to deal with a *domineering* mother; the second method of labeling, on the contrary, gives a guide for action—take distance, stand up, etc.

In order to clarify how therapy can help the patient move beyond mere intellectual acceptance of truth and toward emotional acceptance of it, we need to understand the intersubjective dimension of speech. Freud discusses this in his demand for a *promise* of honesty, and Peirce, in his theory of human beings as semiotic.

Freud's demand that the patient be a moral coworker in achieving true self-revelation. As I have already discussed Freud's view of the patient as a moral coworker, I wish to start this section by clarifying Peirce's thoroughgoing semiotic view of human beings. "When we think," says Peirce, "we ourselves, as we are at that moment, appear as a sign." Furthermore, "everything which is present to us is a phenomenal manifestation of ourselves" (Peirce 1992). Peirce goes on to give such examples as feelings, images, conceptions, and other representations. These phenomenal manifestations of ourselves become signs of ourselves because they become available for interpretation and thus are guiding our actions

in a positive or a negative way. They do not have to be signs in the narrow sense of the word. They become so when we think, when we interpret (Colapietro 1989, 53).

By incorporating feelings, images, and thoughts (conceptions) into his
theory of the sign, Peirce has made his theory applicable to much of what
psychoanalysis is about. Let us therefore see how his description of the
human being as a semiotic being opens up some possibilities for understanding the therapeutic dialogue.

A sign has, of course, some materiality. But it is a materiality that represents. According to Peirce, representing requires "three references: 1st,
it is a sign *to* some thought which interprets it; 2d, it is a sign *for* some object to which in that thought it is equivalent; 3d, it is a sign, *in* some respect or quality, which brings it into connection with its object" (Peirce
1992, 38). For Peirce, a sign is to be interpreted by some thought. However, "to what thought does that thought-sign which is ourself address itself?" (38–39). According to Peirce it addresses itself to another thought.
We are therefore multiple strings of interpreting thoughts. "Each former
thought suggests something to the thought which follows it, i.e., is the
sign of something to this latter" (39). However, each of us has had the experience of stopping one train of thought and pursuing another one.
Here is an example. First thought-series: While making waffles for my children and their friends, I anticipate their chatter, their grateful faces. Second thought-series: Suddenly, I remember not having paid the traffic
ticket now lying on my desk. I am afraid that my payment will be too late.
Maybe I can drive to the Bureau of Traffic Adjudication in person. I hate
the thought. It will take two to three hours, there will be long lines, etc.
Back to the first thought-series: The voice of my son calls me back to the
waffle breakfast. I see the empty table and ask for help setting the table.
I bring the plate with waffles to the table and notice the small chunks of
wood missing from the table legs. Third thought-series: No effort is
needed to remind me that Appollo, our dog, had chewed them off when
he was a puppy. Here and there, the legs of our furniture show marks of
puppy activities. Appollo is cute but he is still a problem.

Peirce does not deny that we do what I have just described, remark-
ing, "Our train of thought may, it is true, be interrupted" (ibid.). But Peirce
is also drawing attention to another aspect of thought interruption. If one
train of thought can be interrupted by another, it must be the case that
there are multiple trains of thought running at the same time. Peirce said
it more radically. Instead of arguing that for one train of thought to be interrupted there must be at least two trains of thought, he simply writes:
"But we must remember that, in addition to the principal element of
thought at any moment, there are a *hundred* things in our mind to which

but a small fraction of attention or consciousness is conceded" (ibid.; my italics). This observation is for Peirce the occasion to redescribe what we called "interruption of a train of thought." Instead of interruption, Peirce describes it by saying that "a new constituent of thought gets the uppermost," and he explicitly denies "that the train of thought which it displaces is broken off altogether." For Peirce *we are,* therefore, *multiple trains of thought at once.*

One could ask why a self does not combine several trains of thought, given that unity is a goal of the self, according to Peirce (Colapietro 1989, 75). The answer might lie in the following consideration. Any thought is an interpretation of some aspect of reality and, as such, is an interpretation of some particular event. In interpreting that particular event, it provides an experience that confirms, contradicts, or is unrelated to previous experience. All semiotic experience for Peirce is providing a guide for action. Semiotic experience unrelated to or contradicting previous experience cannot easily be integrated. This is all the more difficult, because for Peirce, knowledge of particulars leads to the formation of habits because of the successful action that it gives rise to (90). As long as a human being encounters new — unrelated or contradictory — experiences, he or she will not be able to readily integrate them. These new experiences will therefore become the basis for new trains of thought.

The idea that we as human beings are multiple trains of thought goes well with two of Peirce's other views. The first concerns Peirce's denial of the existence of intuition. He writes: "We have no power of Intuition, but every cognition is determined logically by previous cognitions" (Peirce 1992, 30). From this he concludes that "the striking in of a new experience is never an instantaneous affair, but is an *event* occupying time, and coming to pass by a continuous process. Its prominence in consciousness, therefore, must probably be the consummation of a growing process" (39). Thus, for Peirce, the hundreds of trains of thought do not all simultaneously force themselves into consciousness. Rather, trains of thought are processes that follow a logical path toward their consummation. Let us call that invisible path toward consummation the "incubation period" of a train of thought. During that incubation period, these trains of thought do not gain prominence in consciousness. However, just because a train of thought is not prominently present in consciousness does not mean that it has ceased "abruptly and instantaneously" (ibid.). We are bundles of multiple trains of thought, the prominence in consciousness of which shifts over time. Prominence of one train of thought is not to be interpreted as interruption of other ones. Thus, every human being is more thought than he or she appears to be. The talking cure might be considered from this point of view as a technique that allows a train of thought to appear in words before its normal consummation process has taken place. The other side of the coin is that the talking cure allows the emergence of trains of thought that are not ready to be a guide for action.

Peirce adds a second view. He draws a radical conclusion from redescribing an apparent interruption of thought as the coming into prominence of another thought series. That radical conclusion is that the interruption of a train of thought is not possible before death. A train of thought can go into an incubation period, but "there is no . . . thought belonging to this series, subsequently to which there is not a thought which interprets or repeats it" (ibid.). Here Peirce jumps from a possibility to a postulated necessity. Indeed, he writes, "there is no exception, therefore, to the law that every thought-sign is translated or interpreted in a subsequent one, unless it be that all thought comes to an abrupt and final end in death" (ibid.). One way of justifying Peirce's reasoning is to note that what is possible would be actualized, given enough time. If enough time has passed and something that is possible is still not actualized, we need to suppose the existence of a counter-force hindering the actualization of that particular possibility.

Enriched with Peirce's semiotic view of the human being, I now wish to clarify two Freudian ideas. First, there is Freud's understanding of repression as a failure to translate a message (an inscription) from a lower level of consciousness into a higher one. In 1925 Freud published two articles, translated as "A Note upon the 'Mystic Writing-Pad'" and "Negation." In the first, Freud explicitly concludes that a writing-pad is a good model for the functioning of the perceptual apparatus of our mind (*S.E.* 19:232). In "Negation," Freud observed that patients are able to disclose a painful truth upon the condition of being able to deny it as is evident from the following text: "Thus the content of a repressed image or idea can make its way into consciousness, on condition that it is *negated* (235). Let us recall Freud's example of a patient who related a dream with a female figure in it. To the question of who that female could be, the patient answered, "It's *not* my mother." Freud interprets this statement by saying, "So, it *is* his mother." Freud continues, "It is as though the patient had said: 'It's true that my mother came into my mind as I thought of this person, but I don't feel inclined to let the association count'" (ibid.).

In Peirce's semiotic theory, there is a train of thought that produces a female figure, which in turn can be a sign that is to be further interpreted. The thought interpreting this sign is "mother." However, there is a force resisting that thought, preventing it from being allowed to play the function of interpretant. What is the nature of this force which could interfere with a thought becoming an interpretant? For Peirce, that interfering force is another train of thought, such as, "I know that I do not despise my mother that much." As a consequence, the first train of thought goes underground and disappears from consciousness.

Let us call all those trains of thought that are not free to let the next thought perform the role of interpretant "unconscious trains of thought." These unconscious trains of thought will by definition cease to be unconscious when and if a succeeding thought is able to perform the role of interpretant. But, also by definition, there are forces that prevent such interpretative performances (unmediated, unconscious images that dominate a person's psychic life, other conflicting trains of thought, lack of imagination, lack of appropriate words). Peirce says as much in the following text:

> There are, as I am prepared to maintain, operations of the mind which are logically exactly analogous to inferences excepting only that they are unconscious and therefore not subject to criticism. But that makes all the difference in the world; for inference is essentially deliberate, and self-controlled. Any operation which cannot be controlled, any conclusion which is not abandoned, not merely as soon as criticism has pronounced against it, but in the very act of pronouncing that decree, is not of the nature of rational inference — is not reasoning. [*CP* 5.108]

Freud's demand to be honest leaves the task of interpretative performance to the patient alone. He or she is asked to make the commitment to be honest. However, Freud's demand to the patient to make a promise to the therapist to be honest means that the healing interpretative performance becomes a joint moral enterprise. When the patient fails in the required interpretative performance, typically by not finding the appropriate interpretant (sign), that is not the end of the effort. The therapist can allow and help the patient to make detours that prepare the needed interpretative performance, that is, finding the appropriate interpretants.

Helping a patient find the appropriate interpretant is exactly what Freud did in the analysis of forgetting of foreign words. When Freud's friend did not know why he forgot the word *aliquis* in a Latin proverb, Freud invited him to tell what came to his mind. From *aliquis* the patient made associations with St. Simon and ritual blood-sacrifice, St. Augustine, and St. Januarius. Freud then offered the interpretation that the calendar saints and the reference to blood are "a brilliant allusion to women's periods," which, just like *aliquis* in the proverb, should not (better not) disappear (*S.E.* 6:11). It should be noted, however, that even if the therapist is committed to helping the patient to carry out interpretative performance, the therapist is not authorized to perform the semiotic activity for the patient. The promise of truthful semiotic activity was made by the patient, not by the therapist. More importantly, the interpretative activity of the therapist is not semiotic activity of the patient. In the case of Freud's friend, the semiotic activity of the friend took the form of confessing a number of things, such as having a girlfriend, that the lady in question was Italian, and that he went with her to Naples (ibid.).

Freud did not possess or did not apply the above rule of semiotic interpretation early in his career. His failure in the case of Dora can be attributed in part to his attempt to impose his own interpretations upon Dora, namely that Dora herself was in love with her seducer, Mr. K. Later in his career, Freud advocated a much more respectful attitude toward patients when giving interpretations, as is evident from his statement, "We do not pretend that an individual construction is anything more than a conjecture which awaits examination, confirmation or rejection" (S.E. 23:265).

The semiotic rule that the patient herself must do the interpreting was clearly expressed by Freud when he wrote that "one must be careful not to give a patient the solution of a symptom or the translation of a wish until he is already so close to it that he has only one short step more to make in order to get hold of the explanation for himself" (S.E. 12:140). Clearly, the later Freud was closer to Peirce's view of semiotic activity than the Freud who was treating Dora.

Let us now turn to the Freudian claim that therapeutic activity does not end at the moment when the patient is able to acknowledge intellectually a thought connection, for example, that the female figure in the dream is "mother." According to Freud, full intellectual acceptance of the repressed does not mean that the repressive process is removed (S.E. 19:236).

Peirce's pragmatic semiotics allows us to articulate this curious discrepancy between intellectual and emotional acceptance. Peirce rejects an intellectualist semiotics. He argues instead that "the whole function of thought is to produce habits of action" (Peirce 1992, 131). Semiotic activity creates an interpretant that is a *guide to action*. Semiotic activity can be defective when there is no interpretant or when what appears to be an interpretant is not a guide for action (Vergote 1997, 63). Indeed, as I have argued before, Peirce would say that a patient who accepts, intellectually but not emotionally, that the female figure in his dream must be his mother, even though she is also domineering, has not yet made the connection with the thought that his mother is a domineering woman, because knowing that a person is domineering includes the rule for action: be on your guard against such a person. I interpret Peirce to claim that it is false to believe that one *knows* that a particular person is domineering without accepting and acting upon the rule: be on your guard against such a person.

What Peirce explicitly connects, Freud leaves separated. It seems to me that Freud does not interpret the promise to be honest as also including the requirement that the patient be able to find a proper guide for action. He does not do so because he believes that repression makes satisfactory action impossible, because "the patient's condition is such that, until her repressions are removed, she is incapable of getting real satisfaction" (*S.E.* 12:165). Freud is so convinced about the inability of the patient to find a proper guide for action that he demands that treatment be made in a state of abstinence (153–54). Describing the reasons for not allowing the patient to make substantial decisions during psychoanalytic treatment, he writes, "The patient's need and longing should be allowed to persist in her, in order that they may serve as forces impelling her to do work and to make changes, and . . . we must beware of appeasing those forces by means of surrogates" (165). For Freud, the work of true self-revelation is a precondition for satisfactory decision-making.

Freud and Peirce might, however, not be so far apart. Indeed, Peirce sees a connection between semiotic activity and the creation of a guide for action. Freud sees a connection between the inability to discover any guide for action and the inability to produce true self-revelation because of the presence of repression. Freud clearly gives priority to semiotic activity separated from any concerns for immediate action in order to prepare for semiotic activity that once more can provide a guide for action. However, in his later writings Freud develops a position that is similar to Peirce's. He stresses that it is the patient who must find action-directed semiotic activity. Freud advises against the therapist suggesting sublimation possibilities when talking has undone inhibitions: "As a doctor, one must above all be tolerant to the weakness of a patient . . . many people fall ill precisely from an attempt to sublimate their instincts beyond the degree permitted by their organization and . . . in those who have a capacity for sublimation the process usually takes place of itself as soon as their inhibitions have been overcome by analysis" (119).

If we interpret sublimation as successful action, we can affirm that Freud, like Peirce, connects successful human action with the action being grounded in the semiotic context. Freud sees truthful self-revelation as a precondition for such self-directed action. Freud does not fully analyze the nature of successful sublimation as self-directed action. Peirce calls it successful semiotic activity or semiosis.

Conclusion

A structuralist analysis of language sees the liberating possibilities of language mainly in its differentiating function. Freud makes two moral requests of his patients: that they be honest, and that they promise to be honest. Peirce's view of language allows us to make sense of Freud's demand of *honesty*. Peirce affirms that human beings have the capability of performing semiotic activity in which particulars can be labeled truthfully, and thus one can say that commitment to honesty is not an empty commitment. Peirce's view of language allows us also to clarify Freud's moral demand that his patients *promise to be honest*. The promise to the therapist makes the patient and the therapist moral coworkers. The patient accepts the burden of truthful semiotic activity, which, in Peirce's view, leads to the creation of an interpretant that is a guide for action. The therapist accepts the burden of helping the patient toward such liberating semiotic activity. In his later writings, Freud stresses that such help needs to restrain itself in order to allow the patient to perform the semiotic activity him- or herself. The request for honesty affirms in the patient a form of agency that is only fully realized if the patient him- or herself can perform semiotic activity and if that semiotic activity will become action-guiding in a successful way.

Notes

I benefited from suggestions and comments made by Joseph Brent and John Muller and from the editorial assistance of Thane Naberhaus and Joe Kakesh.

1. Lacan went even further and argued that liberating speech not only violates the rules for telling a story, but also violates other rules of language (e.g., lexical rules). Thus, for Lacan, all misspeech is a successful revelation of the unconscious, as Freud also understood when he analyzed the word *familionär* (Lacan 1977, 58).

2. For an interesting example of how difficult it is to execute these demands, see *S.E.* 12:135–36n, where Freud writes, "I once treated a high official, who was bound by his oath of office not to communicate certain things because they were state secrets, and the analysis came to grief as a consequence of this restriction. Psychoanalytic treatment must have no regard for any consideration, because the neurosis and its resistances are themselves without any such regard."

3. See also Lacan (1977), 34 and 40. For a very brief example of a Lacanian analysis based on a structuralist understanding of language see Peraldi (1987): 59–63. The effort at reaching the truth can also be observed there. Peraldi (the therapist) writes, "Mr. D. (the patient) noticed it [the double meaning of the expression] immediately and burst into laughter. Then *he decided to analyze it*

very carefully" (61; my italics) and "then Mr. D. remembered with some uneasiness" and finally "he suddenly remembered" (62).

References

Brent, Joseph. *Charles Sanders Peirce. A Life.* Bloomington: Indiana University Press, 1993.

Colapietro, Vincent M. *Peirce's Approach to the Self: A Semiotic Perspective on Human Subjectivity.* Albany: State University of New York Press, 1989.

Freud, Sigmund. *The Standard Edition of the Complete Psychological Works of Sigmund Freud.* Edited and translated by James Strachey. 24 vols. London: Hogarth, 1953–74.

The Psychopathology of Everyday Life (1901), vol. 6.

"Recommendations to Physicians Practising Psycho-Analysis" (1912), vol. 12.

"On Beginning the Treatment (Further Recommendations on the Technique of Psycho-Analysis I)" (1913), vol. 12.

"Remembering, Repeating and Working-Through (Further Recommendations on the Technique of Psycho-Analysis II)" (1914), vol. 12.

"Observations on Transference-Love (Further Recommendations on the Technique of Psycho-Analysis III)" (1915), vol. 12.

"Negation" (1925), vol. 19.

"A Note upon the 'Mystic Writing-Pad'" (1925), vol. 19.

"An Autobiographical Study" (1925), vol. 20.

"Constructions in Analysis" (1937), vol. 23.

Lacan, Jacques. *Écrits: A Selection.* Translated by Alan Sheridan. New York: W. W. Norton, 1977.

Muller, John P., and Richardson, William J. *Lacan and Language: A Reader's Guide to* Écrits. New York: International Universities Press, 1982.

Peirce, Charles Sanders. *Philosophical Writings of Peirce.* Edited by Justus Buchler. New York: Dover Publications, 1955.

——. *Collected Papers of Charles Sanders Peirce.* Edited by Charles Hartshorne, Paul Weiss, and Arthur W. Burks. 8 vols. Cambridge: Harvard University Press, 1931–58.

——. *The Essential Peirce: Selected Philosophical Writings.* Edited by Nathan Houser and Christian Kloesel. Bloomington: Indiana University Press, 1992.

Peraldi, François. "Krake/Krakra: A Case Study." *PsychCritique* 2, no. 1 (1987): 55–63.

Saussure, Ferdinand de. *Course in General Linguistics.* Edited by Charles Bally and Albert Sechehaye. Translated by Wade Baskin. New York: Philosophical Library, 1959.

Thompson, M. Guy. *The Truth about Freud's Technique: The Encounter with the Real.* New York: New York University Press, 1994.

Ver Eecke, Wilfried. *Saying "No."* Pittsburgh: Duquesne University Press, 1984.

Vergote, Antoine. *La Psychanalyse à l'Épreuve de la Sublimation.* Paris: Les Éditions du Cerf, 1997.

7 Peirce and Psychopragmatics
Semiosis and Performativity

Angela Moorjani

> *I cannot infallibly know that there is any Truth.*
> —Charles Sanders Peirce, *Semiotic and Significs*

In "A Survey of Pragmaticism," Peirce defines semiosis as "an action, or influence, which is, or involves, a coöperation of *three* subjects, such as a sign, its object, and its interpretant, this tri-relative influence not being in any way resolvable into actions between pairs" (*CP* 5.484).

There are many different ways of understanding Peirce's triadic semiosis, and I have found no general agreement among his commentators about what he means by a "sign," "its object," "its interpretant," and the cooperation among the three. Some commentators hold the sign's meaning to be its object, whereas others say the sign's meaning is the interpretant. Those who defend the former position emphasize the sign's semantic properties, relating signifier, signified, and referent.[1] Others, who defend the position that the sign's meaning is the interpretant, stress the sign's pragmatic properties, linking the sign-object relation to interpretive and contextual effects.[2] I agree with still others who hold that both views are correct if taken together, not separately, for the meaning circulates among sign, object, and interpretant, not adhering in any single term or in any related two. Nor does the flow of meaning end there, as every act of semiosis depends on previous interpreting acts and is itself reiterated or translated by subsequent acts of signification (*CP* 5.284; MS 517). What makes Peirce's theory of semiosis particularly productive is that in making a sign's meaning result from the cooperation among the signifier, referent, and effect, he inseparably joins the semantic and pragmatic dimensions of signification and thereby opens up meaning-making to a continuous process of psychological and social overdetermination, stretching from the unconscious mind to the shared values of community.

My purpose in this chapter is (1) to show how Peirce's concept of the interpretant can extend our knowledge of the psyche in terms of semiosis, perhaps Peirce's major legacy to psychoanalysis, and (2) to suggest ways in which a poststructuralist pragmatics could be made more productive by taking into account the Peircean and psychoanalytic models of the workings of the mind. In particular, my discussion relating the Peircean interpretant and the pragmatic performative will probe the effect of semiosis on ethical dispositions.

The Peircean writings I cite date largely from after 1900. In the illuminating concluding chapter of his intellectual biography of Peirce, Joseph Brent discusses the reasons for Peirce's turn to ethical thinking in the last years of his life (1993).

Peircean and Freudian Psychic Semiosis

In this section I focus mainly on the Peircean conception of the interpretant within the context of psychic semiosis. As we know, for Peirce, semiosis and the interpretant are not to be limited to human contexts. Yet, there are passages in which he discusses human semiosis per se, and in these he defines the interpretant in terms of the pragmatic effect of signs on receivers. In the same paragraph of "A Survey of Pragmaticism" of 1907 featuring the definition of semiosis I have just quoted, Peirce defines the "logical interpretant" (about which more in a moment) as the "essential effect upon the interpreter, brought about by the semiosis of the sign" (*CP* 5.484). A year later he wrote in a letter, "The determination of the Interpreter's mind I term the *Interpretant* of the Sign" (1976, 886). More generally, the 1907 paper describes the interpretant as the sign's "proper significate outcome" or "proper significate effects" (*CP* 5.473, 475). These effects are the result of the continuous process I have outlined above in which every sign is repeated and translated by a subsequent sign or interpretant.[3]

Peirce, as he was wont to do, elaborated several trichotomies of interpretants.[4] For a discussion of psychic semiosis, the most useful is the triadic division into "emotional," "energetic," and "logical" interpretants, a division that corresponds to the Peircean categories of firstness, or feeling; secondness, or action; and thirdness, or law (*CP* 5.475–76). Accordingly, the emotional interpretant produces a feeling; the energetic interpretant effects a muscular or a mental effort, and the logical interpretant, in addition to generating feeling and action, is an "interpreting thought" (Peirce 1977, 31). Of the three, I concentrate on the logical interpretant, as it has the capacity to initiate ethical action or "a modification of a person's tendencies toward action" (*CP* 5.476). It is important to note that Peirce continually emphasized that the logical interpretant has the power to modify a disposition to act rather than conduct itself. "I deny,"

Peirce wrote, "that pragmaticism as originally defined by me made the intellectual purport of symbols to consist in our conduct. On the contrary, I was most careful to say that it consists in our *concept* of what our conduct *would* be upon *conceivable* occasions" (*CP* 8.208). The logical interpretant's effect is therefore not on behavior directly but instead on the psychic agency or moral conscience that through its rules tempers future actions.

The *logical* in *logical interpretant* can be explained by Peirce's emphasis on the rational nature of thought, conscience, and communication. For him, logical self-control, or right reason, is the same as the ethical self-control effected by the logical interpretant (*CP* 4.540; 5.419). The ideal of our conduct, he writes, is "to execute our little function in the operation of the creation by giving a hand toward rendering the world more reasonable" (*CP* 1.615). Self-control in all its forms is a psychic activity which for Peirce, following Plato, consists of an internal dialogue, or of signs addressed to an other self one is trying to persuade (*CP* 5.421). This psychic dialogue could be interpreted as a divided ego in discussion with itself or, as we shall see, as different psychic agencies in conversation with each other. Indeed, for Peirce, such self-addressed signs can take the shape of concepts that are the first logical interpretants of unconscious needs and experiences: "Every concept, doubtless, first arises when upon a strong, but more or less vague, sense of need is superinduced some involuntary experience of a suggestive nature; that being suggestive which has a certain occult relation to the build of the mind" (*CP* 5.480). This process of interpretation, then, is to be understood in light of Peirce's conception of the unconscious, which shares features with both the Freudian unconscious and preconscious, and of which Peirce writes, "We have an occult nature of which and of its contents we can only judge by the conduct that it determines, and by phenomena of that conduct" (*CP* 5.440). The first logical interpretants would thus give an *ex post facto* awareness of an unconscious domain by pointing to the habitual tendencies to action it orchestrates.

In relation to percepts, or sense impressions, which can enter awareness only if translated into a sign, or a first logical interpretant, Peirce wrote in a 1902 unpublished manuscript: "perceptual facts are themselves abstract representations . . . of the percepts themselves, and these are . . . representations, primarily of impressions of sense, ultimately of a dark underlying something, which cannot be specified without its manifesting itself as a sign of something below" (MS 599; quoted in Johansen 1993, 77–78).[5]

It is worth noting, too, that for Peirce, unconscious material is translated into preconscious and conscious thought (the logical interpretant) by means of Hume's associational processes of resemblance and contiguity, which enjoyed considerable currency in psychological circles at Peirce's time, and which, along with perception, Peirce considered to be inferential (*CP* 8.71; 7.388–450; 7.377). Additionally, in the case of resemblance, Peirce maintains that it "*consists* in an association due to the occult substratum of thought" (*CP* 7.394). These are the same modes of association which Freud saw at work in the operations of the primary process and the dream work, and which undergird later structuralist and Lacanian divisions of cognitive processes into metaphor and metonymy (*S.E.* 4, 5; Jakobson [1956] 1971; Lacan [1957] 1977).

Peirce's awareness of the unconscious is not surprising, given his overall anti-Cartesian mind-set and the many philosophical and psychological discussions of the unconscious in the nineteenth century: "The doctrine of Descartes, that the mind consists solely of that which directly asserts itself in unitary consciousness, modern scientific psychologists altogether reject. Swarming facts positively leave no doubt that vivid consciousness, subject to attention and control, embraces at any one moment a mere scrap of our psychical activity. . . . The obscure part of the mind is the principal part" (*CP* 6.569).

Not only the somatic unconscious but also our habitual dispositions and systems of belief are for Peirce largely unconscious, and these, too, are brought to consciousness under conditions of need and desire by the first logical interpretants (*CP* 1.593). In "What Pragmatism Is," Peirce says that "belief is . . . a habit of mind essentially enduring for some time, and mostly (at least) unconscious" (*CP* 5.417). Similarly, in a 1908 letter to Victoria Welby, he defines belief as "that which [the believer] is prepared to conform his conduct to, without recognizing what it is to which he is conforming his conduct" (1977, 75). Peircean belief, then, is what cognitive psychologists now term a "cognitive script," the framework of unconscious social beliefs and ideals that members of a community share. Such ideals, Peirce points out, have "in the main been imbibed in childhood . . . and have gradually been shaped to [one's] personal nature and to the ideals of [one's] circle of society" (*CP* 1.592). As such, Peircean belief is akin to Mikhail Bakhtin's "conceptual horizon" ([1934–35] 1981), or Edward T. Hall's "cultural unconscious" (1976), those rules of conduct which we apply in interacting with others of which we remain unaware, or Pierre Bourdieu's "habitus" (1979), or, indeed, Freud's superego—both personal and cultural—with its roots in the unconscious (*S.E.* 19:28–39, 48–49; 21:123–45).

The first logical interpretants, which mediate between conscious and unconscious regions of the mind, in turn stimulate the mind to rehearse actions performed in given contexts. It is this process that may lead to a habit change, making a change of habitus the most advanced form of semiosis. Habits of mind, or the rules governing our conduct, are thus acquired by repetition, either material or imaginary. If in reflecting upon an action, that is, when in dialogue with the critical self after the fact, we feel little or no self-reproach, we infer that the action can be repeated when similar conditions hold. Guilt feelings or self-reproach are of course linked to the ethical norms of a community, as Peirce shows by making blame of others, in his words, a "transference" or a "projection" of primary self-reproach (*CP* 5.418–19). The reiterations—actual or imagined—set in motion by lack of self-reproach result in ordering what would otherwise be random actions under a law, or habit of mind, influencing future behavior. Such imaginary repetitions, leading to a cultural belief or establishing patterns to live by, are further strengthened by direct commands to onself.

> *Reiterations in the inner world—fancied reiterations—if well-intensi-fied by direct effort, produce habits,* just as do reiterations in the outer world; *and these habits will have power to influence actual behaviour in the outer world;* especially, if each reiteration be accompanied by a peculiar strong effort that is usually likened to issuing a command to one's future self. [*CP* 5.487]

Someone accustomed to conceptualizing psychic interaction in terms of Freudian metapsychology, in which the ego seeks to mediate among unconscious drives, or "instinctual representatives" (*S.E.* 14:186), the requirements of the outer world, and the commands of an inner law, cannot fail to see parallels between Peirce's semiotic model of rational self-control and Freud's semiotic model of the psychic apparatus. As we have seen, for Peirce, too, rational self-control involves the effects on an inner interlocutor of instinctual thoughts, sense impressions, moral judgments, reiterations, and ethical commands, all of which are in the form of signs mediated by logical interpretants. The eventual effect of the interpretants is to modulate beliefs or the cultural unconscious via repetition. Repetition and ethical change are inseparable from semiosis.

In drawing attention to what the Peircean and Freudian conceptions of intrapsychic semiosis have in common, I do not mean to underestimate the differences between them. Both, however, posit a conscious rationality evolving from a somatic *it,* the *it* being a philosophic term adopted by both Peirce and Freud (*CP* 1.547; *S.E.* 19:23). (Consequently, *it* rather than *id* would have best translated Freud's *Es.*) Further, the two thinkers agree that conscious and unconscious domains remain linked by processes of association and a continuous chain of translations or interpretations. Most strikingly, in the famous letter to Wilhelm Fliess of December 6, 1896, Freud defined the psychic apparatus in terms of a transcription of signs proceeding from percepts to unconscious and then to conscious or verbal inscriptions (*S.E.* 1:233–34), a semiotic model again taken up in "The Unconscious" of 1915 and "A Note upon the Mystic 'Writing-Pad'" of 1925. This Freudian model of layered psychic transcriptions agrees with Peirce's pragmaticist model of the mind.[6] Additionally, both Peirce and Freud's hypothesis of the unconscious is inferential, not mythological, based as it is on observations of the effects of psychic semiosis. In this connection, it becomes clear that the claim by Lacan (1970, 188) that the unconscious is structured like a language is a questionable formulation of the Peircean and Freudian insights that the entire psyche—not just the unconscious—functions as a continuous process of semiosis.[7]

To continue with the Peircean and Freudian parallels, both thinkers emphasize the role of repetition or of "reiteration," as Peirce puts it. They posit psychic semiosis as a repetition or translation of signs from one psychic level to another and from one self to another self. In addition, for Peirce, ethical dispositions may be modified by means of the reiteration of thoughts or of logical interpretants resulting from such intrapsychic semiosis. For Freud (*S.E.* 18:1–64), the repetition compulsion involves the reappearance of the repressed and unconscious drives, including the death drive, against which the ego attempts to defend itself by equally compulsive repetitions. Although, as stated, there are obvious differences between the two conceptions, it is nevertheless important to note that, for both thinkers, semiotic reiterations permeate the entire psychic process and take the shape of sign translations or interpretations that influence conscience and conduct.

Although it is interesting to note these general agreements, which are no doubt to be explained by the fact that both Peirce and Freud were extending the views of the same precursors and by the fact that we are now reading both thinkers through poststructuralist lenses, it is equally important not to collapse the Peircean and Freudian models.[8] Peirce's unconscious, of course, is not the psychoanalytic unconscious, with much of its content the result of repression, or of what Freud called the "ostrich policy" (*S.E.* 5:600), in which the "psychical representatives" of drives, which operate like Peirce's first logical interpretants, are censored and prevented from becoming conscious and nameable (*S.E.* 14:148). (As we have seen, though, Freud in no way limited the unconscious to the repressed, a point he made explicitly in "The Unconscious" [166].) In many of his writings, too, Freud preferred a dynamic-economic model to the topographical one for the workings of the psyche, whereas Peirce grounded the psyche in the cosmic mind and, further, in the mind of God

(*CP* 7.558; Corrington 1993, 167–204).[9] In some ways, then, Peirce's conception of the psyche is closer to Spinoza's univocity of being or to the absolute ground of the mystics and nineteenth-century German idealist philosophers, such as Schelling, than it is to Freud's. Within the limitations of this chapter, I cannot pursue this question. Instead, I will make a few preliminary stabs at making the notion of the logical interpretant cooperate with a psychopragmatic notion of performativity and at doing so within the context of psychic semiosis discussed so far.[10]

Psychopragmatics

Early in this paper I defined the interpretant as a sign's pragmatic effect on the receiver. The modifier *pragmatic* here refers to *pragmatics* as a branch of semiotics that Charles Morris defined as the study of "the relation of signs to interpreters" ([1938] 1971, 21). It is not surprising that Morris was thinking of *pragmatism* when he coined the term *pragmatics,* so the term *pragmatics* serves to recognize the contributions Peirce, James, Dewey, and other pragmatists made to semiotics. Morris wrote: "It is a plausible view that the permanent significance of pragmatism lies in the fact that it has directed attention more closely to the relation of signs to their users than had previously been done and has assessed more profoundly than ever before the relevance of this relation in understanding intellectual activities" (43).

In relating signs to their interpreters, pragmatics takes into account Peirce's definition of semiosis as an action. Critical, as well, for the field of pragmatics is Peirce's notion of "informational" knowledge, that is, all that interpreters need to know in addition to the meanings of words in order to understand utterances. Peirce's distinction between the two types of interpreter competence, which he called "informational" and "verbal" (MS 664; quoted in Johansen 1993, 147), continues to be drawn in terms of "contextual," or "pragmatic," versus "semantic" meanings.

One of the most influential developments in the field of pragmatics is speech act theory, which at first would appear to have much in common with Peirce's triadic view of semiosis. As is well known, in *How to Do Things with Words,* John L. Austin divides an utterance into a "locutionary act" with a determinate sense, which is accompanied by an "illocutionary act," which performs an intentional action such as promising or commanding, and a "perlocutionary act," which brings about an effect on the receiver (1975, 109ff.). Further, Austin introduced the notion of the "performative" as "doing something as opposed to just saying something" (133). In relating these aspects of speech act theory to Peircean semiosis, one finds that the locutionary act corresponds to the semantic relation between a sign and its object, and the illocutionary and per- locutionary acts parallel the pragmatic relation between signs and their interpretants. The notions of speech act and performativity as such echo Peirce's broader definition, as quoted at the beginning of this chapter, of all semiosis as an action.

Jacques Derrida's critique of Austin, combined with his public and rather acerbic debate with John Searles, has made clear, however, to what extent speech act theory falls short as a pragmatic theory of semiosis in the Peircean sense. Derrida objects to speech act theory primarily be- cause (1) in positing that a sender's intention and a receiver's response are transparent to the interlocutors, the theory omits the role of the un- conscious in semiosis; and (2) in neglecting the reiteration of speech acts through recontextualization, speech act theory excludes alterity, abnor- mality, and change. It is striking to what extent Derrida's objections to speech act theory, then, especially his critique of the unified subject and of the theory's exclusionary moves, depend on the Peircean and Freudian theories of psychic semiosis. It may be suggested, therefore, that speech act theory could with much profit be rethought or reinterpreted by tak- ing into account Peirce's notion of the interpretant and the Peircean and Freudian conceptions of a continuous process of psychic semiosis, as they mutually extend each other. Such a mutual extension is perhaps what Derrida has in part accomplished by his concept of *différance* — difference, or nonidentity with oneself, and postponement of significa- tion — a concept that echoes or, rather, translates, Peirce and Freud's con- tinuous semiosis or the translation of one interpretant by another and then another in an unending process.

In Derrida's texts about the speech act controversy, dating from 1972 to 1988, a Peircean intertext is hard to miss. Two examples follow:

> When I speak here of law, of convention or of invention, I would like not to rely, as it might seem I do, upon the classical opposition between nature and law, or between animals alleged not to have language and man, author of speech acts and capable of entering into a relation to the law, be it of obedience or of transgression. . . . Barring any inconsistency, ineptness, or insufficiently rigorous formalization on my part, my statements on this subject should be valid beyond the marks and society called "human." [1988, 134]

and:

> Every sign, linguistic or non-linguistic . . . can . . . break with every given context, engendering [*and* inscribing itself in] an infinity of new contexts

in a manner which is absolutely illimitable. [79; bracketed addition by Derrida into his self-quoted text]

It is therefore surprising that no direct reference is made to Peirce, as indeed there had been in the 1967 *De la grammatologie.* There Derrida pays tribute to Peirce as a predecessor: "Peirce goes very far in the direction that I have called the de-construction of the transcendental signified, which, at one time or another, would place a reassuring end to the reference from sign to sign" (1974, 49).

A pertinent example of the reinterpretation of speech act theory's notion of performativity in light of Derrida's semiotic critique is found in Judith Butler's *Bodies That Matter* (1993). In this study, Butler examines the discursive practices that form and regulate the social beliefs concerning sexed bodies. For Butler, our access to a sexed body is via the utterances that constitute it in speaking of it, that is, we know it only as an effect of semiosis. The body as a primary given is not available. Taking Derrida's critique of Austin into account, Butler then redefines performativity as the "power of discourse to produce effects through reiteration" (1993, 20). In emphasizing reiteration and the founding role of exclusion, Butler's performativity—via Derrida's semiotic critique— would appear to be a more appropriate interpretant of Peirce's interpretant than of Austin's performative. At the same time, what is emphasized is the power of semiosis to effect change, in the domain, for instance, of the image of the sexed body and its implications for social beliefs and ethical action. It is such reconceptualization of conscience or of the cultural unconscious in terms of psychic semiosis that can have far-reaching effects on both pragmatics and psychoanalytic thought.

Not only speech act theory but other influential developments in the field of pragmatics as well would profit from taking into account the Peircean and Freudian descriptions of psychic semiosis. For example, in *Relevance: Communication and Cognition,* Dan Sperber and Deirdre Wilson, who base their approach to pragmatics on cognitive psychology, indict semiotics for what they take to be its coding-decoding model, which ignores the crucial role of inference in human communication (1986, 1–9ff.). Tracing the inferential model of communication to the contemporary philosopher Paul Grice, they assert, "Pragmatic interpretation seems to us to resemble scientific theorizing in essential respects. The speaker's intentions are not decoded but non-demonstratively [nondeductively] inferred, by a process of hypothesis formation and confirmation. . . . The hearer's aim is to arrive at the most plausible hypothesis about the speaker's intentions" (Wilson and Sperber [1986] 1991, 585). Yet, as we have seen, an inferential model of semiosis is already to be found in the work of Peirce. Similarly, Freud considered dialogue with others and dialogue with oneself as other to be inferential (*S.E.* 14:169).

Unlike Peirce's and Freud's theories of semiosis, however, with which their inferential model agrees, Sperber and Wilson's view of communication excludes the nonintentional. For them, not even the interpretation of a medical symptom, such as a hoarse voice as evidence of a sore throat, is communicative, when it is not intentionally conveyed (1986, 22–23). By extension, those nonverbal messages, which are transmitted outside of awareness, and the types of phenomena examined by Freud as evidence of the unconscious — psychical symptoms and obsessions, slips of the tongue, and the subtexts of dreams, jokes, fantasies, and memories — are not considered to be forms of communication. Specifically, in the case of slips of the tongue, Sperber and Wilson hold that since the goal of hearers is to infer the meanings intended by the speakers, they simply discount slips of the tongue as wrong meanings (23). That wrong meanings are meaningful or that such slips might have meanings of their own, which can, moreover, be derived inferentially, is not considered. I argue that, as in the case of speech act theory, Sperber and Wilson's cognitive models are not as productive as they might be if they included communicative behavior outside of consciousness.

When they turn their attention to the performative effects of language, Sperber and Wilson hold that a communicator's informational intention is to modify not thoughts directly but the audience's "cognitive environment," or store of assumptions (58), which corresponds to what Peirce termed habitual dispositions, or systems of belief. In interpreting an utterance, hearers make a sender's explicitly expressed assumptions interact with a set of already processed assumptions in their own cognitive environment. No less than their inferential model of communication, the description of this process, in which the understanding of an utterance depends on previous acts of interpretation in the hearer's system of social beliefs, recalls Peirce's view of psychic semiosis, in particular the action of the logical interpretants, which in determining the interpreter's mind depends on chains of previous interpretants, or established habits and beliefs. In making their theory of relevance depend on the contextual effects obtained from the interaction of assumptions (or interpretants), Sperber and Wilson have made a major contribution to pragmatics, limited though it is by their exclusion of the nonintentional (119).

There is still another way in which Sperber and Wilson appear to be rediscovering the Peircean concept of the interpretant. For them, every utterance is an "interpretation" of a speaker's thought, of which hearers in turn must construct their own mental "interpretations" (230). Nor do they fail to ask the question of what the speaker's interpreted thought itself represents, and so on (231). It follows that since hearers interpret an interpretation of a thought which itself is an interpretation of a thought, and so on, they have hypothesized another chainlike series of interpretants in the manner of Peirce. Utterance comprehension, then, puts into interaction two series of interpretants, one translating the speaker's thought and the other transcribing the assumptions of the receiver's cognitive environment. Given the astonishing overlap between their cognitive model and Peirce's model of psychic semiosis, the disappointment in semiotics the authors repeatedly express in their book is all the more surprising. Although they are in agreement with Peirce—unknowingly, it would appear—about the ultimately rational nature of communication and the performative action of the logical interpretant, their insistence on the speaker's intentions and disregard of the unconscious, whether personal or cultural, result in their excluding large areas of behavior that both Peirce and Freud submitted to lucid analysis.

It is in the realm of ethics and aesthetics that I would like—if ever so briefly—to point out some consequences of insisting on conscious intentionality and transparency and to argue for a Peircean and psychoanalytically informed approach to pragmatics. For to insist on intentionality as a *sine qua non* of communication has major implications for questions of social justice and an ethics of discourse.[11] Are acts of racial discrimination, for example, that are "unintentional" therefore not to be taken as acts of communication? Is one to ignore their devastating effects? In a defense of affirmative action, law professor Michael Rooke-Ley points out that in civil rights cases in the past thirty years, U.S. courts have, for the most part, required proof of discriminatory intent, whereas "only a small percentage of discrimination occurs at the hands of overt, plain-speaking racists. Rather, most discrimination today is subtle, arguably unconscious and often institutionalized" (1995, A14). Although it is clear that acts of racial discrimination are against the law, the intentionality requirement keeps courts from applying legal sanctions against such acts, which, in their ubiquity and repetitiveness, serve to maintain social inequality as a community norm. Is there a way out of this impasse? I believe that psychopragmatic considerations can be of help. If acts of discrimination are mostly unintentionally committed, this would seem to imply that, for unintentional racists, there are no internal constraints of conscience, no habitual dispositions, no cultural unconscious that has internalized restrictions on discrimination. In psychoanalytic terms, the racism is an effect of a fearful otherness within the self, which can be projected outward because it is uncensored by conscience. That an unjust action, which is moreover legally proscribed, can nevertheless be a generally condoned community norm points to the clash of values that tests the mettle of societies.

From the point of view of performativity and the Peircean definition of semiosis, racist utterances, whether intentional or not, have discriminatory effects that must be considered an integral part of the act of communication. Why should the sender's intention take precedence over the receiver's reaction? The two are inseparable parts of one process of semiosis mediated by a chain of translations or interpretants. Bringing the socially harmful action of discourse into the open, as has been done, for example, for sexual harassment, in which the performative effect on the receiver is taken into account, may be a step in the direction of changing an ingrained community norm. The backlash that has taken place in the wake of sexual harassment guidelines and decisions is proof, however, of the difficulty of effecting a change of habitus. The resistance is no doubt to be understood partly through the reinforcement that external reiterations receive from unconscious repetitions of the terrors of otherness (Moorjani 1992). Until a change of social conscience occurs and sanctions are internalized, there is no alternative but to put in place external constraints—as happened in the case of sexual harassment—in order to preclude the repetition of discriminatory acts, intentional or not.[12]

Another influential reevaluation of performativity in the interest of an ethics of discourse is found in Catharine MacKinnon's ironically entitled *Only Words* (1993). In this slim volume, MacKinnon, too, uses Austin's concept of performativity as a starting point to examine the action of words and images in fostering discrimination and enforcing social inequality. Arguing against those legal interpretations that extend First Amendment protection to pornography and hate propaganda as forms of speech, she cogently maintains that such language and images cannot be reduced to saying, or semantics, but must be viewed as pragmatic doing, with discriminatory effects that violate the equality provisions of the Fourteenth Amendment.

Against speech act intentionalists, however, MacKinnon extends performativity to the unconscious. One of the special effects of pornography, she maintains, is its ability to circumvent consciousness by its direct sexual impact on viewers. She holds that the discriminatory and sexually abusive content of pornography is energized by the direct sexual feelings and bodily responses it has the power to evoke in male viewers (1993, 16ff., 61–62). MacKinnon's analysis of the triple performative action of pornography points to the role of the logical interpretant in semiosis, which in addition to translating ideas, produces energetic (in this case, physical) and emotional effects.

Of major concern to MacKinnon is the proliferation of pornographic discourse through film, video, and the Internet, which by its repetitive force and officially protected status is turning pornography into an acceptable community norm (90 – 102). As in the case of racial discrimination, why, then, would men feel self-reproach about sexual aggression against women? In psychopragmatic terms, the reiterations of pornographic media are reinforced by imaginary repetitions, which, in turn, lean on the interpretants of instinctual drives. And these outer and inner reiterations produce the cultural unconscious that influences behavior. As in the case of Butler's reinterpretation of Austin's performativity, by taking repetition and unconscious effects into account, MacKinnon's analysis of the discriminatory, and therefore illegal, force of pornography moves beyond speech act theory to a psychopragmatically informed call for social change.

I would like to end with a question about aesthetics, to which Peirce, agreeing with the Romantic philosophers, subordinates ethics (Brent 1993, 53, 301). Within the purview of the pragmatic intentionalists, what is one to make of the method of poets and artists who work toward the unknown, the unexpected, the unconscious? Akin to many artists, Gerhard Richter insists on the unintentional dimension of his painting: "My method or my expectation which, so to speak, drives me to painting, is opposition. . . . Just that something will emerge that is unknown to me, which I could not plan, which is better, cleverer, than I am . . . the whole process does not exist for its own sake" (quoted in Gidal 1993, 47). Do we discount such unintentional works as meaningless? Or do we aim "to arrive at the most plausible hypothesis" (Wilson and Sperber 1986, 585) not about the sender's intentions but about the "unknown" of the work itself? Since the work's intentions are as opaque to the sender as to the interpreter, its deciphering involves processes of interpretation in opposition to conscious dispositions, the sender's no less than the receiver's. This method of understanding may involve what Peirce termed a state of "musement" (*CP* 6:458 – 62), which is akin to what François Roustang has described as self-hypnosis, in which our habitual ways of thinking and acting are suspended (1994). In Freudian terms, one might view this state as the interaction of unconscious modes of thinking (*S.E.* 14:194). It is in this mood that the repetitions of our habitual dispositions can be overcome by a change of mind through the emotional, energetic, and logical action of the interpretants. In inhibiting the representation of the intentional, the habitual, the already known, a work's indeterminate signs may render the process of interpretation radically productive, although it may produce unknowingness. In "Endless Finalities," an essay on Gerhard Richter's abstract paintings, Peter Gidal aptly describes what such an interpreting process might be: "Each time you try again to recognise, or try to make a space, or a form, or a colour, or a depth, or a 'painting' through which something could be, you're brought up against impossibility, the end of that process, only to be moved ineluctably to attempt that grasping again. Not that any of this engagement with the painting is undetermined; it is endlessly determined by the material there ballastless" (1993, 45). A pragmatics that fails to take into account aesthetic performativity is in great need of rethinking.

I argue for a reconceptualization of the field of pragmatics and especially of the notion of the performative in terms of Peircean and Freudian psychic semiosis. In particular, I suggest that a tripartite interchange between pragmatics, Peirce's pragmaticism, and psychoanalysis will help to renew our understanding of an ethics of discourse.

Notes

A shorter version of this chapter was delivered at the 1994 Semiotic Society of America Meeting in Philadelphia, Pennsylvania, and appears in the proceedings volume *Semiotics 1994,* edited by C. W. Spinks and John Deely (New York: Peter Lang, 1995). A still more abridged version was presented at the 1995 Conference in Literature and Psychoanalysis in Freiburg, Germany. The paper has been substantially revised and extended for the present volume.

   In citing Peirce's writings of 1860 to 1911, which the eight volumes of the *Collected Papers* group thematically, I have followed the usual practice in Peirce scholarship of using the abbreviated title *CP* and the volume number followed by a period and the pertinent paragraph numbers. Instead of giving the date of publication of the *Collected Papers* volumes, I have included the date of first publication or composition of Peirce's writings in the list of individual volumes under the entry for the *Collected Papers.* Citations of manuscript sources refer to the manuscript numbers used by the Houghton Library at Harvard University.

   1. I have used the terms *signifier, signified,* and *referent* because of their long history in philosophical thought about the nature of signs, with the first two terms originally coined by the Stoics. Peirce, however, unlike Ferdinand de Saussure, invented his own terminology: he spoke of the signified as the inner or "immediate object" of the sign, whereas his outer or "dynamic" object is akin to the referent (*CP* 4.536). For an overview of the different interpretations given to Peircean semiosis, see Colapietro (1989); Deely (1990); Johansen (1993); Morris ([1938] 1971); Murphey (1961); and Savan (1987–88).

   2. Aware of the role of context in utterance interpretation, Peirce writes that "the common stock of knowledge of utterer and interpreter, called to mind by the words, is a part of the sign" (MS 517, 1904).

   3. In relation to symbol and interpretant, Peirce writes, "Now it is of the essential nature of a symbol that it determines an interpretant, which is itself a sym-

bol. A symbol, therefore, produces an endless series of interpretants" (MS 517, 1904).

4. For an excellent discussion of the various Peircean divisions of the interpretant, see Johansen (1993, 145–74).

5. For Peirce, the *ex post facto* awareness of percepts was to be understood in terms of logical inference: "Whatever feature of the percept is brought into relief by some association and thus attains a logical position . . . the attribution of Existence to it in the Perceptual Judgment is virtually and in an extended sense, a logical Abductive Inference nearly approximating to necessary inference" (*CP* 4.541).

6. A contemporary neurologist, who connects reason to its emotional and bodily underpinnings, has come to a similar conclusion as Peirce and Freud about the existence of psychic transcriptions. In *Descartes' Error,* Antonio Damasio holds that mind, or cognition, consists of thought processes that organize and translate verbal and nonverbal mental images, the neural substrate of which in turn consists of topographically organized "neural representations," which on a "nonconscious" level translate innate and acquired "dispositional representations" (instincts, drives, bodily states and schemata, emotions, and the cultural unconscious) (1994, 90ff.). Further, he, too, hypothesizes a link from ethical rules and social conventions to the drives and instincts: "Although such conventions and rules need be transmitted only through education and socialization, from generation to generation, I suspect that the neural representations of the wisdom they embody, and of the means to implement that wisdom, are inextricably linked to the neural representation of innate regulatory biological processes" (125). Obviously, Peirce's logical interpretants, or interpreting thoughts, which translate percepts, emotions, unconscious needs, and experiences, and determine ethical dispositions are apropos for Damasio's theory as is Freud's topographical model. One might also recall Freud's statement in *The Ego and the Id* that "the ego is first and foremost a bodily ego" (*S.E.* 19:26). Damasio's term *representation* brings to mind that it is one of the words Peirce used for a sign.

7. For a semiotic critique of Lacan's conception of the linguistic structure of the unconscious, see Bär (1975, 31–58); for a psychoanalytic critique, see Laplanche ([1987] 1989, 40–45). Similarly, François Roustang (1984, 936) quotes an article by Régnier Pirard, published in the *Revue philosophique de Louvain* (Nov. 1979), in which Pirard states, "If the unconscious takes over language to the point of becoming equivalent to it, we might as well say that there is no longer, nor was there ever, an unconscious." Lacan, of course, is contradicting Freud in contending that the unconscious "is a thinking with words" (1970, 189), since, for Freud (*S.E.* 14:201–2), the translation of "thing-presentations" into words occurs only at the border between the unconscious and consciousness. It is interesting to note that André Green, Pierre Bayard, and Jean Bellemin-Noël hold that Peirce inspired Lacan's thinking about the signifier and the linguistic structure of the unconscious: "En effet, nous trouvons dans Peirce tout le refoulé de la théorie de Lacan. Peirce, qui est un géant!" [Actually, one finds in Peirce all that is repressed in Lacan's theory. Peirce, who is a giant!] (1993, 113; my translation).

On the question of the epistemology of the unconscious, Roustang finds the existence of the unconscious to be an unverifiable hypothesis and its invention a myth (1984). Freud, however, in the essay "The Unconscious," sees his hypothesizing as inferential: "We have no other aim but that of translating into theory the results of observation. . . . We shall defend the complications of our theory so long as we find that they meet the results of observation" (*S.E.* 14:190). Like any hypothesis, the existence of the unconscious is defensible only as long as it is able to predict certain effects. Roustang is right, of course, to emphasize the hypothetical nature of the unconscious and to warn against the tendency to accept it as a fact. Its mythical status, however, is debatable. Perhaps the many recent arguments against granting Freud's hypotheses any scientific status whatsoever have to do with an understanding of the scientific method that excludes the kind of inferential thinking that Freud largely practiced and that Peirce called "abduction," or "hypothetical reasoning." Peirce puts his finger on one of the difficulties with this type of inference in an essay entitled "Our Senses as Reasoning Machines": "[Hypothetical reasoning] consists in the introduction into a confused tangle of given facts of an idea not given whose only justification lies in its reducing that tangle to order. This kind of inference is little subject to control, and so not highly rational; and one reason for this is that when once the facts have been apprehended in the light of the hypothesis, they become so swallowed up in it, that a strong exertion of intellect is required to disembarrass them from it" (MS 831, 1900).

8. Regarding the precursors that Peirce and Freud have in common for their conceptions of psychic semiosis (for there are many other precursors, such as the hypnotists, that they do not necessarily share), I have in mind (1) the psychological associationists, particularly Johann Friedrich Herbart (1776-1841), whose work was familiar to both Peirce and Freud (*CP* 7.393; Jones 1953, 374), and whose ideas can be traced back to David Hume's principles of contiguity and resemblance in *An Enquiry Concerning Human Understanding* (1748); and (2) the nineteenth-century thinkers, writers, and artists whose works give evidence of an understanding of the unconscious. Among the latter, I consider of foremost importance the romantics and symbolists; Kant and the German idealist philosophers, especially Schelling and Schopenhauer; and the founder of experimental psychology, Gustav Theodor Fechner (1801-87), and his disciple Wilhelm Wundt (1832-1920). Ellenberger points out that Freud, who quotes Fechner in several of his major works, was influenced by the latter's concept of mental energy, his topographical view of the mind, and his principles of pleasure-unpleasure, constancy, and repetition (1970, 217-18). Since references to Fechner and Wundt are also scattered throughout Peirce's writings, it is likely that Fechner's repetition principle, for instance, was known to both Peirce and Freud. Strangely enough, Freud seems not to have read Eduard von Hartmann (1842-1906) (Whyte 1960, 166), whose monumental *Philosophy of the Unconscious* of 1869 went through numerous editions and translations. Of Hartmann, Peirce writes, "To my apprehension Hartmann has proved conclusively that unconscious mind exists" (*CP* 7.364) and also refers to Hartmann's belief that the processes of association are unconscious (*CP* 7.395). For an overview of the unconscious before Freud, in addition to Ellenberger (1970), see Whyte (1960). Whyte

appropriately points out that although the existence of the unconscious mind was being established from 1680 to 1880, the discovery of its structure did not begin before the twentieth century (1960, 63).

9. In the discussion period following the presentation of an earlier version of this paper at the 1994 Semiotic Society of America Meeting, Vincent Colapietro suggested that Freud's dynamic-economic model of the psyche, too, can be understood in semiotic terms. I am indebted to him for this perceptive remark.

10. For further examinations of the commonalities between the Peircean and psychoanalytic models of psychic semiosis, see Colapietro (1989), Corrington (1993), de Lauretis (1984; 1994), and Silverman (1983). Although critical of Peirce's "scant attention to the unconscious," this, of course, judged from the published writings, Silverman (1983, 18), for example, holds that "no treatment of the relationship between subject and signifier would be complete without the Peircian scheme, which offers a more satisfactory explanation of the role of the cognitive subject in the signifying process than does that of Freud, Lacan, or Benveniste."

11. In a recent review of a collection of articles on responsibility in oral discourse, Peter Stromberg suggests that speech act theory's assumption that the meaning of an utterance depends on the intentions of the speaker "is part of a much larger system of interlocking notions about moral responsibility. (In part, the point is that Western culture has taken shape in the context of a religious heritage that defines moral worth in terms of individual intentions.)" (1995, 260). The intentionality assumption and the authority it confers on the speaker are, however, not universally accepted. In some non-Western societies, certain categories of speakers are indeed required to take responsibility for how their words are interpreted. I argue that, in specific contexts, this responsibility accrues to Western speakers as well. One might also add that in textual studies, the concept of the "intentional fallacy," which precludes understanding a work through the author's intentions, has long held currency. I thank Thomas Field for bringing the above review to my attention and for dialogue about intentionality in pragmatics.

12. In his chapter on human "extensions," Hall writes of "internalizing" and "externalizing" as two complementary and continuous ways of establishing ethical controls. He adds perceptively that "actions that are under the control of what we call the conscience in one part of the world may be handled by externalized controls elsewhere" (1976, 27). Social justice is endangered, it would seem to follow, when the two controls break down simultaneously, or when the weakening of one is not compensated by the strengthening of the other.

References

Austin, John L. *How to Do Things with Words.* 2d. ed. Edited by J. O. Urmson and Marina Sbisa. Cambridge: Harvard University Press, 1975.

Bakhtin, Mikhail M. "Discourse in the Novel" (1934-35). In *The Dialogic Imagination: Four Essays by M. M. Bakhtin,* translated by Michael Holquist and Caryl Emerson, 259-422. Austin: University of Texas Press, 1981.

Bär, Eugen. *Semiotic Approaches to Psychotherapy.* Bloomington: Indiana University, 1975.

Bourdieu, Pierre. *La distinction: critique sociale du jugement.* Paris: Minuit, 1979.

Brent, Joseph. *Charles Sanders Peirce: A Life.* Bloomington: Indiana University Press, 1993.

Butler, Judith. *Bodies That Matter: On the Discursive Limits of "Sex."* New York: Routledge, 1993.

Colapietro, Vincent M. *Peirce's Approach to the Self: A Semiotic Perspective on Human Subjectivity.* Albany: State University of New York Press, 1989.

Corrington, Robert S. *An Introduction to C. S. Peirce: Philosopher, Semiotician, and Ecstatic Naturalist.* Lanham, Md.: Rowman and Littlefield, 1993.

Damasio, Antonio R. *Descartes' Error: Emotion, Reason, and the Human Brain.* New York: G. P. Putnam's Sons, 1994.

Deely, John. *Basics of Semiotics.* Bloomington: Indiana University Press, 1990.

de Lauretis, Teresa. *Alice Doesn't: Feminism, Semiotics, Cinema.* Bloomington: Indiana University Press, 1984.

—————. *The Practice of Love: Lesbian Sexuality and Perverse Desire.* Bloomington: Indiana University Press, 1994.

Derrida, Jacques. *Of Grammatology.* Translated by Gayatri Chakravorty Spivak. Baltimore: Johns Hopkins University Press, 1974. Originally published as *De la grammatologie* (Paris: Minuit, 1967).

—————. *Limited Inc.* Evanston, Ill.: Northwestern University Press, 1988.

Ellenberger, Henri F. *The Discovery of the Unconscious: The History and Evolution of Dynamic Psychiatry.* New York: Basic Books, 1970.

Freud, Sigmund. *The Standard Edition of the Complete Psychological Works of Sigmund Freud.* Edited and translated by James Strachey. 24 vols. London: Hogarth, 1953-74.

Letter to Wilhelm Fliess of December 6, 1896, vol. 1.

The Interpretation of Dreams (1900), vols. 4, 5.

"Repression" (1915), vol. 14.

"The Unconscious" (1915), vol. 14.

Beyond the Pleasure Principle (1920), vol. 18.

The Ego and the Id (Das Ich und das Es) (1923), vol. 19.

"A Note upon the 'Mystic Writing-Pad'" (1925), vol. 19.

Civilization and Its Discontents (1930), vol. 21.

Gidal, Peter. "Endless Finalities." *Parkett* 35 (1993): 44-48.

Green, André, Bayard, Pierre, and Bellemin-Noël, Jean. "Entretien." *Littérature* 90 (1993): 108-24.

Hall, Edward T. *Beyond Culture.* Garden City, N.Y.: Anchor Press, 1976.

Hume, David. *An Enquiry Concerning Human Understanding* (1748). Indianapolis: Hackett, 1977.

Jakobson, Roman. "Two Aspects of Language and Two Types of Aphasic Disturbances" (1956). In *Word and Language*. Vol. 2 of *Selected Writings*. The Hague: Mouton, 1971.

Johansen, Jorgen Dines. *Dialogic Semiosis: An Essay on Signs and Meaning*. Bloomington: Indiana University Press, 1993.

Jones, Ernest. *The Formative Years and the Great Discoveries, 1856–1900*. Vol. 1 of *The Life and Work of Sigmund Freud*. New York: Basic Books, 1953.

Lacan, Jacques. "Of Structure As an Inmixing of an Otherness Prerequisite to Any Subject Whatever." In *The Structuralist Controversy*, edited by Richard Macksey and Eugenio Donato. Baltimore: Johns Hopkins University Press, 1970.

————. "The Agency of the Letter in the Unconscious or Reason since Freud." In *Écrits: A Selection*, translated by Alan Sheridan. New York: W. W. Norton, 1977. Originally published as "L'instance de la lettre dans l'inconscient ou la raison depuis Freud" (1957). *Ecrits*. (Paris: Seuil, 1966).

Laplanche, Jean. *New Foundations for Psychoanalysis* (1987). Translated by David Macey. Cambridge, Mass.: Basil Blackwell, 1989.

MacKinnon, Catharine A. *Only Words*. Cambridge: Harvard University Press, 1993.

Moorjani, Angela. *The Aesthetics of Loss and Lessness*. London: Macmillan; New York: St. Martin's, 1992.

Morris, Charles. *Foundations of the Theory of Signs*. (1938). In *Writings on the General Theory of Signs*. The Hague: Mouton, 1971.

Murphey, Murray G. *The Development of Peirce's Philosophy*. Cambridge: Harvard University Press, 1961.

Peirce, Charles Sanders. *Collected Papers of Charles Sanders Peirce*. Edited by Charles Hartshorne, Paul Weiss, and Arthur W. Burks. 8 vols. Cambridge: Harvard University Press, 1931–58.

"On a New List of Categories" (1867), vol. 1.545–59.

"Some Consequences of Four Incapacities" (1868), vol. 5.264–317.

Review of William James, *The Principles of Psychology* (1891), vol. 8.55–71.

"Introduction, The Association of Ideas," from the *Grand Logic* (c. 1893), vol. 7.388–450.

"Of Reasoning in General," chapter 1 of "Short Logic" (c. 1893), vol. 7.555–58.

"Psychognosy," from *Minute Logic* (c. 1902), vol. 7.362–87.

"What Makes a Reasoning Sound?" ("Ideals of Conduct") (1903), vol. 1:591–615.

"Issues of Pragmaticism" (1905), vol. 5.438–63.

"What Pragmatism Is" (1905), vol. 5.411–37.

"Logic and Spiritualism" (c. 1905), vol. 6.557–87.

Undated letter to Signor Calderoni (c. 1905), vol. 8.205–13.

"Prolegomena to an Apology for Pragmaticism" (1906), vol. 4.530–72.

Unpublished letter-article to the editor of *The Nation* ("A Survey of Pragmaticism") (c. 1907), vol. 5.464–96.

"A Neglected Argument for the Reality of God" (1908), vol. 6.452–93.

————. Letter to Philip E. B. Jourdain of December 5, 1908. In *The New Elements of Mathematics*, edited by Carolyn Eisele. Vol. 3, part 2. The Hague: Mouton, 1976.

————. *Semiotic and Significs: The Correspondence between Charles S. Peirce and Victoria Lady Welby.* Edited by Charles S. Hardwick. Bloomington: Indiana University Press, 1977.

Rooke-Ley, Michael M. Letter to the Editor. *New York Times,* March 6, 1995, sec. A, p. 14.

Roustang, François. "On the Epistemology of Psychoanalysis." *Modern Language Notes* 99 (1984): 928–40.

———. *Qu'est-ce que l'hypnose.* Paris: Minuit, 1994.

Savan, David. *An Introduction to C. S. Peirce's Full System of Semeiotic.* Toronto: Toronto Semiotic Circle, 1987–88.

Silverman, Kaja. *The Subject of Semiotics.* New York: Oxford University Press, 1983.

Sperber, Dan, and Wilson, Deirdre. *Relevance: Communication and Cognition.* Cambridge: Harvard University Press, 1986.

Stromberg, Peter G. Review of *Responsibility and Evidence in Oral Discourse,* edited by Jane H. Hill and Judith T. Irvine. *Language in Society* 24 (1995): 259–62.

Whyte, Lancelot Law. *The Unconscious before Freud.* New York: Basic Books, 1960.

Wilson, Deirdre, and Sperber, Dan. "Pragmatics and Modularity" (1986). In *Pragmatics: A Reader,* edited by Steven Davis. New York: Oxford University Press, 1991.

8   Peirce and Derrida
From Sign to Sign

David Pettigrew

In the 1950s Jacques Derrida received a grant to spend a year at Harvard, where, among other projects, he studied the work of Charles S. Peirce. Some ten years later, in his text *Of Grammatology*, he referred to Peirce only marginally, stating that Peirce "goes very far in the direction of what I have called the deconstruction of the transcendental signified, which, at one time or another would place a reassuring end to the reference from sign to sign" (Derrida 1974, 49). Coming from Derrida, this sounds almost like praise. But what can this *ancien élève* of L'École Normale Supérieure have in common with Peirce—the self-described American backwoodsman (see *CP* 5.488)? Had Peirce achieved an unintentional deconstruction of the signified *avant la lettre?* This paper will reflect on these questions by investigating the striking, problematic, and improbable convergence of their thought. This chapter focuses on three points. First, I consider the way Peirce and Derrida's treatment of the relation of signs and the problem of meaning entails a notion of *difference.* Second, I consider how, for each thinker, the subject, or that which underlies the human subject most fundamentally and makes it what it is, is itself considered—however problematically—in terms of the operation of signs. Third, each thinker's questioning of the status of the sign is seen as a disruption of the assumptions of traditional metaphysics, particularly with respect to the indivisible, simple substance associated with the Cartesian cogito. It is on the question of this disruption that I conclude this chapter, for it raises questions as to the nature or status of meaning for contemporary thought.

But what does Derrida mean when he says that Peirce goes *very* far in the direction of the deconstruction of the transcendental signified? According to Derrida, the transcendental signified—the so-called condition of the possibility of meaning—has been the preoccupation or obsession of traditional metaphysics, constituting metaphysics as such and, he writes, "all the metaphysical determinations of truth" (1974, 10). For Derrida, the notion of a transcendental signified implies—even demands—an originary and enduring primacy, a foundational standard of meaning. Moreover, and central to his thinking, Derrida asserts that metaphysics has privileged the spoken word—the logocentric—as it implicates the position of a privileged self-presence, and that it has marginalized the written word.

Sign Relations

Here we need to continue the same citation from *Of Grammatology* with which we began. In the same quotation in which he mentions Peirce, Derrida writes, "I have identified logocentrism and the metaphysics of presence as the exigent, powerful, systematic and irrepressible desire for such a signified" (1974, 49). For Derrida, the marginalization of the written word by metaphysics is due to the loss of presence that is so intrinsic to the operation of the sign, and most evident with the written sign. He writes, in this well-known quote, which is, by now, a classical formulation:

> The sign is usually said to be put in the place of the thing itself, the present thing, "thing" here standing equally for meaning or referent. The sign represents the present in its absence. It takes the place of the present. When we cannot grasp or show the thing, state the present, the being-present, when the present cannot be presented we signify, we go through the detour of the sign. We signal. The sign, in this sense, is deferred presence. . . . And this structure presupposes that the sign, which defers presence, is conceivable only on the basis of the presence that it defers and moving towards the deferred presence that it aims to appropriate. [Derrida 1978a, 9]

For Derrida, to speak of the transcendental signified is to appropriate Saussure's use of the term *signified*. Saussure's linguistic sign, as is well known, operates on the basis of the difference between the signifier (the acoustic image) and the signified (the concept), to which the signifier gives rise (Saussure 1966, 99). Yet, while the relation between these two is binary and entails a positive bond, the value or meaning of the signifier is drawn from its relation to the other signifiers in the language—a relation that is itself not necessarily binary. This relation, Saussure asserts, is a *differential* relation. The signifier's value is that it is different from the other signifiers in the language (114). It is a difference, Saussure writes, "without positive terms" (120).

Derrida's approach to Saussure's notion of differential negativity emphasizes that the difference between the signifiers involves a temporal difference, a deferral of presence. What the sign or signifier signifies, then, is not its signified, but rather this necessarily temporal displacement of the signified by the signifier. For Derrida, it is not so much a displacement as it is a total rupturing of the integrity of the relation of a signifier to a signified or even of a signifier to another signifier. Indeed, insofar as it is the nature of the sign to be cut from the thing it signifies, there is an intrinsic indefiniteness of reference of which Derrida's notion of *différance* takes account. Furthermore, this is not an indefiniteness or ambiguity that can finally be reconciled. It must rather be thought of as a "play," Derrida writes, "for the word 'ambiguity' requires the logic of presence" (1974, 71).

Derrida suggests that it is precisely this indefiniteness of reference that brings the tradition of metaphysics to desire the transcendental signified so intensely, while repressing its absence so vigorously. *Différance* reveals the desire for an *impossible* presence. Insofar as this is a presence that the metaphysics of the sign requires, Derrida's treatment of the sign amounts to the destruction, he writes, of the "concept of 'sign' and its entire logic" (7). And to return to the same passage in which he refers to Peirce, Derrida continues, "Now Peirce considers the indefiniteness of reference as the criterion which allows us to recognize that we are indeed dealing with a system of signs" (49). Indeed, for Peirce, there is no meaning that is not mediated, and that mediation takes the form of the sign—the process of *semiosis*. His treatment of the triadic or tri-relative nature of the sign showed that the sign furnishes no direct access to the thing it signifies. In covering this well-trodden ground, one needs to recall Peirce's assertion that the sign can only represent the object and not furnish acquaintance with it (*CP* 2.231). The sign, he writes, "stands for the object not in all respects but in reference to a sort of idea" (*CP* 2.228). Access to the *thing* signified, then, is already mediated by the sign, or *representamen,* while the sign gives rise as well to yet another mediating influence: the *interpretant.* According to Peirce, "A sign, or *representamen,* is something which stands to somebody for something in some respect or capacity. It addresses somebody, that is, creates in the mind of that person an equivalent sign, or perhaps a more developed sign. That sign which it creates I call the *interpretant* of the first sign" (*CP* 2.228).

If one thinks, and for Peirce one *only* thinks in signs, one is caught up in this triadic network of sign relations. Referring to this aspect of Peirce's work, Derrida states, "The self-identity of the signified conceals itself unceasingly and is always on the move. The property of the representamen is to be itself and an other, to be produced as a structure of reference, to be separated from itself" (1974, 49-50). Indeed, it is central to Peirce's work that signs grow and develop with experience. There is, however, an ultimate stage of this process, at least in a provisional sense, which Peirce referred to as the "most proper significate outcome" of the sign. The proper significate outcome of the sign is the interpretant. However, one needs to read Peirce carefully in this respect. The interpretant is not a *terminal*—or, in Derrida's terminology, a *transcendental*—signified. The interpretant is itself triadic, with emotional, energetic, and logical aspects. The logical interpretant provides the widest scope, or general meaning, of the sign insofar as it influences reflection and action. Even the "logical" interpretant, however, as the "general" meaning of the sign, is not a final or transcendental meaning. For Peirce, it is the nature of signs to refer to other signs, to grow. The general logical interpretant is always in relation to another logical interpretant, to which it is related or under which it is subsumed (*CP* 5.476).

Such an infinite progression, however, would seem to impede the possibility that a sign would actually have an ultimate "meaning." Rather, the ultimate proper significate effect of the sign qua interpretant—and as meaningful—is that of a difference or change with respect to the general concept of the logical interpretant, however infinitesimal that difference may be. The difference, more precisely, is the change of habit in which the sign results. The ultimate outcome of the sign, Peirce said, is a change in habit: "the ultimate logical interpretant of the concept . . . that is not a sign but is of a general application is a *habit-change*; meaning by a habit-change a modification of a person's tendencies toward action" (*CP* 5.476). That the thematic of a change or difference in lived activity is what is significant or meaningful exemplifies a meaning that moves or grows. Its "cash value," to borrow James' term, is its "difference," its transformation. It is not that meaning is inaccessible, but rather that it has an "ineradicable probabilistic" element about it, to borrow a phrase from Kuhn, as it changes and develops (Kuhn 1972, 28).

Common to Derrida and Peirce, then—to summarize the first point briefly—is the notion that fundamental to the relation of signs, and the operation of signs as such, is a notion of difference which makes problematic the simple binary relation of a sign to the thing it signifies. With Derrida, *différance* took the form of an irreconcilable break or rupture, resulting in the destruction of the sign as such, while in the case of Peirce, the triadicity of signs is paradoxically "complete" insofar as it results in a difference or change in habit.[1]

Subjects of Signs

The second point of our engagement of Peirce and Derrida considers the extent to which the operation of signs underlies the human subject: the substratum of the subjectum — its substance. For Derrida, the "problematic of the sign" as a deferral of presence does indeed incorporate a problematic of the human subject. This occurs explicitly in "Freud and the Scene of Writing" (in Derrida 1978b), with his appropriation of a Freudian thematic. As in the case of what is perhaps his misappropriation of Saussurian thinking with respect to the sign (wherein he pushes the theme of temporal delay, which is not explicitly present in Saussure), Derrida enters the Freudian register indirectly and strategically. Derrida's reading of Freud finds that "psychical content will be represented by a text whose essence is irreducibly graphic. The *structure* of the *psychical apparatus* will be *represented* by a writing machine" (1978b, 199).

Derrida's work has chronicled the emergence of this motif in Freud's thought. In "Project for a Scientific Psychology" and in letter fifty-two to Fliess, Freud writes of the psyche as a field of differential memory traces, or signs (1954, 361, 173). By the time of *The Interpretation of Dreams,* Freud had made clear that the energetics of the psyche are nothing if not represented by signs, images, and symbols. The manifest content of the dream is read, for example, as a transcription of the latent dream thoughts.

With his foray into the Freudian scene and his consideration of the psyche-as-writing-machine, Derrida treats of the psyche in the context of the same loss of presence that the written sign "represents" most fundamentally. Derrida shows that central to Freud's work is the notion that the psyche sets up and binds its memory traces in a differential system in order to retain a certain order or quiescence, a quiescence that is ultimately its telos (1978b, 202–3). According to this logic of loss, memory traces are bound in the system, not for what they represent in terms of a particular memory or object, but for the loss, absence, or quiescence that they represent, for that quiescence is what is desired. The psychic memory trace represents "that memory in its absence." For Derrida, the psyche desires the loss (or the originary nonexistence) that the trace represents, for the quiescence that the psyche desires most fundamentally is the loss of itself (although this is a desire that is not without its concomitant anguish). It is in this sense, then, that he asserts that death is at the origin of life, and

> there is no life present *at first* which would *then* come to protect, postpone, or reserve itself, in *différance.* The latter constitutes the essence of

life. Or rather: as *différance* is not an essence, as it is not anything, it *is not* life, if Being is determined as *ousia,* presence, essence/existence, substance or subject. Life must be thought of a trace before Being may be determined as presence. This is the only condition on which we can say that life *is* death. . . . It is a *non-origin* which is *originary.* [203]

Of this desire for self-erasure located in the problematic of the sign, Derrida asserted, "Representation is death. Which may be immediately transformed into the following proposition: death is (only) representation" (277). This mark of difference is, moreover, "the erasure of selfhood, of one's own presence, and is constituted by the threat or anguish of its irremediable disappearance, of the disappearance of its disappearance" (230). Derrida's problematic of the sign, then, has an intrinsic relation to the question of the subject. As *différance* amounts to the destruction of the sign, so it cleaves and erases the self as simple presence to itself.[2]

Similarly, for Peirce, the relation of signs was not simply a matter of an account of meaning, or an epistemology: what is at stake is the question of the constitution of the self. For Peirce, the person is a sign. Thought itself, as we have seen, must take the form of a sign, and moreover, "when we think, then, we ourselves as we are at that moment, appear as a sign" (*CP* 5.283). He explained that "the entire phenomenal manifestation of mind, is a sign resulting from inference" (*CP* 5.313). Peirce asserted that the word or sign a person uses is the person him- or herself, and that one's language is his or her "sum total" (*CP* 5.314). The status of this *person-sign* must be seen in terms of Peirce's treatment of the growth and transformation of signs—that process he interrogates under the heading of semiosis. As such, the person-sign, or what underlies the human subject is something, but qua sign is something which is only represented, triadically fragmented, and caught in the movement of its difference. It must be *futural-conditional,* that is to say, not fully formed in the present, depending rather on the "hereafter," and in a way other than itself. Vincent Colapietro underlines this in his text *Peirce's Approach to the Self* when he asserts that "since personality [for Peirce] is *essentially* temporal, it is not only always incomplete but also *inherently unrealizable*" (1989, 76; my italics).

Moreover, as Colapietro points out, Peirce's account of human semiosis presupposed that the subject is a member of a linguistic community. The formation of the self is dependent on the future thought and experience of the community (*CP* 5.316). Hence, Colapietro's claim that for Peirce, "the individual self is, in its innermost being, not a private sphere but a communicative agent" (1989, 79). This self caught up in this matrix of communication is, as solitary, "illusory," and only becomes authentic in its communication with others (ibid.). This is because "what really is," as well as the identity of humans, depends, as Peirce wrote, "on the ultimate decision of the community: so thought is only what it is by virtue of addressing a future thought which is in its value as thought identical with it, though more developed. In this way, the existence of thought now depends on what is to be hereafter; so that it has only a potential existence, dependent on the future thought of the community" (*CP* 5.316). Hence, Peirce's remarkable assertion that "individual man . . . is only a negation" (*CP* 5.317).

For Peirce and Derrida, then, to discuss the operation of signs is at one and the same time to make problematic the traditional concept of the constitution of the subject. As the notion of difference disrupts the relation of signs, so it rends the fabric of the subject, overturning or decentering the simple self-certainty that would be thought to be at the archic center of the self.

The Disruption of Traditional Assumptions:
Concluding Provocations

Perhaps we can reflect better now on the citation at the beginning of the chapter: Our discussion of Derrida's assertion that Peirce goes very far in the direction of the deconstruction of the transcendental signified has thematized that deconstruction in at least two senses. The first is in the sense that the interactive triadicity of signs deconstructs the transcendental signified as a master-sign or touchstone of originary meaning. The second is that insofar as, for Peirce, the process of semiosis constitutes the subject, its intrinsically conditional, futural, and communal properties deconstruct the solipsistic, simple substance and self-certainty that the philosophical tradition has associated with the Cartesian cogito.

Derrida's thematic of *différance* has similarly been identified as a disruption of meaning as well as of the Cartesian cogito. Derrida calls into question no less than the relations *between* signs that Peirce's project requires. This thematic of a semiotic rupture does indeed signal a dramatic divergence of their thought. In spite of the co-problematic with respect to a disruption of metaphysics suggested here, there is a notion of continuity fundamental to Peirce's project that is not present in Derrida's work. The continuity of signs and the attendant growth of meaning are part of Peirce's reading of the continuity of lived experience. "Personality is not apprehended in an instant," he wrote, "it has to be lived in time" (*CP* 6.155). But Derrida's gaze, as we have seen, is directed rather at the gap produced by a disruption that metaphysics has tried to repress. His project takes account of the manifestations of the repression of the absence of presence.

But in spite of this gap between Peirce and Derrida—which should not be minimized—the disruption of metaphysics of presence and of substance is shared, at least in some respects, by the two thinkers. This disruption raises the concluding point of inquiry here. It is a proposal for an inquiry which is sketched here in the broadest possible strokes. That is, in the light of their interrogation of metaphysics, the ground of meaning, and the status of the human subject, what becomes of this meaning-in-crisis? What seems to be at stake is the question of what we might call the "isness" of the self, or that which underlies the self. For Peirce, this was, after all, a legitimate question for metaphysical inquiry—an inquiry that, he said, excludes a hasty resolution by its nature (*CP* 6.6). Peirce introduces what we have called an "ineradicable probabilistic" element into knowledge in general, as well of the subject, with his formulation of habit change and difference. It is not that truth is inaccessible, but that he transforms the status of the known. In the case of Derrida, it is not perhaps that there is simply *no* meaning, but that any meaning as traditionally embodied in a substantial cogito, for example, is but revealing of its own erasure. Is the ground of meaning to be the "veritable abyss" of Kant's first critique (Kant 1965, 513)? Is the new significance a lack of a "ground"?

With Peirce, we might consider that the subject itself is a kind of foundation when we see his striking assertion that "the one intelligible theory of the universe is that of objective idealism, that matter is effete mind, inveterate habits becoming physical laws" (*CP* 6.25). But in this case, if we return to the subject that is the ground of meaning, we find the pivot of the triadic unfolding of semiosis. As we have seen (and at this point it goes without saying), the subject is a sign. We can consider Peirce's assertion that

> the word or sign man uses *is* the man himself. For, as the fact that every thought is a sign, taken in conjunction with the fact that life is a train of thought, proves that man is a sign; so that every thought is an external sign, proves that man is an external sign. That is to say the man and the external sign are identical, in the same sense in which the words *homo* and *man* are identical. Thus my language is the sum total of myself; for the man is the thought. [*CP* 5.314]

Moreover, we know that as a sign the subject must be considered as that triadic unfolding of semiosis, a "tri-relative influence not being in any way resolvable into actions between pairs" (*CP* 5.484). It is due to this tri-relative relation that Peirce wrote that "man is a sign developing according to the laws of inference" (*CP* 5.312). Indeed, in this respect Peirce claimed even more dramatically that all mental functioning can be reduced to "a *formula* of valid reasoning" (*CP* 5.266; my italics).

To say that the subject develops according to the laws of inference and can be reduced to a formula of valid reasoning is to say that the subject must be considered, most properly, as a logical function at the juncture of semiosis. Such an assertion does not deny what Peirce classified as the subject's emotional or energetic/physical aspects. It does, however, underline the fact that only the logical form of triadicity produces meaning as such.[3] The meaning of the person-sign, therefore, must be located or nested most fundamentally in the networking matrix of the logical relations of signs.

With this characterization of the person as a logical function, or as that which can only be understood as it conforms to a certain logical rule or formula, there is an interesting return to Descartes, for in some sense the subject would have to be said to be at the source of a *mathesis universalis,* an origin of reasoning. Yet to immediately draw the necessary distinction: in this case it is not an origin that is a simple substance, but a purely mathematical or logical function that produces a form of contingent and mediated knowledge. In this more radical sense, the subject does not simply project its *mathesis,* but is no more than that very *mathesis.* As such, this thematic of what we might call the "person as calculus" reduces the subject to the status of an algorithm, which gives rise to a formal projection.[4] That we find such efficient relations generating a form recalls Saussure's assertion that the relations of signs "*produces a form, not a substance*" (1966, 113) which amounts to saying that language is, at root, a system of formal differential relations.

Derrida's notion of *différance* should, no doubt, be more difficult to reduce to such a Cartesian frame, except for the fact that Derrida himself asserts that *différance* gives form, in the sense that it is "the formation of form" (1974, 63). In his essay entitled "*Différance,*" he also writes that *différance* is the "possibility of conceptuality, of a conceptual process" (1978a, 11) and of the "unfolding of Being" (22). Such a formal conceptuality is established on the paradoxical basis of the mark of *différance,* or trace, which, as we have seen, is its very death or disappearance in its presentation. Derrida writes that such a "(pure) trace" must be presupposed. "*The (pure) trace is différance.* It does not depend on any sensible plenitude. . . . It is on the contrary, the *condition* of such a plenitude. Although it does not exist, although it is never a being present outside of all plenitude, its possibility is *by all rights anterior* to all that one calls sign" (1974, my italics). In "Freud and the Scene of Writing" in *Writing and* Différance, Derrida underlines this notion that the trace, in its very erasure, is a kind of "structure" which is the condition of the possibility of the repression of its loss. He writes, "It is the very structure which makes possible, as the movement of temporalization and pure *auto-affection,* something that can be called repression in general" (1978b, 230). But in deference to Derrida we need to take account of his assertion that this "anteriority," or "structure," is, after all, a paradoxically nonoriginary origin: a function that is the erasure of its own function.[5]

Nonetheless, it is a function, he writes, "in a structure of generalized reference" (1978a, 24). In this case, the *mathesis* of Descartes, or even the logic of Peirce, could be read as a form that is built on the "structure" of *différance,* but it is a form that is the deliberate attempt to repress the inaccessibility of its origin. Or, we could say that, for Derrida, such a form, whether logical or linguistic, is an attempt to repress the idea that there is no transcendental signified, and no necessary relation between signs. We can certainly recall his assertion that his treatment of the sign amounts to its destruction. This deference notwithstanding, the notion of *différance* remains a pure and necessary possibility, or something like a logical necessity. But how do we take account of this contradiction? On the one hand, Peirce and Derrida extol the play of signs, while, on the other, they seem to reduce that very play to a formal algorithmic function. And this is a "play" and a function, after all, in which the status of meaning is at stake.

To the extent that this formal systematicity is essential for the process of semiosis, the play from sign to sign seems exhausted, deflated, and reduced to a formal function—or at least thereby challenged. The meaning and *subjectness* that Peirce's and Derrida's treatments of semiosis interrogate, and perhaps reduce to a logical function, is exhausted and deflated in the sense that it is rendered abstract and emptied of its empirical contents: Peirce reduces semiosis to an abstract logical form, and Derrida thematizes the trace as an empty, nonoriginary origin. Given the importance of the purely logical and abstract function at the heart of semiosis, it seems that Peirce's and Derrida's projects propose the paradox of an *exhaustion* of meaning that is nonetheless the basis of meaning, whether that meaning corresponds to a triadically unfolding form, in the case of Peirce, or to the deconstruction of that very form by Derrida.

Insofar as Peirce's and Derrida's treatments of the relation from sign to sign share in this disruption of metaphysics that regrounds meaning and the subject in what seems to be an empty algorithmic function, their work suggests a distinctive continuity as well as an interesting tendency in modern thought. It is the question of this link in their work, and this tendency, which, I suggest, calls for further inquiry. I am thinking of the term *tendency* here as itself a relation to something, a movement toward something—a purpose. The word also holds within it the sense of the drift or trend of a discourse, a discourse with a purpose that is not explicitly expressed.

The perdurance of this tendency in their work suggests that as modern thinking reflects on its form and its origins, it is led to thematize an origin in the sense of what we have described as the "empty function" of the Peircean semiosis and the "(pure)" nonoriginary origin of Derridean *différance*. It is as though contemporary thinkers require—even cling desperately to—such a basis, such an empty algorithmic function as the condition of the possibility of thought repetitively reflecting on itself. Insofar as this is the case, we propose the need for its recognition as such as well as its interrogation. Perhaps such a tendency was what Heidegger had in mind when when he stated that "cybernetics" had taken the place of philosophy, suggesting that a certain "technicity" had come to master our lives and thinking. Heidegger suggested that humanity was threatened by this "epoch" of "technicity" and by a world in which "all our relationships have become merely technical ones." In the *Spiegel* interview of 1966, Heidegger stated that "everything is functioning. That is precisely what is awesome, that everything functions, that the functioning propels everything more and more toward further functioning, and that technicity dislodges and uproots humanity from the earth" (Sheehan 1981, 56).

Are Peirce's and Derrida's ideas with respect to the sign an unexpected manifestation of the technicity of which Heidegger spoke? Does their thinking reduce the subject to a logical function that is its uprooting and the exhausting of its humanity? Is it a case of a latent and unexpressed tendency of modernity? To the extent that this is the case, the engagement of Peirce and Derrida in this chapter suggests the pervasiveness of the technicity of which Heidegger spoke, and raises questions about exactly what is, after all, at stake in the relation from sign to sign.

Notes

"Peirce and Derrida: From Sign to Sign" was originally presented at the Charles Sanders Peirce Sesquicentennial International Congress, September 5–10, 1989, Harvard University. A subsequent version has appeared in *Peirce's Doctrine of Signs: Theory, Applications, Connections,* edited by Vincent Colapietro and Thomas Olshewsky (Berlin: Mouton de Gruyter, 1995). I am grateful to Sheila Magnotti, secretary of the Department of Philosophy at Southern Connecticut State University, for her preparation of the electronic manuscript of the revised and expanded version for publication in this volume.

1. On pages 326 and 327 of his text *Heidegger's Being and Time: A Reading for Readers* (1988), E. F. Kaelin reflects on the relation of Peirce to Derrida:

The most vocal spokesman for this movement (post structuralism), the Frenchman Jacques Derrida, was moved to reject both formalism and structuralism on the grounds that both these earlier schools suffered what Heidegger called the failure of the metaphysics of presence. . . . Not only did a set of signifieds not become present as a signification for the signifiers we read, not only were they not made present by our perception of the words of a text, but these signifiers themselves, which were at best blips on a preconscious screen, left only traces. . . . But to the structural difference between the signifiers of our language, Derrida added temporal difference—an indefinite deferral of meaning, since for every written text there is another constructed to be further deconstructed. The idea is not new for Americans, for American philosophers have been aware of it since Charles Peirce's theory of signs: what holds together a sign vehicle serving as a representamen and its object as represented is an *interpretant,* which itself may become an object for another sign, and will for that reason call for another interpretant.

Here it seems that Kaelin emphasizes the very progression or sliding of interpretants that Peirce seeks to avoid through his formulation of the notion of the habit-change. As we have seen, the real and living logical conclusion of the sign, its proper significate outcome, is the change in habit in which it results (*CP* 5.491).

2. Derrida has, of course, published numerous books and articles after the publication and translation of "Freud and the Scene of Writing" in *Writing and* Différance. One such text, which bears particular mention in conjunction with the appearance of this revised chapter, is *Archive Fever: A Freudian Impression,* translated by Eric Prenowitz (Chicago: University of Chicago Press, 1996). (*Archive Fever* originally appeared as *Mal d'Archive: une impression freudienne,* Éditions Galilée, 1995.) In *Archive Fever,* Derrida returns to his own archive, as it were, by citing passages from "Freud and the Scene of Writing." The passage Derrida cites on page 14 of *Archive Fever,* for example, reevokes the image of the psyche as a writing machine. In addition, the passage emphasizes that "the machine—and consequently representation—is death and finitude *within* the psyche." This passage emphasizes, then, the theme of negativity at the heart of the psyche that is discussed here. However, for Derrida, the passage is related to his interest, in part, in a critical comparison between Freud's writing machine found in "A Note upon the 'Mystic Writing-Pad'" and "archival machines" of our own time. He wishes to show that the archival machines and institutions of our own time are plagued, in spite of their technological advances, by the anguish of the same pervasive loss that operates at the core of the psyche. The "archive drive," as Derrida calls it, will always be frustrated by an inability to remember, always plagued by its limits or finitude. As the *psyche* was threatened by "the erasure of selfhood, of one's own presence, and constituted by the threat or anguish of its irremediable disappearance, of the disappearance of its disappearance" (1978b, 277), so the *archive* would necessarily face the same anguish of disappearance, the erasure of the archive, its memory and its promise (see n. 5 below).

3. This suggestion does question Vincent Colapietro's insistence on placing the Peircean self in a biological organism, an enduring human organism (see 1989, 84–87). That the self is or is part of a biological organism, is not disputed. What is being suggested by my account here is that both the self and its form of

embodiment are only intelligible and self-reflective, with Peirce, as agencies of function in a logico-mathematical matrix.

4. The term *algorithm* is due in this sense, of course, to Lacan, but its use in this context is closer to that of Lacoue-Labarthe and Nancy ([1973] 1992). With respect to the notion of "person as calculus" it is interesting to note that on page 203 of *Freud and the Scene of Writing,* while discussing the operation of *différance* in relation to the psyche, Derrida asserts that *différance* must be conceived of "in other terms than those of a calculus or mechanics of decision." In the translator's footnote on page 329 of the same text Alan Bass writes, "Since *différance* subverts meaning and presence, it does not *decide.*" We suppose that Bass and Derrida mean that neither *différance* nor the psyche calculate. Our point is not that *différance* or the psyche calculates, but that its operation or activity is best described in terms of an automatic mechanical function which repeats itself in spite of itself. Such a function, in the case of Peirce and Derrida, leads to the form of semiosis. Indeed, Derrida writes on page 227 of *Freud and the Scene of Writing* that "the subject of writing is a system of relations between strata."

5. Derrida returns as well to what we might refer to as this motif of the "non-originary origin" in *Archive Fever;* of the motif of a trace, that, in its very erasure, engenders a kind of "structure" which is the condition of the possibility of the repression of its loss. In *Archive Fever,* the archive (as indicated in n. 2 above), operates or springs from its own erasure. Discussing Freud's concept of the "death drive" Derrida writes that the drive "operates in silence, it never leaves any archive of its own. It destroys in advance its own archive." This effacing of its own traces would be its propriety. The drive "incites forgetfulness, amnesia." Yet this self-effacement is the paradoxical condition of the archival function. "The archive takes place," Derrida writes, "at the place of the originary and structural breakdown of the said memory" (1996, 11). The archive would seem to demand—by virtue of its "internal contradiction"—then, the repetitive and impossible task of remembering. The archive "always works" Derrida reflects, "and *a priori against itself*" (ibid.; my italics). This self-effacing and "burning" of the archive is an algorithmically repetitive condition of the desire for the archive, and the attendant archival institution. For Derrida, we "burn with passion," we are "in need of archives" because we "search for the archive where it slips away" (91). For Derrida, then, it seems that this *arch-différance* (what he calls, in another context, "archiviolithic," or "archive-destroying") lies at the core of any archival institution.

References

Colapietro, Vincent M. *Peirce's Approach to the Self: A Semiotic Perspective on Human Subjectivity.* Albany: State University of New York Press, 1989.

Derrida, Jacques. *Of Grammatology.* Translated by Gayatri Chakravorty Spivak. Baltimore: Johns Hopkins University Press, 1974. Originally published as *De la grammatologie* (Paris: Minuit, 1967).

————. *Margins of Philosophy.* Translated by Alan Bass. Chicago: University of Chicago Press, 1978a.

————. *Writing and* Différance. Translated by Alan Bass. Chicago: University of Chicago Press, 1978b.

————. *Archive Fever: A Freudian Impression.* Translated by Eric Prenowitz. Chicago: University of Chicago Press, 1996.

Freud, Sigmund. *The Origins of Psychoanalysis.* Translated by Eric Mosbacher and James Strachey. New York: Basic Books, 1954.

Kaelin, E. F. *Heidegger's* Being and Time: *A Reading for Readers.* Gainesville: University Presses of Florida, 1988.

Kant, Immanuel. *The Critique of Pure Reason.* Translated by N. Kemp-Smith. New York: St. Martin's, 1965.

Kuhn, Thomas. *The Essential Tension.* Chicago: University of Chicago Press, 1972.

Lacoue-Labarthe, Phillippe, and Nancy, Jean-Luc. *The Title of the Letter: A Reading of Lacan* (1973). Translated by David Pettigrew and François Raffoul. Albany: State University of New York Press, 1992.

Peirce, Charles Sanders. *Collected Papers of Charles Sanders Peirce.* Edited by Charles Hartshorne, Paul Weiss, and Arthur W. Burks. Cambridge: Harvard University Press, 1931–58.

Saussure, Ferdinand de. *Course in General Linguistics.* Translated by Wade Baskin. New York: McGraw-Hill, 1966.

Sheehan, Thomas, ed. "Only a God Can Save Us." Translated by William Richardson. In *Heidegger: The Man and the Thinker.* Chicago: Precedent, 1981.

9   Further Consequences of a Singular Capacity

Vincent Colapietro

My purpose here is to supplement ideas presented in "Notes for a Sketch of a Peircean Theory of the Unconscious" (Colapietro 1995b).[1] Teresa de Lauretis has explored some of the same territory, though in an angle quite different from the one that I adopted in "Notes for a Sketch." While I used Peirce's categories of firstness, secondness, and thirdness as a set of interrelated heuristic clues for exploring the phenomenon of the unconscious,[2] de Lauretis used his general concept of interpretant and specific notion of habit change to suggest how Freud might be read in light of Peirce and, conversely, how Peirce might be read in light of Freud. Her approach and mine are by no means exclusive; it is reasonable to suppose that they are complementary. But, whereas my own categoreal approach begins at a high level of generality (the categories being by definition concepts of the utmost generality [see, e.g., 5.43]), de Lauretis's approach commences at a more specific and more specifically semiotic level.

In this chapter, I (1) approach the unconscious from the angle of de Lauretis's highly suggestive reading of Freud vis-à-vis Peirce (i.e., her reconfiguration of the psychoanalytic notion of the unconscious vis-à-vis the Peircean notion of interpretant); and (2) relate, though only briefly, the results of this pointedly semiotic investigation to the conclusions of my prior categoreal inquiry. Accordingly, I revisit here the Freudian notion of the unconscious, and I do so once again from a distinctively Peircean perspective. But rather than relying primarily upon Peirce's heuristic set of categories, I follow de Lauretis's lead and turn principally to his nuanced conception of interpretant (Shapiro 1983; Savan 1987–88; Liska 1990).

Setting the Stage: Disentangling Two Classifications

Peirce offers several distinct classifications of the interpretant, but he returned to two in particular time and again in his efforts to identify the effects wrought by semiosis. In both *Alice Doesn't* (1984) and *The Practice of Love* (1994), however, de Lauretis apparently limits her attention to but one classification, that of the emotional, energetic, and logical interpretant. In fact, she does implicitly bring into play the other classification, but does so in such a way as to blur the distinction between the final or ultimate interpretant, on the one hand, and the logical interpretant, on the other (1994, 300). For she focuses on the final logical interpretant without noting that this notion results from the intersection of two distinct classifications of what Peirce calls "significate effects." In one classification (the one upon which de Lauretis explicitly draws), the *logical* interpretant is distinguished from both the *emotional* and the *energetic* interpretants; in the other, the *final* interpretant (also called the ultimate, or normal interpretant) is distinguished from both the *immediate* and the *dynamical* interpretants. In what is perhaps Peirce's best-known articulation of the former classification, he himself presents the ultimate logical interpretant as though it were simply the name of a class of interpretants within a single classification rather than that of an intersection between two distinct classifications. But this intersection is not appreciated if these classifications are conflated.

Only confusion can result from the fusion of what should be kept distinct, even (perhaps especially) if what is conceptually distinct can be concretely united. The ultimate logical interpretant names the unity of that which is in principle distinguishable, to wit, the interpretant as general in nature and the interpretant as the destined terminus of the deliberative process. By drawing explicitly upon Peirce's two distinct classifications of the interpretant rather than simply the one on which de Lauretis focuses (by considering the unconscious in light of immediate, dynamic, and normal or final interpretants as well as emotional, energetic, and logical interpretants), and also by emphasizing that the notion of final logical interpretant is a conceptual node resulting from the intersection of the two classifications (Short 1996, Savan 1987–88), we will be in a better position to appreciate what is involved in reading the Freudian unconscious in light of Peircean semiotic. Moreover, rather than simply relying on the conceptual resources provided by this Peircean framework, we will introduce the notion of a quasi-ultimate logical interpretant. Such an interpretant is one that in some respects enjoys the status of a truly ultimate logical interpretant but that in other respects fails to be a "deliberately formed, self-analyzing habit" (*CP* 5.491). The notion of such an interpretant is implicit in both Peirce's own writings (see, e.g., *CP* 5.479) and de Lauretis's use of those texts, but it needs to be made explicit.

Like de Lauretis, I too stress the personal unconscious as a nexus of constitutive dispositions, a set of habits by which the unconscious and, more inclusively, subjectivity are constituted as such (see, e.g., *CP* 6.228).[3] That is, both the unconscious and the subject are constituted by a unique history of concrete involvements with other human agents and, significantly, through the mediation of these agents, with the natural world. Repression no less than subjectivity emerges as a result of the way others intervene in one's life and, in turn, the way one responds to such interventions and indeed solicits them in the first place (think here of the young child endangering itself and thus eliciting a response from a care giver). Both emerge and take determinate shape as an inevitable consequence of social interactions. Consequently, I also emphasize that the personal unconscious is an evolved and evolving nexus implicated in a unique history, and that this irreducibly singular history is,[4] in its turn, embedded in a wider social history (de Lauretis 1994, 303).[5] But this nexus evolves largely by means of signs. The crucial connection here is brought into focus when de Lauretis makes the following suggestion:

> When Laplanche and Pontalis explain that in Freud "unconscious wishes tend to be fulfilled through the restoration of signs which are bound to the earliest experiences of satisfaction" and that the "restoration operates according to the laws of primary processes" (*The Language of Psycho-Analysis* 481), I see no reason why it would be wrong to infer that those early experiences could have resulted in signs whose final interpretants were unconscious habits. Unconscious wishes, therefore, might be thought of as the significate *effects* of those early experiences as well as *causes* for the re-presentation—be it through symptom-formation, hallucination, dream images, or fetishes—of the signs that fulfill(ed) them. [302]

There is, in fact, no reason for contending that such an inference is illicit. But a final interpretant of the sort suggested in the passage just quoted needs to be distinguished sharply from what Peirce intended by the ultimate logical interpretant.[6]

This point of disagreement rests upon substantial agreement regarding important matters. My agreement with de Lauretis resides partly (but only partly) in seeing (1) that the Peircean notion of interpretant is an extremely fruitful one, (2) that the Peircean construal of logical interpretant as habit-change is equally fecund, and (3) that almost all of the sorts of habit change most important for understanding subjectivity involve imagination and fantasy. In effect, de Lauretis is tracing out some of the consequences of the human capacity to forge certain associations, to link certain images with one another, and then to connect this image with that feeling, this fantasy with that desire—in sum, the distinct human capacity to take habits of a highly complex character. But there is a need to trace out these consequences in stricter accord with some pivotal notions in Peirce's semiotic theory.

At least in anthroposemiosis (Deely 1994), the taking of habits includes acquiring propensities to real-ize certain fantasies (de Lauretis 1994, 309) and also to imagine certain realities. But these specific tendencies are, at bottom, highly complicated instances of a ubiquitous tendency, the habit *found throughout nature* of taking habits. What distinguishes the various kinds of natural beings from one another is the habits they exhibit, including the degree, manner, and rapidity with which they divest themselves of old habits, arm themselves with new ones, and integrate the new with the old. According to Peirce, "The highest quality of mind involves greatest readiness to take habits, and a great readiness to lose them"; this quality "implies a degree of feeling neither very intense nor very feeble" (*CP* 6.613). In other words, this capacity entails a measure of consciousness below that of the most acute sensations (e.g., intense pleasure or pain) but above that of our quasi-automatic reactions resulting from the unimpeded operation of effective habits in familiar circumstances.[7] The sharpness of such sensations is likely to arrest action, whereas the fluidity of such reactions is likely to require minimal consciousness. The most manifest characteristic of matter is the seemingly absolute reluctance to lose old habits and to take new ones. What links matter and mind—what provides the *tertium quid* between material and mental substances or agencies—is the presence of habits and, beyond this, the tendency (however slight and thus imperceptible) to take new habits (Savan 1987–88). What is manifest in the case of mind is minutely true, but largely hidden, in the case of matter.[8] The truly cosmic (or universal) tendency to acquire novel dispositions is, when we turn to Homo sapiens, a truly dramatic tendency.[9] The focus of de Lauretis's interpretation is to trace out the consequences of certain aspects of this dramatic tendency. Here I trace out some further consequences of this singular capacity.[10]

Classifying Signs, Objects, and Interpretants

Peirce devised numerous classifications of signs (see, e.g., Burks 1949; Sheriff 1989). His general theory of signs is nothing if not a record of taxonomic experiments, focusing above all else on the sign itself (see, e.g., *CP* 2.254–64 and 8.343). But, in addition to these taxonomies, we encounter in his writings a classification of the object and also several classifications of the interpretant.[11] He insists that "it is clearly indispensable to start with an accurate and broad analysis of the nature of a Sign" (Peirce 1977; cf. *CP* 8.343). But this very analysis yields components (the object and the interpretant) which themselves call for classification, and the classifications of sign, object, and interpretant intersect to generate possibilities of drawing fine-grained distinctions among semiosic phenomena.

The Sign in Itself. A sign can be taken as a first: it may be considered in itself, apart from anything else — in particular, apart from either its object or the series of interpretants flowing from the interaction between the sign and its object. According to Peirce, "A Sign may *itself* have a 'possible' Mode of Being" — or "its Mode of Being may be Actuality: as with any barometer" (1977, 83). Finally, it may be that mode characteristic of habits, would-be's or would-do's. In other words, the sign in itself may be a tone, token, or type: qua possibility, it might be called a *tone* (though Peirce was not entirely satisfied with this locution); qua actuality, a *token;* and qua would-do, *type.*

The Sign in Relation to Its Other. Anything functions as a sign, in part, only insofar as something else generates, constrains, or determines the functioning of that thing (e.g., the sunflower turning toward the sun bears witness to the presence of the sun, the function of its turning being essentially linked to the function of sunlight [*CP* 2.24; Esposito 1979]). The sign is, in other words, essentially related to something other than itself.[12] Though semiosis is a process exhibiting an irreducibly triadic structure, it is one encompassing irreducibly dyadic relationships; the most important of these dyads is the relationship between sign and object. The secondness inherent in semiosis is most manifest in this relationship. Moreover, the two grades of secondness — degenerate and genuine — are discernible in this relationship, for "it is usual and proper to distinguish two Objects of a Sign, the Mediate without, and the Immediate within the Sign" (Peirce 1977, 83). The relationship between sign and its immediate object is one of degenerate secondness, whereas that between sign and its dynamical object is one of genuine secondness.

The classification of the object is truly central to Peirce's approach to the semiotic; but it is, in contrast to the various classifications of signs and the two principal classifications of interpretants, readily comprehensible and largely uncontroversial (cf. de Lauretis 1994, 304). The *immediate* object is the object as it is represented by some sign or (since every sign ideally generates an interpretant-sign until it generates an interpretant-habit) by some sequence of signs, whereas the *dynamical* object is the object insofar as it can act as a functionally independent constraint on the process of interpretant-generation. The distinction between immediate and dynamical object is a formal distinction, since one and the same being can be both kinds of object. If such a formal identity were precluded, then truth in a sense strenuously advocated by Peirce would also be precluded.[13]

For many purposes, our representations of reality, especially if granted the degree of vagueness and generality requisite for the purpose(s) at hand, coincide with the realities represented. For our more refined purposes, it is crucial to keep in mind the distinction between the way reality is represented by us and the way it is apart from our representations (in Peirce's terminology, the distinction between the immediate and the dynamical object, respectively). Peirce's formal distinction between the two kinds of semiosic object makes his theory of signs the tool of a fallibilist: our representations of reality are always potentially other than the realities represented (Colapietro 1997). What we say about things might be quite different from the way those things would reveal themselves to us: the way we take things to be may be mis-takings. So, commonsensical realism and a still all-too-unfamiliar fallibilism are both given their due in the Peircean conception of the semiotic object,[14] an object at once representable within the modest limits imposed by most mundane purposes potentially mistaken within these same limits. By using the adjective *mundane* here, I intend to underscore the down-to-earth character of what is being championed in this context.

The distinction between the immediate and dynamic object is, thus, intended to secure the status of a standard by which our assertions and, more generally, our representations might be judged. If our assertions and representations are self-enclosed—if the very possibility of exposure to corrective influences is ruled out—then processes of self-correction are also ruled out. Self-correction requires corrective others; it demands the bold yet humble willingness to expose oneself to the other as other. Though scientific inquiry is a self-consciously fallible process, all semiosic processes are—no matter how blindly groping, no matter how unconsciously executed—ones in which something analogous to the distinction between immediate and dynamical object can be discerned. Though scientific investigation characteristically involves deliberate experimentation, human semiosis always involves unwitting trials and unconscious processes: the scientist is the self-conscious, practical fallibilist, whereas human agents are generally unwitting and unconscious fallibilists. This is the reason they are *im*practical fallibilists! Their errors are too costly: time, energy, and their very selves are spent too freely for so little. Their negotiations with their inner drives and outer circumstances extract from them a payment which more courageous, attentive, sustained agents might avoid.

Interpretants as Significate-Effects of Signs and *Their Objects.* In *The Sense of Grammar: Language as Semeiotic,* Michael Shapiro describes Peirce's theory of the interpretant as "the most important part of his semeiotic" (1983, 45). "The theory of the interpretant is," according to David Savan in his *Introduction to C. S. Peirce's Full System of Semeiotic,* "the most extensive and important of Peirce's theory of signs. His pragmatism and his theory of method . . . fall within it. Many other aspects of his philosophy . . . are closely related to it" (1987 – 88, 40).[15]

In general, the interpretant is (to use one of Peirce's own descriptive expressions) the "proper significate effect" of a sign-process: it is the upshot of such a process. The results of semiosis are ordinarily multiform, for signs prompt *feelings,* incite *actions,* and produce *other signs* as well as other forms of generality (e.g., desires, hopes, fears, expectations, and habits [*CP* 5.486]). Here the word *actions* designates not only outward, bodily actions but also those purely inward exertions, those mental soliloquies strutting and fretting on the stage of imagination. Signs, through the complex mediation of these feelings, exertions, and further signs, shape the sensibility and condition the character of the sign-user. Insofar as feelings are proper significate effects of a sign-action, they merit the name of *emotional* interpretant; and insofar as exertions are such effects, they merit the name of *energetic* interpretant. But neither the immediacy of feeling nor the singularity of action can, either itself or solely in conjunction with the other, explain meaning. For meaning is inherently general; in contrast, immediate feeling is unique and therefore ineffable, while brute action is singular and thereby antigeneral. The *logical* interpretant must be of a general nature, otherwise the logical processes would be impossible.

Whereas the logical interpretant is marked by its inherent generality, the *ultimate* logical interpretant is defined by its provisional stability. The ultimate logical interpretant is the *terminus ad quem,* the point at which semiosis terminates, for the time being. What proves sufficient for the time being might, in fact, also prove so for the indefinite long run, especially if the logical interpretant is that of a sign of a high degree of vagueness and generality. But the more determinate a sign is in these two respects (i.e., the less vague and general a sign is), the more open any actually established ultimate interpretant is to being modified or even eradicated.

One way to clarify further what Peirce intends by the ultimate logical interpretant of a sign is to contrast this interpretant with "the first logical interpretants" (*CP* 5.480 – 81). Whereas readiness "to act in a certain way under given circumstances and when actuated by a given motive is [what we generally mean by] a habit, the word *belief* might be reserved for 'a deliberate, or self-controlled, habit'" (*CP* 5.480).[16] In a sense, the first step toward the formation of cognitive habits is conjecture, or hypothesis. Peirce goes so far as to suggest that "every concept, every general proposition of the great edifice of science, first came to us as a conjecture. These ideas [guesses] are the *first logical interpretants* of the phenomena that suggest them, and which, as suggesting them, are [themselves] signs" (*CP* 5.480). But between these first logical interpretants and any ultimate one there can be discerned or, at least, must be posited intervening logical interpretants:

> In the next step of thought, those first logical interpretants stimulate us to various voluntary performances in the inner world. We imagine ourselves in various circumstances and animated by various motives; and we proceed to trace out the alternative lines of conduct which the conjectures would leave open to us. We are, moreover, led, by the same inward activity, to remark different ways in which our conjectures could be slightly modified. The logical interpretant must, therefore, be in a relatively future tense. [*CP* 5.481]

If not arrested or deflected, this process of interpretant-generation terminates in a relatively stable cognitive (or intellectual) habit.[17] But, given the remarkable plasticity of human physiology, and also given the inevitable conflicts among the objects desired and thus pursued by human agents, the habit-interpretants generated by sign-actions are often only very problematic orientations of the agents in whom they are inscribed to some sphere of engagement. In light of their actual experience, it is more often than not understandable why these, rather than other, habits were generated; but, in light of wider experience and deeper reflection, it is frequently clear that other dispositions would better serve these agents. The circumstances in which their habits were formed did not provide sufficient opportunity for deliberative imagination. At the very least, what I am saying here concerns agents from the perspective of *their own* motives and aims. But it might also concern these motives and aims themselves. For given more inclusive experience and adequate reflection, these might show themselves to be infantile or self-debilitating or deficient in some other way.

As noted earlier, Peirce offers an alternate classification of interpretants. He classifies interpretants not only as emotional, energetic, and logical, but also as immediate, dynamic, and normal (*CP* 8.343). Some interpreters of Peirce suppose that these are but two different ways of expressing the same classification; others recognize that the classifications are different but disagree with one another about how the two schemes are related. But the best expositors of Peirce's semiotic (e.g.,

Ransdell, Savan, Shapiro, and Short) respect the differences between these two classifications. They are correct in doing so.

Most relevant to our purposes is the possibility that only the two classifications taken together can provide the conceptual resources for describing the complex processes to which I have just alluded, namely, those processes in which sign-actions generate self-frustrating or self-destructive interpretant-habits. A dramatic example of such self-frustrating interpretant habits is repetition compulsion. My concern is not with specific phenomena but with the general mechanism(s) by which such habits are formed or, more exactly, with the Peircean notions through which the formation of these habits might be described and, to some extent, explained.

Semiosis, as an irreducibly triadic process, generates an irreducibly triadic result (the interpretant), the character of which is unintelligible apart from the processes out of which the result emerges and also the processes made possible by this result.[18] To be sure, Max H. Fisch is correct when he asserts that "the fundamental conception of semeiotic is not that of sign but that of semeiosis" (1986, 330). But sign-action is frequently effective action; when it is effective, it modifies the agent-medium by and in whom it occurs.[19] (In calling any action effective, all that I mean to convey is that it produces results, it makes a difference, not that it produces desirable results or makes a beneficial difference.) In Peirce's semiotic, then, the emphasis on process does not result in an eclipse of product. For the triadic structure of semiosis replicates itself above all in the structure of its result — its interpretant, or, more precisely, the open-ended series of three-termed forms generated by the dynamic interaction between sign and object. Parallel to the distinction between immediate and dynamical *object,* Peirce distinguishes between an immediate and dynamical *interpretant:* "It is . . . requisite to distinguish the *Immediate Interpretant,* i.e., the Interpretant represented or signified in the Sign, from the *Dynamical Interpretant,* or effect actually produced on the Mind by the Sign" (*CP* 8.343). It is also necessary to recognize, in addition to these two kinds of interpretant, "*the Normal Interpretant,* or effect that would be produced on the mind by the Sign after sufficient development of thought" (*CP* 7.343).

All forms, but especially the distinctively human forms, of semiosis are *essentially* fallibilistic. By their very nature they are liable to error. Since lying implies an intent to deceive, signs in general are misleadingly defined as anything that might be used to lie (cf. Eco 1992); however, since signs by their very nature secure the possibility of error (they *are* that by which the possibility of error comes into being), they are in general properly defined as anything that might generate an illusion or instigate a mistake. But, in order to account for the process of generating mistakes and illusions, it is necessary to articulate the ways in which the evolution of interpretants can be arrested or, in other ways, maimed.

This task itself presupposes that there is, albeit within *very* wide margins, a *normal* course of development, one more or less destined to take place.[20] Given, on the one hand, the constitution and exigencies of human organisms and, on the other hand, the contours and constraints of the environment in which such organisms are required to secure their existence and enact their impulses, the development of interpretants is subjected to various, frequently contradictory, pressures.[21] But the cumulative effect of these persistent pressures, physiological and psychological as well as environmental, operates in such a way as to favor—at least in the long run—certain habits of feeling, action, and habit-taking. Semiosis is a process that always rests on the operation of established habits and occasionally culminates in the formation of new habits or, at least, the alteration of existing ones (even if the alteration amounts to nothing more than the strengthening or weakening of those habits). But some habits are debilitating while others are facilitating.

The ultimate logical interpretant is the habit that ultimately *would be* generated by semiosis, though the ultimacy here is merely provisional. It marks the provisional, yet nonetheless real, closure of a process, albeit a closure which itself opens possibilities and thereby exposes the newly established habit to unforeseeable vicissitudes and even fatal challenges. In addition, the habit that happens to be established by a particular semiosic process is not necessarily a suitable or facilitating habit. It might poorly serve the human agents in just that immediate environment in which it was generated and to which they suppose it to apply. In contrast to whatever habit just happens to be established, we might imagine the habit that given sufficient experience and reflection would be established. Peirce calls this the *normal* interpretant and characterizes it as the "effect that would be produced on the mind by the Sign after sufficient development of thought" (*CP* 8.343; cf. Savan 1987–88 and Short 1996).

If we use the Peircean notion of interpretant to interpret the psychoanalytic conception of the unconscious, we ought to look beyond the ultimate logical interpretants of signs. As necessary as the idea of such interpretants is for framing a distinctively Peircean understanding of the unconscious, it is not sufficient. There are instinctual tendencies and acquired habits that block the formation of ever more flexible, nuanced, and effective habits of feeling, acting, and imagining. The defense mechanisms are, at once, unavoidable, effective, and futile strategies by which the body-ego attempts to conduct an ongoing series of incredibly complex negotiations.[22] These mechanisms are *unavoidable* in the straightforward sense that, given the force of instinctual tendencies, the influence of cultural forces, and our extended ineptness in negotiating harmonious agreements among these ubiquitous pressures, we cannot help but devise all too hasty and all too crude strategies for coping with these pressures. These mechanisms are generally *effective* in the minimal sense that they allow the conflict-ridden organism to escape being a paralyzed agent: they permit the body-ego to continue its ongoing negotiations with these conflicting demands, even if only in a precarious and even debilitated manner. In brief, they permit the body-ego to go on. Finally, these mechanisms are ultimately *futile* and worse—self-frustrating—in the sense that the minimal successes attained via the all too partial, precarious, and costly negotiations of the body-ego are destined to prove to be useless or self-stultifying as one moves through the world. What Peirce says about the instinctual beliefs might profitably be recalled here: The critical commonsensist acknowledges that "our indubitable beliefs refer to a somewhat primitive mode of life" (*CP* 5.511). In fact, their authority is limited to such a sphere: "While they never become dubitable in so far as our mode of life remains that of somewhat primitive man, yet as we develop degrees of self-control unknown to that man, occasions of action arise in relation to which the original beliefs, if stretched to cover them, have no sufficient authority" (ibid.). We might say that their power far outstrips their authority.[23]

A quasi-final interpretant of this sort occupies the functional position but does not exercise sufficiently the defining functions of such a habit; in many cases, it may be a randomly formed, self-concealing disposition. Often, these hidden dispositions result in deformed deliberations or simply debilitating actions; hence, not a deliberately formed habit of action, but deeply deforming acts of deliberation (including acts by which the very possibility of deliberation is undermined) characterize so many quasi-ultimate logical interpretants. Any habit that would arrest or, worse, destroy opportunities for cultivating deliberately formed, self-analyzing habits, but which would do so in its role as quasi-final interpretant, would have a very important status within the economy of our psychic lives.

Psychoanalytically understood, the unconscious encompasses the repressed; in turn, the repressed is itself both the effect of largely unconscious processes and the cause of a vast portion of our mental life. In order to get at the unconscious in this sense, it is crucial to establish a distinction between the repressed and the unrepressed (i.e., the repressed insofar as it becomes available to the conscious deliberative agency of those essentially problematic beings—enculturated human organisms).[24] Indeed, apart from such a distinction, the repressed is devoid of meaning. One way to establish and maintain this distinction is by recourse to Peirce's notion of normal interpretant, the habit-interpretant which would result from sufficient experience and reflection (from experience sufficiently wide and deep, from reflection sufficiently sustained and courageous). Peirce contrasts the normal interpretant to both the immediate and the dynamical interpretant: whereas the *immediate* interpretant is "the Interpretant represented or signified in the Sign," the *dynamical* interpretant is the "effect actually produced on the mind by the Sign" (*CP* 8.343). The actual effect might be and, in fact, ordinarily *is* different from both what is immediately presented to unreflective consciousness and what would be deliberately adopted by reflective subjectivity.

Experience marks and, indeed, maims us in ways more complex and less accessible than those noted by the inevitably superficial consciousness of the experiencing subject. Ordinarily, the headlong rush of lived experience provides insufficient opportunities to note much beyond the immediately salient features of the complex situations in which the vulnerable body-ego is precariously situated and selectively preoccupied.[25] Also, the purpose at hand channels attention and activity in some more or less definite directions, deflecting it from countless other possible ones. Finally, there is hardly ever simply one, perspicuous purpose channeling attention and activity: unavowed tendencies are intertwined with conscious objectives to produce complex patterns within the psychic tapestry. The immense egoism involved in elevating voluntary attention (the body-ego insofar as it is a conscious source of its own purposive exertions) to the status of absolute authority, even over its own doings and resistances, is an immense error, especially since it blocks the road of inquiry.

Consciousness includes far more than the field of voluntary attention; in turn, mind encompasses far more than the operations and forms of consciousness. Psychology is, accordingly, too narrowly defined as the science of consciousness, let alone of that specific form designated as voluntary, reflexive attention. Not simply the forms, functions, and fissures of consciousness, but primarily the operation, acquisition, and integration of habits (processes with which consciousness is only sometimes interwoven) are the foci of this science. Peirce asserted, "For if psychology were restricted to the phenomena of consciousness, the establishment of mental associations [including dissociations; cf. *CP* 5.476ff. and de Lauretis 1994, 301], the taking of habits, which is the very market-place of psychology, would be outside its boulevards" (*CP* 7.367).

The Taking of Habits and the Habits of Imagining

As noted above, Peirce maintained that the capacity to acquire new habits and, as part of this, to shed old ones is found throughout nature, not only in the biological world (cf. de Lauretis 1994, 302). He insisted that "habit is by no means exclusively a mental fact. Empirically, we find that some plants take habits. The stream of water that wears a bed for itself is forming a habit. Every ditcher so thinks of it" (*CP* 5.492; cf. Savan 1987–88). At the very center of Peirce's guess at the riddle of the universe is his generalization that "three elements are active in the universe," namely, chance, law, and habit-taking (*CP* 1.409). "Such is our guess of the secret of the sphinx" (*CP* 1.410).

Biological evolution is only a relatively recent and rare exemplification of a cosmic process. Human development, ontogenetic as well as phylogenetic, needs to be seen against a backdrop of evolutionary processes, ranging from the most inclusive level (the evolution of the cosmos itself) to the most immediate level (that of the particular cultures in which the individual organism is implicated). What distinguishes the human animal from other species is the manner in which humans acquire habits as well as the manner in which contingent, unstable yet paradoxically inescapable, tenacious habits constitute human subjectivity.[26] The habits constitutive of our subjectivity are, at once, contingent and unstable *as well as* inescapable and tenacious. Although it is, for example, contingent upon circumstances that we acquire one language rather than another, it is inescapable that we acquire the language spoken to us as infants (etymologically, nontalkers). Furthermore, although even our most deeply rooted habits can be uprooted and, to that extent, cannot be counted as absolutely secure (e.g., the loss of one's capacity to recognize one's own name), all habits exercise a tenacity, a capacity to take growing hold (sometimes tyrannical control) of the body-ego.

The inescapability of contingent habits and the tenacity of alterable tendencies are salient features of our psychic development. So too is our acquisition of habits not only by means of repeated outward exertions but also as the result of singular private fantasies. This acquisition of habits is frequently mediated by the exercise of imagination: fantasy — the dream of possibility, of what might be — continually, persistently, seductively intervenes in our psychic lives in such a way as to influence both what is and what would be (*CP* 8.216; de Lauretis 1994, 309). In Peirce's words, "The *will be's,* the actually *is's,* and the *have beens* are not the sum of the reals. They cover only actuality. There are besides *would be's* and *can be's* that are real" (*CP* 8.216). In general, what we count as real is ordinarily a complex intersection of these three distinct modes of being (the possible, the actual, and the real as distinct from the inclusively Real). The book on the table is an actuality. But it is also a possibility — say, the possibility of being entertaining and at the same time instructive. We *imagine* that the book might be nothing less than and perhaps even more than that; it *might be* the work destined to change one's life. Finally, it is a set of what are, in effect, habits: the letters and other marks (including the spaces) on the page are themselves would-do's and would-be's.[27] In their presence, the competent reader would be induced to trace series of interpretants in some directions and not in others; though the marks on the page are not rigidly and narrowly determinative of the directions (let alone a single direction) in which interpretants are generated, they *dispose* competent readers to move along certain paths and not others (cf. Eco 1992; also Rorty 1992).

To repeat, what we count as real is usually a complex intersection of all three modes of being. But, in the distinctive phases of our actual experience, one or another ontological modality is likely to be predominant. For example, when the book is first perceived as one object among several others on the table (when it confronts us most forcefully as an object—a *Gegenstand,* that which stands over against us), even if the object is immediately, unhesitatingly, recognized as a book, it is above all else an actuality. In contrast, when we take the book in hand as a complex pattern of interwoven symbols—as an integrated set of interpretant-generators—it confronts us predominantly as a reality in the narrow sense (not the inclusive sense of Reality, the sense encompassing possibility and actuality as well as reality). Our perceptual experience of the book as an actual object in our visual field is an experience marked by secondness: the book confronts us as *both* other than the objects with which it is immediately juxtaposed and other than ourselves. Our experience of imagining the book as a source of enjoyment and illumination is one marked by firstness: it confronts us as a possibility. Finally, the experience of reading the book is, especially if the process attains the fluency of pleasurable activity (*CP* 5.113), one marked by thirdness: the book is a stream of interpretants in whose currents we are caught up and carried along (cf. Ransdell 1979).

The imagining of possibility is rooted in our instinctual nature and nourished by our cultural inheritances and individual experiences. According to Peirce, "Human instinct is no whit less miraculous than that of the bird, the beaver, or the ant. Only, instead of being directed to bodily motions, such as singing and flying, or to the construction of dwellings, or to the organization of communities, *its theater is the plastic inner world,* and its products are the marvelous conceptions of which the greatest are the ideas of number, time, and space." (MS 318: 44; my italics; Colapietro 1989, 114–15).

The imagining of what *might be* is fantasy in its most rudimentary sense. The imagining of what might be in such a way that the image of the possible absorbs and controls attention with the same force and authority as the percept of the actual is fantasy in its most characteristic form.[28] Such imagining is itself an experience; it is a process of actually *living through* something (cf. Schrag 1969). Experience, in this basal sense, is appropriately named by the German word *Erlebnis*. But dreaming is an experience in which the most salient feature of experience—the confrontation of self and not-self—is highly attenuated; in other words, it is an experience in which the self is so thoroughly absorbed in its own images that the sense of otherness, of actuality, is eclipsed by the sense of intimacy, and also that of involvement. The phenomenology of fantasy would reveal that, for the experiencing subject, the dream is not felt to be in the dreamer but that the dreamer is in the dream (as we so significantly say, "she is lost in her dream"). Of course, this is in line with Peirce's own insistence that thought is not so much in us as that we are in thought; that is, we are enveloped in signs. The dreamer is so thoroughly *in* the dream—so intimately absorbed in the concrete images of the particular fantasy—that she does not feel that she is in the dream. Such a feeling would require a felt sense of difference between dreamer and dream; but what distinguishes, above all else, the experience of dreaming from other modes of experience is exactly the absence of such a felt distance, the lack of the two-sided consciousness so generally predominant in virtually all other modes of experience. As with the dancer and the dance, the dreamer and the dream are one. Their actually being one renders possible other possibilities (one fantasy engenders countless others). Beyond this, their actually being one tends to render actual both the tendency to reimagine this absorbing experience (to return to this lived fantasy) *and* the tendency to actualize our private fantasies in our social relationships. Or, if not to actualize such fantasies in these relationships, at least to allow these fantasies to color these relationships. Insofar as the fantasies are unconscious, they of course operate quite apart from the consciousness and control of the person in whom they have taken root.

We acquire habits through imaginary as well as actual exertions. A singular imaginative flight might establish a habit as effectively as repeated outward actions. In its distinctively human form, then, the capacity to take habits encompasses both the capacity to acquire habits by means of imaginative experience (experienced fantasies, lived dreams—call them what you will) and the capacity to develop habits of imagining (Colapietro 1989). My habits of action bear the stamp of the acts of my imagination. But this is so largely because I am instinctually and culturally disposed to live imaginatively, to become absorbed in fantasies, and indeed to be transformed by images. One way in which Peirce himself makes this point is to assert that "every sane person lives in a double world, the outer and the inner world, the world of percepts and the world of fancies" (*CP*

5.487). Our actual lives involve ceaseless transitions from an order of insistent percepts and irrevocable exertions and also, conversely, from an order of pliable images and reclaimable deeds. Just as the shock of actuality can prompt a withdrawal into imagination, an imaginary performance might influence our actual engagements (*CP* 5.486, n. 10).

According to Peirce, "The whole business of ratiocination, and all that makes us intellectual beings, is performed in imagination" (*CP* 6.286). It might even be that ratiocination is properly described as a species of imagination, distinguished from other species by its function (the representation of reality) and form (the criticism, correction, and control of its own products and processes). To imagine that reality might be different than we habitually imagine it to be is, on the one side, to put imagination in the service of reality and, on the other, to envision reality itself as something accessible only through imaginative processes. At the second, or abstract, level of clarity, the real and the merely imagined are sharply distinguished (the real being defined in opposition to a figment of anyone's imagination); at the third or pragmatic level of clarification, however, the interplay between reality and imagination comes into focus. For what is real at this level of clarity is *not* independent of thought in general; it is not knowable apart from the wild flights of theoretical imagination so prominent in the actual history of scientific investigation.

In one sense, then, dreams *are* such stuff as meanings are made on; and it is a sense Peirce himself would not hesitate to endorse. But, in another respect, it is to the generation and kinds of interpretants that we must turn, if we are to make sense out of meaning. It is also these semiotic processes and functional varieties to which we must turn to make sense out of our very selves.

Toward a Formally Semiotic Approach to the Unconscious

While a categoreal description of the unconscious prepares the way for a semiotic approach, such a description certainly does not constitute such an approach. In order to undertake an explicitly and formally semiotic approach to the unconscious, it is necessary to draw upon the definitions and classifications proper to the self-conscious study of sign-generating processes. One of the virtues of Teresa de Lauretis's creative appropriation of Peircean semiotic is the way that this appropriation explicitly draws upon the central notion of the ultimate logical interpretant. But, in the best tradition of American pragmatism, she puts Peirce to work: she uses the tools that she finds in his semiotic toolbox. The specific focus of what she does not hesitate to call a theoretical fantasy is the complex semiotic processes by which lesbian subjectivity is constituted.

Even though my account in this chapter is at a more specific and specifically semiotic level than the categoreal approach of my earlier paper, it is quite far from the level of specificity on which de Lauretis is, for the most part, working. But my principal objective has been primarily to make more fully available to psychoanalytic and other theorists the conceptual resources of the Peircean semiotic. At a yet later time, I do hope to work out in greater detail a semiotic explanation of human subjectivity. But like Peirce himself, I am "a convinced Pragmaticist in Semeiotic"; in part what this means is that the notion of habit (including an account of how habits are formed and the ways they are deforming) must play a central role in working out the details of this explanation. Accordingly, this chapter might be viewed as a sketch of a part of that more ambitious undertaking.

Conclusion

The plasticity of our biological constitution is revealed in various ways, not the least of which is that our instinctual impulses—even the most tyrannical of these—do not drive us in any fixed direction. In other words, our instinctual impulses have variable objects, variable across different cultures and even across the exceedingly short span of an individual's personal history. The habits inscribed within our physiological beings by the centuries-long struggles of our biological ancestors are, in their characteristic functioning, largely nothing more than the rudimentary structures out of which more complex habits are generated. Our instincts are incomplete and inchoate; they evolve in the direction of more determinate dispositions via semiotic processes. Signs give rise not only to other signs of the same character but also to habits of a markedly different nature than these seemingly ephemeral processes. What is in itself transient is, in its effect (its proper significate effect), often far from transient.

Unquestionably, then, our instinctual impulses are *radically* transformed by the inescapable pressures of cultural practices. The pressures of these practices are staggeringly vast and various. On the one hand, the prohibitions, admonitions, encouragements, etc., of the authoritative representatives of these cultural practices and, on the other, the promptings, aversions, fascinations, etc., of our largely opaque instinctual nature thrust us into an ongoing series of complex negotiations and renegotiations. The fabric of our very subjectivity is woven out of these renegotiations. The habits of our being are the more or less lasting stitches in this fabric. While these stitches are among the most intimate aspects of our selves, they are in great measure the work of other, often hidden, hands. The recognition of this fact does not entail the denial of our agency;

rather, it identifies one of the principal tasks to which human agency must commit itself, if it is to approximate the Peircean ideal of self-mastery.

Notes

1. These ideas were originally presented on June 13, 1994, in Berkeley, California, at the Fifth Congress of the International Association for Semiotic Studies–Association Internationale Sémiotique (IASS-AIS). At that same meeting, Teresa de Lauretis presented her own provocative and insightful reading of Peirce in light of Freud and, in turn, Freud in light of Peirce. While my earlier "Notes for a Sketch" focused on the Peircean categories, this chapter focuses on the crucial notion of interpretant. Hence, this treatment draws more explicitly on Peirce's semiotic conceptions, as the earlier treatment drew more heavily on his phenomenological categories.

2. This expression, "the phenomenon of the unconscious," is curious, if not oxymoronic, for the unconscious is that which by its very nature refuses to put in an appearance. It is the antiphenomenal.

3. Human subjectivity is here understood to be a split being, a being split into a multilevel consciousness (*CP* 7.540) and an unfathomable unconscious (*CP* 7.554). In this view, subjectivity includes the unconscious. Augusto Ponzio correctly stresses that "in Peirce alterity is found within the very subject who is an open dialogue between the sign and interpretant" (1985, 23). Indeed, the unconscious is a system of habits included within a wider system of dynamically interacting dispositions.

4. In *The Practice of Love,* de Lauretis brings the historical character of human subjectivity into sharp focus when she explains that, by history, she means "the particular configuration of discourses, representations, and practices—familial and broadly institutional, cultural and subcultural, public and private—that the subject crosses and that in turn traverse the subject, according to the contingencies of each subject's existence in the world" (1994, 303).

5. Often Peirce appears to slight and, on occasion, even to deny the importance and efficacy of individual agents. The individual as such appears to be reduced to a process or function controlled by forces other than itself. According to Peirce, there are laws that more or less determine how material and cultural circumstances influence human existence and conduct. "But these laws are not of the nature of mechanical forces, such that the individual and the spirit of man is [*sic.*] swallowed up in cosmical movements, but on the contrary it is a law by virtue of which lofty results require for their attainment lofty thinkers of original power and individual value. You cannot silence or stifle or starve one of them without a loss of civilization from which it never can wholly recover" (*CP* 7.275).

6. Peirce leads himself to misinterpretation here, for he in one place defines the ultimate logical interpretant as a self-analyzing habit. More fully, he declares that "the deliberately formed, self-analyzing habit—self-analyzing because formed by the aid of the exercises that nourished it—is the living definition, the veritable and final logical interpretant" (*CP* 5.491). So understood,

it is difficult—if not impossible—to distinguish between the ultimate logical interpretant and the normal interpretant. But it is imperative to insist upon this distinction, even if some texts *seem* to imply their identity and, beyond this, if they happen in some cases to overlap or entirely coincide. The ultimate logical interpretant is formally distinct from the normal interpretant; even so, there are some instances in which what counts as the one will also count as the other.

7. In Peirce's writings, one of the principal meanings of *consciousness* is feeling: to be conscious is to be sentient (Colapietro 1989).

8. Peirce characterized himself as a Schellinglike idealist. In this conception of matter and mind, Peirce's affinity to Schelling is evident.

9. This tendency is dramatic in a twofold sense: in the sense, first, of what is noteworthy or remarkable and, second, of what exhibits the structure of a story.

10. For readers unacquainted with Peirce, let me point out that one of his most important essays was an early paper entitled "Some Consequences of Four Incapacities." In "Certain Faculties Claimed for Man," Peirce launched a critique of Cartesianism and, in particular, of our alleged capacities (or "faculties") to know reality intuitively, to know ourselves introspectively, to think without signs, and to frame a conception of an unknowable thing-in-itself. In "Some Consequences," he traced out some of the important implications of denying that we possess such faculties. The title of this chapter is obviously a play on the title of Peirce's article.

11. To say that Peirce offers his classification of objects and of interpretants *in addition to* his classification of signs themselves is somewhat misleading, for it does not convey the extent to which his taxonomies of object and interpretant are devised in conjunction with his taxonomy of signs; for example, in a letter to Victoria Lady Welby, he asserts—immediately after, first, distinguishing the immediate and dynamical object and, then, distinguishing the immediate, dynamical, and normal interpretant—that these distinctions provide the bases for recognizing "ten respects in which Signs may be divided" (*CP* 8.343).

12. This point requires qualification, for all that is necessary is that a sign be formally and functionally other than its object (not that it be actually other than its object). Peirce in effect qualifies this point when he asserts that

> in order that anything should be a Sign, it must "represent," as we say, something else, called its Object, although the condition that a Sign must be other than its *Object* is perhaps arbitrary, since, if we insist upon it we must at least make an exception in the case of a Sign that is a part of a Sign. Thus nothing prevents the actor who acts a character in a historical drama from carrying as a theatrical "property" the very relic that the article is supposed merely to represent, such as the crucifix that Bulwer's Richelieu holds up with such effect in his defiance. On a map of an island laid down upon the soil of that island there must, under all ordinary circumstances, be some position, some point, marked or not, that represents *qua* place on the map, the very same point *qua* place on the map. [2.230]

13. In a manuscript from ca. 1906 (i.e., at the time when Jamesian pragmatism was gaining a wide audience), Peirce stated, "It appears that there are certain mummified pedants who have never waked to the truth that the act of knowing a real object alters it. They are curious specimens of humanity, and as I am one of them, it may be amusing to see how I think" (*CP* 5.555).

14. Foundationalists persist in seeing fallibilism as a variety of skepticism, while skeptics tend to view it either as a form of crypto-foundationalism or as a skepticism afraid to accept the implications of its own insights. But, from the perspective of fallibilism itself, neither of these characterizations are, by a long measure, fair.

15. To Lady Welby, Peirce describes his own investigations of signs as broader than hers: while her significs focuses on the relationship of signs to their interpretants (Peirce 1977), his own work in semiotic was primarily concerned, at least at the outset, with the relationship of symbols to their objects. But he was "forced to make original studies into *all branches* of the general theory of signs" (Peirce 1977, 80–81, my italics). Even so, Savan's claim stands.

16. Peirce is not consistent in this usage, for on more than a few occasions he uses the term *belief* to designate any cognitive habit, no matter how that habit is formed.

17. The reason for qualifying these habits as cognitive or intellectual is made clear by Peirce's insistence that "it is not all signs that have logical interpretants, but only intellectual concepts and the like; and these are all either general or intimately connected with generals. . . . This shows that the species of future tense of the logical interpretant is that of the conditional mood, the '*would-be*,'" or would-happen (*CP* 5.482).

18. Teresa de Lauretis contends that "Peirce names interpretant the dynamic structure that supports the nexus of object, sign, and meaning, as well as the process of mediation itself. A series of interpretants, or 'significate effects' (I insist on this term which conveys the processual and open-ended nature of meaning), sustains each instance of semiosis, each instance of the unending process of mediations and negotiations between the self and the world" (1994, 300).

19. The human organism is not simply a passive medium in and through which sign-actions take place of their own inherent dynamic; nor is it in absolute control of even its own cognitive processes. The human organism is, at once, a *medium* in and through which sign actions take place to a significant degree of their own accord and an *agent* from which self-controlled actions emanate and, thus, to which deeds are properly attributed (cf. Colapietro 1989, 38).

20. The Peircean notion of destiny is central but problematic: it is central to his theory of inquiry and, indeed, his vision of the cosmos, but it is problematic in at least a twofold way. First, it is not easy to understand exactly what Peirce intends by his advocacy of this notion; second, it is not clear that the notion is tenable.

21. The exigencies to which I am referring here are both constitutional and adventitious exigencies. Examples of the former are the need for food, water, activity, stimulation, and the like; examples of the latter are the imperative desires for sexual stimulation of a certain sort, etc. In between constitutional and ad-

ventitious exigencies are such needs as those for enduring companionship, for esteemed work, and so on.

22. Teresa de Lauretis uses the term *negotiation* to describe the processes of semiosis by which the human organism comes to terms with the now conflicting, now complementary, demands of its world and its own being. The word also connotes the work of diplomats. For a development of a connection between semiosis and diplomacy, see Colapietro (1995a).

23. My friend and, in this instance, editor, Joseph Brent, objects that this construal of the unconscious does not work. He further suggests that to make it work one would have to reconstruct either Freud or Peirce. Of course, he is right. So I must acknowledge that the account being offered here entails a reconstruction of Freud, but little or no modification of Peirce's own views regarding semiosis and mentality.

24. One reason to describe enculturated human organisms as "essentially problematic beings" is that such organisms are problems unto themselves; another reason is that the problematic character of their own existence is itself problematic (Is the problem itself the solution or the solution to be found in the jettisoning of the problem?).

25. William James, who was a friend and supporter of Peirce, offers several brilliant metaphors to evoke this aspect of experience. In one place, he states, "Life is in the transitions as much as in the terms connected; often, indeed, it seems to be there more emphatically, as if our spurts and sallies forth were the real firing-line of the battle, were like the thin line of flame advancing across the dry autumnal field which the farmer proceeds to burn" (James 1977, 212-13).

26. After identifying eight or so levels of self-control, Peirce concludes that "there are certainly more grades than I have enumerated. Perhaps their number is indefinite. The brutes are certainly capable of more than one grade of control; but it seems to me that our superiority to them is more due to our greater number of grades of self-control than it is to our versatility" (*CP* 5.533; Colapietro 1989, 109ff.). He goes on to claim that language itself is a faculty explicable as "a phenomenon of self-control" (*CP* 5.534).

27. Just as silence is constitutive of spoken language, space is essential to written language.

28. Three fine treatments of Peirce's theory of perception are Bernstein (1964), Hausman (1990), and Santaella (1993). No one of these, however, considers the extent to which perception is a fantasy-laden process. I do not know of any scholar who has worked out the details of construing perception as such a process.

References

Alexander, Thomas M. "Pragmatic Imagination." *Transactions of the Charles S. Peirce Society* 26, no. 3 (1990): 325-48.

Bär, Eugen. "The Unconscious Icon: Topology and Tropology." In *Iconicity: Essays on Nature and Culture,* edited by Paul Bouissac, Michael Herzfeld, and Roland Posner. Tubingen, Germany: Stauffenberg Verlag, 1986.

Bernstein, Richard J. "Peirce's Theory of Perception." In *Studies in the Philosophy of Charles Sanders Peirce,* Second Series, edited by Edward C. Moore and Richard S. Robin, 165 – 89. Amherst: University of Massachusetts Press, 1964.

Burks, Arthur. "Icon, Index, and Symbol." *Philosophy and Phenomenological Research* 9 (1949): 673 – 89.

Burks, Arthur, and Weiss, Paul. "Peirce's Sixty-six Signs." *Journal of Philosophy* 42 (1945): 383 – 88.

Colapietro, Vincent M. "Dreams: Such Stuff As Meanings Are Made On." *Versus: Quaderni di studi semiotici* 49 (1988): 65 – 79.

———. *Peirce's Approach to the Self: A Semiotic Perspective on Human Subjectivity.* Albany: State University of New York Press, 1989.

———. 1995 "Mediating Opposition and Opposing Mediation: The Interplay between Secondness and Thirdness" in *Semiotics 1994.*

———. "Notes for a Sketch of a Peircean Theory of the Unconscious." *Transactions of the Charles S. Peirce Society* 31, no. 3 (1995b): 482 – 506.

———. "The Dynamical Object and the Deliberative Subject." In *The Rule of Reason: The Philosophy of Charles Sanders Peirce,* edited by Jacqueline Brunning and Paul Forster, 262 – 88. Toronto: University of Toronto Press, 1997.

Deely, John. *The Human Use of Signs or Elements of Anthroposemiosis.* Lanham, Md.: Rowman and Littlefield, 1994.

de Lauretis, Teresa. *Alice Doesn't: Feminism, Semiotics, Cinema.* Bloomington: Indiana University Press, 1984.

———. *The Practice of Love: Lesbian Sexuality and Perverse Desire.* Bloomington: Indiana University Press, 1994.

Eco, Umberto. *Interpretation and Overinterpretation.* Edited by Stefan Collini. Cambridge: Cambridge University Press, 1992.

Esposito, Joseph L. "On the Origins and Foundations of Peirce's Semiotic." *Peirce Studies,* 19 – 24. No. 1. Lubbock, Tex.: Institute for Studies in Pragmaticism, 1979.

Fisch, Max H. *Peirce, Semeiotic, and Pragmatism.* Bloomington: Indiana University Press, 1986.

Hausman, Carl R. "In and Out of Peirce's Percepts." *Transactions of the Charles S. Peirce Society* 26, no. 3 (1990): 271 – 308.

James, William. *The Writings of William James: A Comprehensive Edition.* Edited by John J. McDermott. Chicago: University of Chicago Press, 1977.

Kruse, Felicia E. "Nature and Semiosis." *Transactions of the Charles S. Peirce Society* 26, no. 2 (1990): 211 – 24.

Liska, James. "Peirce's Interpretant." *Transactions of the Charles S. Peirce Society* 26, no. 1 (1990): 17 – 62.

Peirce, Charles Sanders. *Collected Papers of Charles Sanders Peirce.* Edited by Charles Hartshorne, Paul Weiss, and Arthur W. Burks. 8 vols. Cambridge: Harvard University Press, 1931 – 58.

———. *Semiotic and Significs: The Correspondence between Charles S. Peirce and Victoria Lady Welby.* Edited by Charles S. Hardwick. Bloomington, Indiana University Press, 1977.

Ponzio, Augusto. "Semiotics between Peirce and Bakhtin." *Kodikas/Code: Ars Semeiotica* 8, nos. 1/2 (1985): 11–28.

Ransdell, Joseph. "The Epistemic Function of Iconicity in Perception." *Peirce Studies*. No. 1. Lubbock, Tex.: Institute for Studies in Pragmaticism, 1979.

Rorty, Richard. "The Pragmatist's Progress." In *Interpretation and Overinterpretation,* edited by Stefan Collini, 89–108. Cambridge: Cambridge University Press, 1992.

Rosenthal, Sandra B. "Peirce's Ultimate Logical Interpretant and Dynamical Object: A Pragmatic Perspective." *Transactions of the Charles S. Peirce Society* 26, no. 2 (1990): 195–210.

———. *Charles Peirce's Pragmatic Pluralism.* Albany: State University of New York Press, 1994.

Santaella, Lúcia. *A Percepção: una teoria semiótica.* São Paulo, Brazil: Experimento, 1993.

Savan, David. *An Introduction to C. S. Peirce's Full System of Semeiotic.* Toronto: Toronto Semiotic Circle, 1987–88.

Schrag, Calvin. *Experience and Being.* Evanston, Ill.: Northwestern University Press, 1969.

Shapiro, Michael. *The Sense of Grammar: Language As Semeiotic.* Bloomington: Indiana University Press, 1983.

———. *The Sense of Change: Language As History.* Bloomington: Indiana University Press, 1991.

Sheriff, John K. *The Fate of Meaning.* Princeton: Princeton University Press, 1989.

Short, T. L. "Interpreting Peirce's Interpretant: A Response to Lalor, Liszka, and Meyers." *Transactions of the Charles S. Peirce Society* 32, no. 4 (1996): 488–541.

10   Gender, Body, and Habit Change

Teresa de Lauretis

*That a famous library has been cursed by a woman is a matter
of complete indifference to a famous library.*
—Virginia Woolf

W ith very few exceptions, gender and the body have been a matter
of complete indifference to semiotics, but a central concern of psychoanalysis. As I have argued elsewhere that Peirce's notion of habit effectively
bridges the theoretical divide between semiotics and psychoanalysis (de
Lauretis 1984), here I explore the relation of habit to gender.

In the 1970s and up to the early 1980s, the study of gender was virtually an exclusive concern of feminist studies, as was the notion of sexual
difference, with which it was initially synonymous. Men, whether straight
or gay, did not write about gender then; the first scholarly works in gay
studies were works of history and sociology. Gender was women's problem, as was "sexual difference," and these were the terms by which
women analyzed and articulated the sociosexual definition of Woman as
different from the universal standard that was Man. In other words, gender was the mark of woman, the mark of a sexual difference, women's difference, which entailed women's subordinate status in society and a set
of character traits derived specifically from their anatomical/biological
sex. Gender was the sum of those traits, whether they were thought to be
innate, supplied by nature, or imposed by culture and social conditioning.

The single most influential feminist essay on gender, Gayle Rubin's
"Traffic in Women," which defined the mutual implication of sex and gender in the concept of a "sex-gender system," was published in 1975 in a
volume by the explicit title *Toward an Anthropology of Women.* Rubin
begins her essay by stating that "a 'sex-gender system' is the set of arrange-
ments by which a society transforms biological sexuality into products
of human activity, and in which these transformed sexual needs are satisfied" (1975, 159). And, after a brilliant discussion of Lévi-Strauss and La-

159

can, she concludes her synopsis of Freud's account of female sexuality with the statement—now rather surprising—that "psychoanalysis is a theory of gender" (198). Surprising indeed, for it was again Rubin who, in a later essay, drastically disjoined gender from sex, arguing that "an autonomous theory and politics specific to sexuality must be developed" in separation from the feminist critique of gender as the social structure of women's oppression (1984, 309).

It was in that context that my *Technologies of Gender* (1987) was written. In it I argued that gender was not the simple derivation of anatomical/biological sex but a sociocultural construction, a representation, or better, the compounded effect of discursive and visual representations which, following Foucault, I saw emanating from various institutional apparatuses: not from only the family, the educational system, the media, medicine, and law, but also from less obvious ones—language, art, literature, film, and theory. However, the constructedness or discursive nature of gender does not prevent it from having concrete effects or "real" implications, both social and subjective, for the material life of individuals. On the contrary, the reality of gender is precisely in the effects of its representation; gender is real-ized, or becomes "real," when that representation becomes a self-representation, or is individually assumed as a form of one's social and subjective identity.

Thus, I wrote, the subject is *en-gendered*—that is, produced or constructed, and constructed-as-gendered—in the process of assuming, taking on, and identifying with the subject positions and meaning effects specified by a particular society's gender system. Put another way, the social subject is effectively en-gendered in an interactive subjection to what I called the technologies of gender. I wrote *en-gendered* with a hyphen: I was punning on the verb *to engender*—which means "to produce or bring into existence" and comes etymologically from *genus* and *generare,* and hence does not have feminine (or masculine) connotations— and the word *gender* in its feminist usage, meaning the mark of woman. By *en-gendered* I meant that the social subject was produced or constituted *as a woman or as a man,* and that is to say that gender was inscribed or implanted in each subject from its inception, from the very beginning of subjectivity, even before the apperception of sexual difference.

While I, too, saw the validity of distinguishing gender from sex and sexuality, I did not see that distinction as absolutely as Rubin did, but only as theoretically necessary. For it seemed obvious to me that, in social, subjective, and psychic reality, gender and sexuality are in fact interrelated. However, more important is that the elaboration of the concept *gender* occurred within feminist studies, well before the shift to what is now called gender studies. I stress this because that history is already disappearing: in another decade or so, perhaps no one will remember that the critical concept of gender and the notion of the gendered subject did not exist before feminists analyzed it, theorized it, and *named* it.

As feminist research became institutionalized in undergraduate women's studies programs, institutionalization brought about certain constraints, like the need to sustain enrollments, the constitution of curricular sequences of courses, and thus the constitution of a sort of canon, a corpus of texts representative of the legitimate approaches to "the study of women." It also brought about an odor of ideological and intellectual enclosure. As women's studies went "mainstream," it acquired a measure of legitimacy but also began closing down its borders, so to speak, and not allowing entrance to texts or views that were considered "offensive to women." Freud, for instance, was a targeted exemplar of misogynist "male theory" in my university's women's studies program, and so was, consequently, Irigaray's *Speculum de l'autre femme,* which was not only about Freud but also about Plato, Aristotle, and other "European male philosophers." And never mind that she was reading them "against the grain."

Two solutions were found by those who for different reasons disliked this institutionalization of women's studies. One solution, if one was a feminist but unwilling to wear an intellectual chastity belt, was to integrate one's feminist critical perspectives into one's disciplinary or regular teaching. The other solution, adopted by those to whom feminism was something of an embarrassment or an undesirable association, was to distance oneself from the specific concern with women by looking instead at the relations of women and men in a larger, usually sociological, frame; for instance, examining the construction of masculinity or masculinities, gender formation patterns in adolescence, or alternative models of gender (e.g., the Native American berdache). The latter solution led to gender studies.

Today, the rubric *gender studies* covers a variety of topics that range from the more conservative, such as the family and the relations of women and men, to the more "sexy," such as gender crossing, drag, transvestism, and what has been called neosexualities (active bisexuality, sadomasochism, transsexuality, and transgender, among others). And the rubric could be stretched further to include practices of bodily modification such as piercing, tattooing, scarification, or bodybuilding—all of which are seen as ways to "deconstruct" gender and to blur or dissolve the boundaries of "traditional" sexual identities ("traditional" including heterosexual *and* homosexual identities). To the more sophisticated or intellectually ambitious writings in this genre is given the name *queer theory,* wherein the word *theory* signals a higher academic status—or the aspiration to it.[1]

In a semiotic view of gender studies, then, it can be said that the relation of gender to sex has gone from contiguity to similarity, or from metonymy to metaphor: in the early feminist studies of the sex-gender system, it was a syntagmatic relation on the axis of combination. In those studies in which gender is understood as culturally specific and constructed, whereas sex is assigned by nature, it remains a strict binary opposition. More recently, as both gender and sex are often understood as discursive constructions that are neither natural nor fixed for each individual, but can be resignified in performance or surgically reassigned, the relation of gender and sex is a metaphoric, paradigmatic relation on the axis of substitution. The newly coined term *transgender* goes one step further: although modeled on *transsexual,* and thus carrying the sexual reference, *transgender* seems to refer to a transformation that is not, or not only, the bodily transformation from one anatomical sex to the other (as the term *transsexual* is usually, if simplistically, understood), but a transformation into a being who is beyond the two traditional genders (masculine and feminine), beyond the two traditional sexes (male and female), and beyond the two allegedly "traditional" forms of sexual organization (heterosexual and homosexual).[2] In referring to, but eliding the corporeal (i.e., the *sexual* of *transsexual*), *transgender* effects a total projection of the axis of combination onto the axis of selection, which, in Roman Jakobson's schema, is the true nature of self-referential or poetic language (Jakobson 1960). And indeed *transgender* is a trope that fully realizes the nature of the signifier; that is to say, it is meaningful only as a sign. It signifies "I am a signifier," and bears no reference to a gender, a sex, a sexuality, or a body; no reference to anything but its own discursive nature.

The body, however, has lately become the focus of much attention. To judge from published titles such as *Volatile Bodies, Sexy Bodies, Spectacular Bodies, Posthuman Bodies, The Figural Body,* or the way in which Judith Butler's book *Bodies That Matter* revises her earlier *Gender Trouble,* the body has become itself a symptom of the trouble with gender. This is not new, of course, in psychoanalysis, where the body has always been the site of symptomatic production and expression, the organ of speech of a particular language: initially that was the language of the unconscious speaking in neurotic symptoms, and subsequently, following from the popularization of psychoanalysis in the culture at large, the body also speaks the more accessible language of the preconscious, known to us from common-usage expressions such as, "My body is telling me something."

I will return to psychoanalysis and its relation to semiotics, but for the moment I'd like to consider the body as gender symptom in the work of a young German sociologist, Gesa Lindemann, author of a book on gender difference and transsexuality entitled *Das Paradoxe Geschlecht* (The Paradox of Gender). The German word *Geschlecht* is not semantically coextensive with the English *gender* but segments the continuum in such a manner as to convey the meaning of both gender and anatomical/biological sex. Consequently, gender difference [*Geschlechterdifferenz*] also means sexual difference—and not by metaphoric substitution; moreover, gender as *Geschlecht* is directly contiguous with the body.

In a recent essay translated into English with the title "The Body of Gender Difference" (note how this reverses the commonsense understanding of gender as based on body difference), Lindemann asserts that "bodies differ in gender as a result of social practices" and "the material conditions of the body are to be comprehended entirely as a socially created reality" (1996, 341). However, this is not to say that gender and body are effects of a purely discursive production or a disembodied performativity; for, in Lindemann's phenomenological perspective, on the one hand it is "untenable to assume a natural gendered body," but on the other hand—and this is the paradox of gender—it is "imperative to recognize an inherent logic of the body and the sensory reference of bodies to their environment." As Lindemann defines it, therefore, "gender difference"— which, I remind you, in German includes sex difference—is a historically variable "social form" that imposes a distinction between bodies "insofar as they are experienced and treated as gender-defined bodies." This entails that the local realization of the gender distinction in each body "is broken down by the inherent logic of that which is physical or sensory"; and the latter is further differentiated between "the inherent logic of the visual perception of gestalt" and "the inherent logic of feeling" (341–42).

This interesting distinction, which addresses not only the material dimension of the body but also the specificity of diverse sensory registers—the modalities of sight, hearing, taste, touch, and smell through which the body relates to the environment—owes to another peculiarity of natural language: the fact that German, unlike English, has two words for body, *Körper* and *Leib*. The first refers to the body as a form, "a visible and concrete gestalt," while *Leib* refers to the body as it experiences the environment through the senses and as it is experienced subjectively in feeling; in short, *Körper* is the body as imaged and *Leib* is the body *as it feels*. In the essay *Körper* is translated with "objectified body" and *Leib* with "living body," further subdivided into "experiencing body" and "experienced body" (349).

I cannot go into this lexical distinction in greater detail except to add that objectified body and living body stand in a "reflexive relationship" to each other that is also "a normative meaning relationship" or, in other words, "a modern living body is disciplined by the objectified body's pictorial form" (353). In certain contexts, the objectified body, its image or representation as gestalt (analogous to what Lacan described in the child's experience at the mirror stage), becomes dominant and overrides the perceptions that belong to the living body, the body experiencing and experienced, so that perception itself becomes gendered (or perhaps more exactly, in English, gendered and sexed). The example Lindemann gives is the following:

> A transsexual woman [a male-to-female transsexual], whom I call Verena, who at the time of this depiction had not yet had genital surgery, described a visit to a women's public toilets.
>
> *Verena:* I was sitting on the toilet. I was relaxing and about to pee . . . and then another woman came in and I was startled—what'll happen if she notices something? She went into the stall next to me and she was rather loud, the way she was peeing, so I was relieved. Yeah, well, and then—I just went ahead and started peeing too.
>
> [Lindemann comments:] Verena is sitting in a cubicle in a public toilet. She cannot be seen by the person who enters—presumably a woman. Verena is startled. Her reaction is immediate and does not come from a fear of being "exposed as a man" upon leaving. This reaction implies that a relationship must have been established between Verena and the person who entered such that it is immediately clear to Verena that she is out of place in terms of gender. In order to analyze this relationship it is necessary to understand what it means to sit on a toilet in a relaxed manner. You relax, feel in your abdomen the development of a region of the experienced body, the relative location of which overlaps with the urogenital area of the objectified body. As a result of the socialization of the experienced body, it exists in a reflexive meaning relationship to this part of the objectified body. [But at this moment, that relationship is inactive: while Verena is sitting on the toilet, alone in the restroom, she does not feel inappropriate in terms of gender.] As soon as another person/woman enters the toilet, the situation is fundamentally changed. Verena perceives—she hears the other person—and she evidently feels perceived, since she wonders whether the other person notices anything, i.e., whether the other person perceives Verena as a man. [353–54]

This happens, explains Lindemann, because, "in the experience of being perceived, the felt region of the experienced body abruptly clicks into a meaning relationship with the objectified body. The genital form of the objectified body, which Verena knows that she has [Verena is a male-to-female transsexual *before* genital surgery], becomes the intense reality of the felt region of the experienced body." If Verena fears she may be perceived as a man it is because she perceives herself as gender-different in relation to the other person. (Note, however, that in the interview Verena describes that person as "*another* woman.") Phenomenologically, the process goes something like this: the shock and startled reaction cause tension in the experienced body; what was "the relaxed felt region of the experienced body . . . suddenly ceases to exist" and is replaced by the internalized image of the objectified body with its male genital form. At the same time, the startled reaction "weakens the perceiving reference of the living body to the environment [and] serves to destroy spontaneously the inappropriately gendered living body" (355), that is, corrects the perception of having a male-gendered body.

Lindemann concludes, "To the extent that objectified body and experiencing body click into a reflexive meaning relationship, perception itself becomes gendered, since it is the living body that is felt and that perceives" (354). The conclusion I would draw requires a slight rephrasing. It is the social representations of the body (*Körper*), with their inherent binary logic, that normalize the generic form and discipline the living body by inscribing gender in the sensory registers of perception, thus implanting gender/sex in the body *as it feels.* To put it in the words I used in *Technologies of Gender,* gender is a representation and a self-representation. I now can add that *the body is a gender symptom in that it bears the inscription of gender and speaks it back through the subject's very senses, through the perceptual apparatus that constitutes the bodily ego.*

I want to anticipate an objection that might be raised. The example of transsexuality to demonstrate the process of the gendering of the body might appear far-fetched or exceptional. It is not. In this case, transsexuality merely makes more conspicuous the general process of subjectivation by its singular focus on gender (as *Geschlecht*) — singular in the sense that the medical regulation of transsexuality, what Lindemann calls "the choreography of transsexual gender change," requires a more "obsessive focus on the form of gender distinction" (345 – 46) than any other social institution (although the family into which I was born was a close second). It requires an exclusive attention to gender which, in other situations, may be diverted or even preempted by the pressure exerted on subjectivation by other social forms such as race, ethnicity, class, and so on. However, here is another example, in the words of a British feminist theorist:

> The term the body sounds to me bounded, whereas the corporeal is more like the word bodily; it's something to do with a register of sensations and possibilities. I'm compelled more and more by those feminist arguments

that there is an irreducible feminine *corporeal* specificity. . . . It's an historically accumulated deposit of the manner in which you experience certain things aided by the specificity of that body. . . . How can you deal with such incommensurate experiences [as menstruation] never ever having anything comparable to blood pouring out of your body without it being some kind of wounding? . . . I am not saying that this kind of event determines what you experience by it, but it is predicate of a radically different register of experience, i.e. the material for inscribing and engendering representation. . . . So I can't go back to a materiality that is un-differentiated and I can't go through simply constructed differentiation. [Pollock 1995, 157–58]

The context of this statement is a discussion among five people on the question of the materiality of the body. It was prompted by Judith Butler's book *Bodies That Matter* and held at the University of Leeds Center for Cultural Studies. I would like to remark a couple of points that make this statement resonate with what has been said so far. First, although the author of the statement I have just quoted, Griselda Pollock, is an English speaker, she *hears* a distinction that English doesn't make explicit, as German does, between the two valences of the body described by Lindemann: *Körper* and *Leib,* the objectified body and the living body. Pollock says, "The term the body *sounds* to me bounded, whereas the corporeal is more like the word bodily; it's something to do with a register of sensations and possibilities" (my italics). Second, Pollock's last sentence, "I can't go back to a materiality that is undifferentiated and I can't go through simply constructed differentiation," is also consonant with Lindemann's argument that gender is embodied and "the diversified inherent logic of the body as an objectified, experiencing, and experienced body . . . cannot be reduced to [abstract] social forms" (Lindemann 1996, 358). In other words, gender cannot be reduced to the idea of a subjectless process that reproduces itself discursively, for example, in the manner Butler designates as citationality.

Pollock's sense of the corporeal as "a radically different register of experience, i.e. the material for inscribing and engendering representation" reminds me of the concept of experience that I articulated years ago in *Alice Doesn't.* There, in fact, I appealed to Peirce's theory of the interpretant, and in particular the concept of habit-change, to redefine experience as a complex of habits, dispositions, associations, perceptions, and expectations resulting from the continuous semiosic interaction of the self's "inner world" with the "outer world," in Peirce's terms. For Peirce, what bridges or connects outer and inner worlds is the chain of interpretants, an ongoing series of semiotic mediations linking objects, signs, and events of the world to their "significate effects" in the subject—

a subject that can thus be said to be "the place in which, the body in whom, the significate effect of the sign takes hold and is real-ized" (de Lauretis 1984, 182–83).

I suggest that, in Lindemann's example of the gendering of perception (how the living body bears and speaks the inscription of gender, or, in Pollock's words, how the body is "the material for inscribing and engendering representation"), what happens to Verena is a chain of interpretants.

Peirce names interpretant the dynamic structure that supports the nexus of object, sign, and meaning, as well as the process of mediation itself. A series of interpretants, or "significate effects" (I insist on this term that conveys the processlike and open-ended nature of meaning), sustains each instance of semiosis, each instance of the unending process of mediations or negotiations between the self and the world. In other words, each moment of what, for the subject, is an imperceptible passage from event (in the outer world) to sign (mental or perceptual representation) to meaning effect (in the inner world) is conceptualized by Peirce as an interpretant. Interpretants are not only mental representations: there are, of course, "intellectual" interpretants (concepts), but there are also "emotional" and "energetic" interpretants.

For example, the significate effect produced by a sign such as the performance of a piece of music may be only a feeling; such a feeling is an *emotional* interpretant of that sign. However, through the mediation of the emotional interpretant, a further significate effect may be produced, which may be a mental or a "muscular exertion"; this would be an *energetic* interpretant, for it involves an "effort" whether mental or physical. The third type of effect that may be produced by the sign is "a *habit-change*"; this, in Peirce's own words, is "a modification of a person's tendencies toward action, resulting from previous experiences or from previous exertions." This is the final or "ultimate" significate effect of the sign, he writes, and designates it the *logical interpretant.* According to Peirce, "The real and living logical conclusion [of the series of mediations that makes up this particular instance of semiosis] *is* that habit." But he quickly qualifies the designation "logical":

> The concept which is a logical interpretant is only imperfectly so. It somewhat partakes of the nature of a verbal definition, and is as inferior to the habit, and much in the same way, as a verbal definition is inferior to the real definition. The deliberately formed, self-analyzing habit — self-analyzing because formed by the aid of analysis of the exercises that nourished it — is the living definition, the veritable and final logical interpretant. [*CP* 5.491][3]

It is important to keep in mind that the logical interpretant is not logical in the sense in which a syllogism is logical, or because it is the result of an intellectual operation like deductive reasoning, but rather it is logical because it makes sense out of the emotion and muscular/mental effort that preceded it by providing a conceptual representation of that effort.

Now, think of Verena sitting on the toilet, relaxed and about to pee. Then:

1. Verena hears another person/woman enter the restroom and is startled.
2. As Verena wonders, "What'll happen if she notices something?" the relaxed felt region of the experienced body suddenly ceases to exist and is replaced by the unexpected perception of a body with a male genital form.
3. At least temporarily, Verena is unable to pee—until the noise made by the other person relieves her fear of being heard peeing like a man. The startling perception of having an inappropriately gendered (i.e., male) body subsides, and Verena is able to relax and pee.

Analysis:

1. An event in the outer world, the person/woman entering, produces an *emotional* interpretant, a feeling, in the inner world: Verena is startled and apprehensive.
2. The startled reaction causes a muscular exertion in the experienced body; it produces an *energetic* interpretant that involves physical and mental effort: Verena's body contracts and is unable to pee.
3. This, in a split-second time, leads to a third interpretant in the chain: Verena experiences her body in male-genital form. This is a *logical interpretant* because it gives meaning to the emotion and muscular/mental effort that preceded it by providing a conceptual representation of it; or rather, by providing a mental image of what Lindemann calls the objectified body. But, in this case, the logical interpretant is not the final interpretant. Since Verena thinks of herself as a woman (she went into the women's restroom in the first place, and in the interview she states that "*another* woman" came in), experiencing her body in male-genital form is a temporary logical interpretant and does not constitute a habit *change*. Indeed it is soon superceded by what Peirce calls "the living definition, the veritable and final logical interpretant," that is, "the deliberately formed, self-analyzing *habit*" (I am a woman). It is this *living* habit

that, in fact, restores Verena's ability to act and the normal functioning of her *living* body.[4]

Similarly, I would argue, the experienced event of menstruation produces a chain of emotional, energetic, and logical interpretants that inscribe in the living body the perception of an objectified, female-gendered/sexed body, and thus en-gender the subject. The cyclical recurrence of the experience reiterates the process and reaffirms the habit to the point of naturalizing it; that is to say, to the point of making the living body *feel* female, with all the diverse implications that such a feeling has for the subject according to her sociocultural positioning. However, one's sociocultural positioning is not necessarily fixed; in fact, it is often unstable or variable over time with life contingencies and, at the very least, with age. And hence the possibility of habit-change, in spite of the permanence or monthly recurrence of the event of menstruation. In other words, the meaning-effects of being female-gendered/sexed and the perception of one's living body as female-gendered/sexed are both overdetermined and subject to change for everyone—not only for Verena.

I have stressed that Peirce's habit is not a purely mental, rational, or intellectual result of the semiosic process. While it is a mental representation, it is so in the sense in which Freud speaks of mental life as psychic reality, a domain where the mental is always implicated with the somatic. One could say that habit or habit-change is the final interpretant or representative of a somatic-mental process (semiosis), not unlike the way in which, in Freud's theory of the sexed-and-gendered body, the drive becomes perceptible in its representations or signifiable through its representatives.

Because Peirce's theory of semiosis joins subjectivity to the social as a confrontation with material reality, and in particular the materiality of the body, I see a homology between the subject of semiosis and Freud's bodily ego. Both theories suggest that subjectivity, and therefore subjectivation, involve somatic, material, and historical dimensions. This makes it possible to analyze gender and sexuality as resulting from a continuous series of semiosic processes or overlapping chains of interpretants. Thus, reading Freud with Peirce in a book that I entitled *The Practice of Love* (1994), I speculate that sexuality is a particular instance of semiosis, in which objects and bodies are displaced from external to internal or psychic reality through a chain of significate effects: interpretants, habits, and habit changes.

The concept of habit, in particular, emphasizes the material, embodied component of desire as a psychic activity whose effects in the subject constitute a sort of knowledge of the body, what the body "knows" or comes to know about its instinctual aims. The somatic, material, and historical dimensions that the Peircean notion of habit inscribes in the subject reconfigure sexuality as a *sexual structuring,* a process overdetermined by both internal and external forces and constraints, which produce the subject as their shifting point of intersection. At the moment described by Lindemann, Verena is precisely at such a shifting point; we might call it a point of habit change, or habit instability.

I have used the word *subject* advisedly. For if sexual or gender structuring, like subject formation in general, is an accumulation of effects that does not accrue to a preexisting subjectivity or to a primal, original, natural body, nevertheless the process takes place in what Freud calls a bodily ego, and it takes place for a subject. The body-ego is not coextensive with the subject, part of which is unconscious, but is the material ground of each subject's subjectivation. Freud states, "The ego is first and foremost a bodily ego; it is . . . ultimately derived from bodily sensations, chiefly from those springing from the surface of the body. It may thus be regarded as a mental projection of the surface of the body" (*S.E.* 19:27).

As I read Freud, the body-ego is a projected perceptual boundary that does not merely delimit or contain the imaginary morphology of an individual self, but actually enables the access to the symbolic. The body-ego is a permeable boundary—an open border, so to speak—a site of incessant material negotiations between, on one side, the external world, the domain of the real, comprising other people and social institutions, and, on the other side, the internal world of the psyche, the drives, the unconscious, and the ego's mechanisms of defense—repression, disavowal, and so forth.

In *The Practice of Love* I suggested that the Peircean concepts of interpretant and habit change may serve to articulate Freud's psychosexual view of the internal world with Foucault's sociosexual analysis of the discursive practices and institutional mechanisms that implant sexuality in the social subject. Here I have sketched out something of the process through which the implantation takes, as it were, producing for the subject a sexed and gendered body.

A Note on Interpretants

The following remarks represent the continuation of a fruitful dialogue between my reading of Freud with Peirce and Vincent Colapietro's reading of Peirce with Freud. Our conversation began with my "Semiotics and Experience" in *Alice Doesn't* and his "Notes for a Sketch of a Peircean Theory of the Unconscious" and has continued through various professional meetings and by correspondence.

In his essay in this volume, Colapietro points out that, in the passage I quoted from *CP* 5.491 (see n. 3 below), Peirce's definition of the ultimate logical interpretant as a self-analyzing habit is misleading in that, elsewhere in Peirce, the "final logical interpretant is a conceptual node resulting from the intersection of . . . two classifications," namely, (1) logical/emotional/energetic interpretants and (2) final (also called ultimate or normal)/immediate/dynamical interpretants (Colapietro, "Further Consequences of a Singular Capacity," p. 137). The point of his objection is that I, misled by that particular Peircean passage, blur the distinction between the two classifications and thus fail to distinguish what Peirce intended by the ultimate logical interpretant from the kind of interpretant "that in some respects enjoys the status of a truly ultimate logical interpretant but that in other respects fails to be a 'deliberately formed, self-analyzing habit' (*CP* 5.491)" (ibid.).

To make the distinction sharp, since it remains implicit in Peirce's writings as well, Colapietro introduces the notion of "a quasi-ultimate logical interpretant" (ibid.). With this term, he designates, for example, "instinctual tendencies and acquired habits," such as psychic defense mechanisms or repetition compulsion, which may actually prevent the formation of deliberate, self-analyzing habits. Quasi-ultimate logical interpretants, he writes, reflect "a randomly formed, self-concealing disposition" that often results in self-destructive habits, "deformed deliberations, or simply debilitating actions; hence, not a deliberately formed habit of action, but deeply deforming acts of deliberation" (p. 146).

Thus Colapietro's *quasi-logical* or *quasi-final* interpretant would account for what elsewhere I have hypothesized as *unconscious habit* (de Lauretis 1994, 302), whereas the logical interpretant would always be in the realm of consciousness and would always be ego-syntonic. Although I would not subscribe to the implicit view that only logical interpretants produce cognitive habits and thus are suited to positive human aims, and that, conversely, quasi-final interpretants tend to be debilitating or destructive of the self, I see value in Colapietro's distinction, especially toward the elaboration of the notion of unconscious habit.

Perhaps where he and I finally diverge is on the issue of a substantive distinction that seems to adjudicate goodness to the truly ultimate logical interpretants (consciousness) and destructiveness to the quasi-ultimate or quasi-logical ones (unconscious). To my questions, "Does this not amount to drawing a line between conscious and unconscious that casts the former as positive or user-friendly, so to speak, and the latter as random or self-destructive to the subject? Doesn't the designation *quasi-logical* imply that logic as cognitive (rational) process is the ultimate human good?" Colapietro replies, "Perhaps, but . . . whatever the ultimate human good for any actual individual or community might be, it is in some manner and measure obtained via deliberation, including communal deliberations in which unspoken assumptions get articulated and inherited or (traditional) relationships of power get questioned. . . . Logical here, then, must not be understood in a narrow or formal sense, but rather taken as the equivalent of the deliberate, the willingness to subject oneself, one's very desires and fantasies even, to an ongoing critique" (personal communication, January 5, 1997).

I have no difficulty taking *logical* beyond the narrow sense of formal logic, but I would still question the emphasis on *deliberate* as a "willingness to subject oneself, one's very desires and fantasies . . . to an ongoing critique," as Colapietro puts it. It is not that self-knowledge and self-critique, individual and communal, are unworthy ideals (although my faith in communal deliberations has worn thin, and I no longer share his belief that they can truly make a personal and political difference; in these times, alas, the pessimism of the intelligence is stronger than the optimism of the will). It is rather that will, self-knowledge, and self-critique time and again collide with, precisely, fantasy and desire, as well as with what may be thought of as unconscious habits (e.g., symptoms): they run up against the intractability of the unconscious, its negativity, its being, for better or for worse, irreducible to will, self-knowledge, or self-critique.

To be sure, as Colapietro argues, a distinction is to be maintained between the unconscious and the conscious, but I think we disagree about the terms of the distinction. When Colapietro states that "it is crucial to establish a distinction between the repressed and the unrepressed (i.e., the repressed insofar as *it becomes available* to the conscious deliberative agency of [human beings])" (p. 146; my italics), he suggests a continuity between the unconscious and the conscious that corresponds to the semantic contiguity of *quasi-logical* to *logical*. In my view, the unconscious as a psychic agency (the system *Ucs.*, in Freud's specification) is not homogeneous or contiguous with the agency of consciousness and is not amenable to that part of consciousness that pertains to deliberative agency.

The bodily ego, I have argued, is a site of negotiations between the external world, with its rapidly shifting universe of cultural meanings and social practices, and the internal world of stubborn, obdurate instinctual drives (de Lauretis 1994, 21–22), which Colapietro aptly calls "our largely opaque instinctual nature" (p. 152). But I see such negotiations often take the form of symptoms, parapraxes, compulsive behavior—in short, what he would call deformed deliberations, destructive habits, or quasi-logical interpretants. The passage from these to the normal or logical interpretants ("the habit-interpretant which would result from sufficient experience and reflection" [p. 145]) is what is at issue. In my understanding of the unconscious, the event of such a passage is at best random; it is unpredictable on the basis of either experience or reflection. In Colapietro's view, on the other hand, it is the task of the ego to promote that passage. For him, then, deliberate/ultimate/final/logical interpretants can lead to the ultimate individual and communal good insofar as they prevail over the quasi-logical ones, in a process or ongoing struggle framed by a vision of human perfectibility and "the Peircean ideal of self-mastery" (p. 153).

I do not share such a vision, nor did the "inventor" of the unconscious, who knew that a psycho-analysis is interminable because of the patient's simultaneous desires to be well and to continue to be ill. Hence the indefinite deferral of the cure, or what Freud called "the asymptotic termination of the treatment" (*SE* 23:215).[5] Here I can do no more than suggest how I would explore further the notion of unconscious habits or significate effects of signs: it would be in the terms of Jean Laplanche's theory of the unconscious as enigmatic signifier and of subjectivity as a work of continuous, partial, and ever imperfect translation.

To conclude these inconclusive remarks, I return very briefly to my minimalist "case history" of Verena. If her/his gender symptoms are a function of habits, who is to say whether such habits result from logical or quasi-logical interpretants, are self-analyzing or deformed deliberations?

Notes

A version of this chapter was delivered as a keynote address to the Semiotic Society of America at its annual meeting in Santa Barbara, California, on October 18, 1996.

1. Incidentally, since I was the one who first used the term "Queer Theory" (as the title of a conference I organized in Santa Cruz in 1990, and then of a special issue of the journal *differences* which I guest-edited in 1991), in an effort to articulate a more complex understanding of homosexuality in its intersections with both social and subjective forms of fantasy, identification, and desire, I marvel at the transformation and dissemination of the term *queer theory* over the last six years. But don't ask me to be more precise about its meaning, its referent, or its interpretants: a few months ago in a major San Francisco bookstore (A Different Light), I noticed that the shelf labeled "Queer Theory" aligned Michel Foucault and Samuel Delany with Gilles Deleuze and Julia Kristeva, Judith Butler and bell hooks, and, I'm embarrassed to say, myself and Umberto Eco, among others.

2. Cf. Leslie Feinberg's heroine in *Stone Butch Blues* (1993), a half-way trans-

sexual, and the self-styled transgender narrator of Minnie Bruce Pratt's *S/HE* (1995).

3. In his chapter in this book, Vincent Colapietro points out that this Peircean definition is misleading. I take up his objection later on, in the section "A Note on Interpretants."

4. My reading of Verena in the framework of the Peircian chain of interpretants emphasizes the temporal dimension of perception, whereas Lindemann's analysis stresses the spatial extension of embodied gender, in which objectified body and living body are two distinct topographies, two differently structured spaces. For Lindemann, therefore, Verena's startled reaction is *simultaneously* the result of the unexpected perception of her body in male-gendered form, and the destruction of that perception (personal communication, January 21, 1997).

5. "The asymptotic termination of the treatment is substantially a matter of indifference to me," Freud wrote. One would think that such a statement appears in "Analysis Terminable and Interminable," a paper of 1937 that reflects Freud's later pessimistic view of the therapeutic effectivity of psychoanalysis, his loss of confidence in the complete success or even the possibility of a cure. But the statement actually appears in a letter to Fliess written on April 16, 1900 (quoted in the Editor's Note to "Analysis Terminable and Interminable" [*SE* 23:215]), the year of publication of *The Interpretation of Dreams,* when Freud was just embarking enthusiastically in his project and had not yet surmised the existence of a death drive or its role in undermining the ego and sustaining the resistance to its therapeutic alteration, the resistance to the cure.

References

Butler, Judith. *Bodies That Matter: On the Discursive Limits of "Sex."* New York: Routledge, 1993.

Colapietro, Vincent M. "Notes for a Sketch of a Peircean Theory of the Unconscious." *Transactions of the Charles S. Peirce Society* 31, no. 3 (1995): 482–506.

de Lauretis, Teresa. *Alice Doesn't: Feminism, Semiotics, Cinema.* Bloomington: Indiana University Press, 1984.

——— . *Technologies of Gender: Essays on Theory, Film, and Fiction.* Bloomington: Indiana University Press, 1987.

——— . *The Practice of Love: Lesbian Sexuality and Perverse Desire.* Bloomington: Indiana University Press, 1994.

Feinberg, Leslie, *Stone Butch Blues.* Ithaca, N.Y.: Firebrand Books, 1993.

Freud, Sigmund. *The Standard Edition of the Complete Psychological Works of Sigmund Freud.* Translated and edited by James Strachey. 24 vols. London: Hogarth Press, 1953–74.

Jakobson, Roman. "Concluding Statement: Linguistics and Poetics." In *Style in Language,* edited by Thomas A. Sebeok, 350–77. Cambridge: M.I.T. Press, 1960.

Laplanche, Jean. *Seduction, Translation and the Drives.* A dossier edited by John

Fletcher and Martin Stanton. Translated by Martin Stanton. London: Institute of Contemporary Arts, 1992.

Lindemann, Gesa. *Das Paradoxe Geschlecht: Transsexualität im Spannungsfeld von Körper, Leib und Gefühl.* Frankfurt: Fischer, 1993.

————. "The Body of Gender Difference." Translated by Allison Brown. *European Journal of Women's Studies* 3, no. 4 (1996): 341–61.

Peirce, Charles Sanders. *Collected Papers of Charles Sanders Peirce.* Edited by Charles Hartshorne, Paul Weiss, and Arthur W. Burks. 8 vols. Cambridge: Harvard University Press, 1931–58.

Pollock, Griselda, Rifkin, Adrian, Easton, Richard, Gabriel, Herta, and Suriano, Toni. "A Conversation on Judith Butler's *Bodies That Matter." parallax: a journal of metadiscursive theory and cultural practices,* no. 1 (Summer 1995): 157–58.

Pratt, Minnie Bruce. *S/HE.* Ithaca, N.Y.: Firebrand Books, 1995.

Rubin, Gayle. "The Traffic in Women: Notes on the 'Political Economy' of Sex." In *Toward an Anthropology of Women,* edited by Rayna R. Reiter, 157–210. New York: Monthly Review Press, 1975.

————. "Thinking Sex: Notes for a Radical Theory of the Politics of Sexuality." In *Pleasure and Danger: Exploring Female Sexuality,* edited by Carole S. Vance. Boston: Routledge and Kegan Paul, 1984.

Woolf, Virginia. *A Room of One's Own.* San Diego: Harcourt Brace Jovanovich, 1929.

Index of Names

Index of Subjects

abduction, 91; as guessing right, 5; as originating knowledge, 7–8; as third type of inference, 4; dangers of, 117n. 7
action, 103; tendency to, 104
aesthetics, 112, 114
affect: in child development, 38; as correlated with tempo of speech, 46; signal function of, 68–70; as evanescent, 69, 79; and firstness, 71; and the three categories, 77; as isolated, 79; as always conscious, 79; as guiding thought, 80
alexithymia, as firstness, 60
algorithm 131, 134n. 4
ambivalence, in psychosis, 19
analytic neutrality, 38
anxiety, 79
architectonic system, 8, 50

beliefs, 146; as unconscious, 105; as habit, 111
bipolar disorder, in Charles Peirce's life, 2, 4
blank space, in inner experience, 44
blathering, 42–43
body, 165; as sexed, 110; as gender symptom, 163
body-ego, 148, 169, 172; and access to symbolic, 170
body language, 39

categories, 63–64, 103, 149; of relation, 50, 55, 56. *See also* firstness; secondness; thirdness

chance, 148
child development: and semiosis, 31–35, 37; as framed by the Third, 32; phase of babbling, 42; as epigenetic, 50, 59; semiotic line of development in, 56
communication, hierarchy of modes of, 53
community, 102, 113, 127, 172; of inquirers 9, 56; and thirdness, 51; and ideals, 105; and norms, 114; and truth, 128
complexity theory, 59
conjecture, 143
consciousness, 147, 154n. 7; as individual, 9; and quality, 69–70, 72; of relationships, 79
context, 32, 49; of psychoanalytic theory, 50; and general system theory, 54; and informational knowledge, 108
contiguity, 105, 117; of index and object, 51
continuity, 128; of mind and nature, 5; and thirdness, 51
control parameters, 59
convention, as relating symbol to object, 52
conversion symptom, 13, 57; as requiring translation, 62
countertransference, 38, 52
culture, 32, 63, 152; as unconscious, 106, 112

death drive, 73, 134n. 5
deconstruction, 110; of the transcendental signified, 122, 128